Praise for *If We Can Put a Man on the Moon . . .*

"Eggers and O'Leary may have created a new genre—the Government Policy Thriller. We couldn't get enough of the stories—good policies gone bad, great ideas that flew off the rails, and, occasionally, the stunning triumph that gives us hope that we can get to the moon again."

—Chip and Dan Heath, coauthors of
Made to Stick: Why Some Ideas Survive and Others Die

"A clear-eyed look at how to get the best out of our public institutions. Instead of easy answers, the authors offer practical suggestions for successful execution in a very challenging and complex environment. A must-read for political leaders."

—Kay Bailey Hutchison, U.S. Senator from Texas

"As we sort out the cross-pressures in twenty-first-century government, this book is a useful and lively guide to how to make things work. Driven by practical cases and pragmatic lessons, it's an invaluable road map to the government of the future."

—Donald F. Kettl, Dean, School of Public Policy,
University of Maryland

"*If We Can Put a Man on the Moon* is the rare book that made me both shake my head in disbelief and nod my head with possibility. Eggers and O'Leary offer a trenchant analysis of how good government intentions can go awry. But they also show how sharper thinking and keener attention to design can help governments at all levels serve citizens better. Pick up two copies—one to read yourself, the other to send to your favorite elected official."

—Daniel H. Pink, author of *A Whole New Mind*

"After serving as a mayor, a congressman for twenty years, and as a secretary of two cabinet-level departments in two administrations from different political parties, I can attest that the challenges of executing successful government programs exist at all levels of government, in all parties, and in all locations. Eggers and O'Leary present exactly the most common traps that lead to a failure of execution, but more importantly they present ways to help avoid those traps. Their ideas should be presented to all government employees."

—Norman Mineta, former U.S. Secretary of Transportation

"This engagingly written book tells the story of numerous notable public policy successes and failures as it draws out some important lessons about how to make government at all levels work better. Filled with interesting facts and important insights, Eggers and O'Leary's book has lessons for both public and private sector leaders who want to get more accomplished."

—Jeffrey Pfeffer, Thomas D. Dee II Professor of
Organizational Behavior, Stanford Business School,
and author of *What Were They Thinking? Unconventional
Wisdom About Management*

"The most important book on government since James Q. Wilson's *Bureaucracy*, published more than two decades ago."

—Dr. Wade Horn, former Assistant Secretary
of the U.S. Department of Health and Human Services

"Just as *Reinventing Government* sparked public-sector innovation in the 1990s, so this groundbreaking new analytical framework can and should spark fresh approaches to the most challenging problems of our times. Eggers and O'Leary remind us that while people are often blamed for government failures, bureaucratic systems are really at fault—and the authors offer a carefully researched methodology for avoiding the mistakes that too often plague public-sector initiatives."

—Tim Clark, Editor in Chief,
Government Executive magazine

"In my line of work, success requires that the risk of failure be taken seriously. This important book shows how government can accomplish its biggest challenges, like putting a man—or a woman—on the moon."

—Sally Ride, professor at the University of California,
San Diego, and the first woman astronaut in space

"*If We Can Put a Man on the Moon* is the classic affirmation that good ideas are not enough. The post-9/11 security environment has challenged government in ways unseen since World War II. This book offers enormous insight into answering those extraordinarily difficult 'how' questions. Avoiding O'Leary and Eggers' 'traps' will make for more efficient and more effective decisions."

—Admiral James M. Loy, former Coast Guard Commandant
and former Deputy Secretary of DHS

"*If We Can Put a Man on the Moon* is essential reading, and it deftly illustrates that competence and accountability in government is critical for success."

—Tom Daschle, former U.S. Senator from South Dakota

"This is an excellent book on a pressing and critical subject. The examples used and the stories told are terrific. I either had forgotten about them or never knew the story behind the story. This not only is solid analysis, but superb reporting. If you care about how well—or poorly—we are governing ourselves, read this book."

—Peter A. Harkness, Founder and Publisher Emeritus,
Governing magazine

"Innovation, transformation, and change can happen in government, but success doesn't always come easily. John O'Leary and Bill Eggers smartly uncover some of the common pitfalls and how to avoid them. It's an indispensable guide to anyone interested in government that works."

—Mitt Romney, former governor of Massachusetts

"This book is a gem—insightful, practical, and beautifully presented. Eggers and O'Leary distill decades of experience with complex public programs. They show us what can go wrong—and remind us about the great things that can be accomplished when design and execution are done well."

—Alasdair S. Roberts, Jerome L. Rappaport Professor of
Law and Public Policy, Suffolk University Law School

"At a time when diatribe often substitutes for thinking, Eggers and O'Leary have written a thoughtful analysis of the hidden forces at play in the public sector. This book will change the way you look at government."

—Tom Ridge, former governor of Pennsylvania

If We Can
Put a Man on
the Moon...

If We Can Put a Man on the Moon...

Getting Big Things Done in Government

William D. Eggers
John O'Leary

HARVARD BUSINESS PRESS
Boston, Massachusetts

The opinions expressed in the book are those of the co-authors and not of
Deloitte. Deloitte refers to one or more of Deloitte Touche Tohmatsu, a Swiss Verein,
and its network of member firms, each of which is a legally separate and
independent entity. Please see www.deloitte.com/about for a detailed description
of the legal structure of Deloitte Touche Tohmatsu and its member firms.

Library of Congress Cataloging-in-Publication Data

Eggers, William D.
  If we can put a man on the moon—: getting big things done in government /
William D. Eggers, John O'Leary.
      p. cm.
  Includes bibliographical references and index.
  ISBN 978-1-4221-6636-9 (hardcover : alk. paper)
  1. Administrative agencies—United States—Management. 2. Government
productivity—United States. I. O'Leary, John, 1962- II. Title.
  JK421.E44 2009
  351.73—dc22

                                                            2009021183

The paper used in this publication meets the requirements of the American National
Standard for Permanence of Paper for Publications and Documents in Libraries and
Archives Z39.48-1992.

Contents

Preface

The Conflict Behind the Cliché

It started as a challenge issued by President John F. Kennedy in 1961. If we can put a man on the moon before the Soviets, Kennedy reasoned, we can prove to the world that democracy works better than socialism. The race to the moon was a contest between two systems of government, and the question would be settled not by debate, but by who could best execute on this endeavor.

When Kennedy issued his challenge, the Soviets had a sizable head start in the space race. They had more powerful rockets, and cosmonaut Yuri Gagarin had just become the first human in space. But America pulled together. In July of 1969, Neil Armstrong planted an American flag on the moon. In Moscow, Soviet officials could only glare at the sky and mutter in Russian.

Instantly, a new cliché entered the lexicon. If we can put a man on the moon, the saying went, then surely we can achieve anything we set our minds to. We had just overcome perhaps the most difficult scientific, administrative, and organizational challenge of all time, and the newly minted phrase expressed boundless confidence in the ability of our country and its government to successfully execute anything it attempted.

While Neil Armstrong was walking around on the moon, such confidence was understandable. In the preceding quarter century, democracy had achieved a series of great triumphs. An alliance of democracies, with a belated assist from the Soviet Union, defeated Nazism, Fascism, and Imperialism in World War II. The free men and women of the Manhattan Project, including refugees from the autocratic regimes, split the atom. The Marshall Plan helped the democratic nations of Europe rebuild that war-torn continent. Democracy confronted its ideological opposite during the Berlin Airlift, the Korean War, and the Cuban missile crisis. America's booming economy and strong military showed that democracy could deliver both guns and butter. A track record of effective execution showed that democracy wasn't just morally superior to collectivism in a theoretical sense—it could actually get the job done as well. This was recognized at the time by the man who led NASA (the National Aeronautics and Space Administration) to this great achievement, James Webb:

> *As astronauts walked the moon, Webb proclaimed to all who would listen that Apollo's real achievement lay in demonstrating that a democratic nation could outmanage an authoritarian state. He said that if the United States could go to the moon, it could solve its other public problems.*[1]

Events of the late 1960s tested this confidence, however. Critics pointed to urban poverty, racial strife, and a deteriorating situation in Vietnam as evidence that government "of the people" wasn't so capable after all. In August 1969, just three weeks after Neil Armstrong's lunar stroll, Richard Nixon became the first American president to cite the success of the Apollo program as proof of government's ability to execute when he unveiled his proposal for welfare reform to a skeptical nation:

> *We face an urban crisis, a social crisis—and at the same time a crisis of confidence in the capacity of government to do its job. . . It is no accident, therefore, that we find increasing skepticism—and not only among our young people, but among citizens everywhere—about the continuing capacity of government to master the challenges we face. . .*
>
> *Abolishing poverty, putting an end to dependency—like reaching the moon a decade ago—may seem to be impossible. But in the spirit of Apollo we can lift our sights and marshal our best efforts.*[2]

The lunar landing had become a rhetorical trump card—who would dare argue that American government wasn't capable after it had put a man on the moon?

The 1970s: From Pride to Malaise in a Decade

If we can put a man on the moon, why can't we put metal in the microwave?

—FRASIER CRANE, *CHEERS*

Unfortunately, the 1970s didn't exactly showcase government as a source of national pride. Nixon's welfare reform proposal came to naught and was followed by a series of disappointments: wage and price controls, Watergate, "Whip Inflation Now" buttons, defeat in Vietnam, an energy crisis, stagflation, the Iran hostage situation, and so on.

In July of 1979, President Jimmy Carter gave a nationally televised address on the mood of the nation. His famous (or infamous) malaise speech cited a "crisis of confidence" that threatened our faith in democracy:

> *Our people are losing that faith, not only in government itself but in the ability as citizens to serve as the ultimate rulers and shapers of our democracy . . . What you see too often in Washington and elsewhere around the country is a system of government that seems incapable of action. You see a Congress twisted and pulled in every direction by hundreds of well-financed and powerful special interests.*[3]

Just as Nixon had done a decade earlier, President Carter then played the Apollo card. After all, said Carter, "We ourselves are the same Americans who just ten years ago put a man on the moon." By this point, the appeal fell on deaf ears. As Frasier Crane's question shows, the once proud boast about reaching the moon had morphed into a grumpy expression of frustration, often combined with a cruel taunt about the failure of our government: if we can put a man on the moon, why can't we fix our schools, or end poverty, or keep inflation under control?

In America, and in other western democracies, attitudes toward government had shifted. In his inaugural address in 1981, President Reagan starkly summarized the philosophy that had gotten him elected: "In this present crisis, government is not the solution to our problem. Government *is* the problem." Reagan's legendary optimism was reserved for America's people, not her government. In less than twenty years, boundless faith in the federal government's ability to solve problems—embodied by Kennedy's bet on the moon and by LBJ's Great Society—had yielded to skepticism bordering on scorn. It was as if the success of the moon landing made the subsequent disappointments of the 1970s all the more difficult to swallow.

The Execution Imperative

We never should have landed a man on the moon. It's a mistake. Now everything is compared to that one accomplishment. "I can't believe they could land a man on the moon . . . and taste my coffee!"

—JERRY SEINFELD, COMEDIAN

Putting a man on the moon sets a high expectation of competence, and disappointment follows whenever government falls short of that mark. For example, in the months that followed the invasion of Iraq, America struggled to impose civil order—to the dismay of many Iraqis. As television journalist Charlie Rose put it, "When the United States arrived a lot of people were saying, 'You know, this is the country that went to the moon, for gosh sakes, they know what to do.' "[4]

By 2008, poll after poll showed unprecedented levels of dissatisfaction with government. The reason was a litany of high-profile stumbles that made the 1970s look like the good old days: Iraq, Boston's Big Dig, Hurricane Katrina and the drowning of New Orleans, Abu Ghraib, the Walter Reed Army Medical Center, and the massive economic meltdown.

When we surveyed members of the Senior Executive Service, the elite ranks of federal managers, 60 percent said that government was *less capable* of executing large projects today than it was thirty years ago. Our survey of fellows of the National Academy of Public Administration echoed these views, with only 16 percent describing the federal government as proficient at designing policy that can actually be implemented. (See Appendixes B and C for more survey results.) Such dim assessments from those who have dedicated their careers to public service should be a wake-up call for anyone who cares about our democratic institutions.

Some have sought to pin the blame for all our problems on President George W. Bush. But George W. Bush cannot be blamed for wage and price controls, or the failed immigration reform bill of 1986, or the failure to enact health care reform in 1994. It's hard to blame Bush for an urban education crisis going into its fourth decade. As the quotes from presidents Nixon, Carter, and Reagan suggest, our execution struggles did not spring into being when George W. Bush took office in 2001.

There is indeed ample historical evidence that democratic governments can achieve great things. There is also ample evidence that democratic governments can fail in their attempts. The requirements for achieving great things are two simple but far from easy steps—wisely choosing which policies to pursue and then executing those policies. The difference between success and failure is execution.

This book is about executing large, important, public initiatives. We use a systems perspective to examine the misunderstood and underappreciated discipline of how democracies actually succeed or fail on large undertakings.

Visit any bookstore. Titles on policy, politics, and how to succeed in business abound. But you won't find many books that address the real-life challenge of executing in the public sector. Yet it is skillful execution that delivers the desired results, while faulty execution produces disastrous results.

The public failures that have plagued our recent history don't need to condemn its future. As this preface is being written in early 2009, the situation appears dire. Like leaders around the globe, newly elected president Barack Obama faces massive challenges. He inherits two wars, an economy in meltdown, and a fiscal tidal wave of red ink rushing toward us as entitlement spending threatens to swamp the federal government. Add to this the enduring policy challenges of immigration, health care, education, and the environment, and it quickly becomes apparent that there is no margin for error. Competent execution has never been more critical, in part because of government's unprecedented role in rescuing banks, auto makers, and state governments. Politicians face a groundswell of anger and distrust that is creating an unhealthy gulf between citizens and their government. Right now, neither the economy nor the treasury nor the citizenry have much tolerance for failure.

Without question, making sound policy choices is critical. Determining what government ought to do is of paramount importance in a democracy. Choose a destructive policy, and the most competent execution in the world won't help. By the same token, however, brilliant policies poorly executed will likewise disappoint. This is not to imply that all our problems are merely technical in nature or that political beliefs are unimportant. But whatever your political beliefs, the execution challenge merits attention. Whether you're a liberal seeking universal health care or a conservative promoting greater choice in education, sound execution matters.

In taking the oath of office, President Obama, like the forty-three presidents who preceded him, promised to "faithfully execute the office of president." President Obama's inaugural address tried to strike a balance between the somber reality of our current circumstances and the hope for better days ahead. Like Kennedy, Obama came to office with bold plans, and had a message for the skeptics in the crowd who questioned the ability of American government to achieve these grand ambitions: "Their memories are short. For they have forgotten what this country has already done," said the new president. Like putting a man on the moon. Obama hasn't forgotten. His inaugural parade was the first in forty years to include astronauts, and also featured NASA's newest lunar rover prototype.[5] Born in 1961, President Barack Obama has told of being a young boy, "sitting on my grandfather's shoulders and watching the Apollo astronauts come ashore in Hawaii. People cheered and waved small flags, and my grandfather explained with pride and assurance how we Americans could accomplish anything we set our minds to do."[6]

This book is about accomplishing what we set our minds to do. It doesn't present any easy answers because there are no easy answers. The journey to success in public sector undertakings is perilous, strewn with traps and snares that bedevil the efforts of the best and brightest.

This book is not about our past. It is about the future that we are about to create. Back when President Kennedy issued the challenge to go to the moon, success depended on execution. In the same way, our future success hinges on both wisdom in charting a course and excellence in carrying out that vision. Look to the moon for a reminder of what is possible. Let that achievement of forty years ago challenge us to create anew a nation capable of such triumphs. There is much work to be done.

Introduction

The Seven Deadly Traps on the Journey to Success

CHAPTER GUIDE

- The Big Dig and the Red Herring Bolt
- Missing the Evidence of Recurring Failure
- Blaming People Versus Blaming the System
- Katrina and the Separation of Powers
- A Map for the Journey to Success
- A Process Perspective
- The Marshall Plan: A Process View
- The Seven Deadly Traps on the Journey to Success
- The Importance of Invisible Systems
- The Delicious Cause of Cholera in London

L'essentiel est invisible pour les yeux.
("The essential is invisible to the eyes.")

—ANTOINE DE SAINT EXUPÉRY, *LE PETIT PRINCE*

The Big Dig and the Red Herring Bolt

On September 8, 1999, a worker on the Big Dig, Boston's mammoth road and tunnel project, noticed a problem. Several recently installed anchor bolts were slipping out of the roof of the tunnel, displacing about one-sixteenth of an inch. These bolts, secured by an epoxy, held up large concrete ceiling panels, and if the bolts separated from the roof, the heavy concrete panels would fall directly onto the roadway below.[1]

Over the next several weeks, workers noticed the displacement increasing.

In December 1999, the management duo of Bechtel and Parsons Brinckerhoff, the private consortium overseeing the Big Dig, and Modern Continental, the company installing the ceiling, agreed on a plan to address the problem. They would replace all the failing anchor bolts using the same design, the same process, and the same epoxy. The only difference would be that now the bolts would be tested to a load of 6,350 pounds—higher than previous testing had required.

In an internal e-mail, a structural engineer noted something disturbing: "Glaringly absent from the [deficiency report] is any explanation why the anchors failed and what steps are proposed to ensure the problem does not reoccur."[2]

Big Dig management had decided to repeat the past in hopes of achieving different results. Their "fix" wouldn't necessarily fix anything.

To be sure, the bolts and epoxy would now be tested with more weight. But what if weight wasn't the problem? Because if weight wasn't the problem, something else was.

That something else was creep. Certain epoxies, when subjected to pressure over time, can "flow," or slowly yield, even at relatively low pressures. You can observe this phenomenon yourself when pulling a paper label off a glass bottle. If you pull hard and fast, the glue will hold and the paper will rip. If you pull slowly and gently, however, the glue will yield and you can remove the entire label intact. In the same way, the epoxy holding the bolts could withstand a heavy load—but only for a short time. Even a lighter load applied over several months could cause creep, allowing the bolts to gradually slip out of the ceiling.

The bolts were reinserted using the same process.

Not surprisingly, the same process yielded the same results. In December 2001, a field engineer noted *more* anchor bolts slipping out of the roof. Some were recently installed bolts, which had been tested at the higher loads. This should have been a huge red flag. As a National Traffic Safety Board (NTSB) report later noted: "At this point, it should have been obvious to B/PB and to Modern Continental that the remedy . . . had not been effective, as anchors that had passed proof tests at higher values were still displacing . . . The companies apparently considered the continuing failures as isolated instances and took no action to address the problem in a systemic way."[3]

A report was filed, which again noted that the "reason for failure is unknown." Once again, slipping anchor bolts were reinstalled using the same design, the same process, and the same epoxy.

The Big Dig leaders ignored evidence of a recurring problem. Why?

One reason may be what we call the "red herring bolt." One of the very first slipping bolts discovered, the red herring bolt exhibited multiple flaws, including insufficient epoxy, excess concrete dust, and improper mixing of resin and hardener. The red herring bolt supported a variety of theories related to improper installation technique. The many flaws of the red herring bolt allowed Big Dig management to believe what they wished to be true— namely, that the slipping bolts were an anomaly caused by somebody's shoddy construction work. It was easier to believe someone had screwed up rather than believe a trail of evidence pointing toward systemic failure.[4]

The tunnel was opened to traffic in January of 2003.

According to the NTSB report, if the Massachusetts Turnpike Authority, the public agency ultimately responsible for the Big Dig, had performed a visual inspection of the tunnel ceiling, slipping bolts could have been seen with the naked eye. But between the road's opening in January 2003 and July 2006, the NTSB could find no evidence that any such inspections were performed.[5]

Among other factors, epoxy creep is exacerbated by high temperatures. On July 10, 2006, the mercury hit 87 degrees in Boston.

That night, at 11:01 p.m., Angel Del Valle was driving his wife Milena to Boston's Logan Airport through one of the new Big Dig tunnels. Without warning, the ceiling of the tunnel collapsed, dropping twenty-six tons of concrete and steel onto their 1991 Buick sedan. Milena Del Valle, a thirty-eight-year-old mother of three, was killed; her husband Angel miraculously escaped with only minor injuries.

Ten concrete ceiling panels, each eight feet by ten feet and weighing 4,700 pounds, had fallen when the epoxy-secured bolts slipped out of the roof. As each anchor bolt gave way, it placed greater weight on the remaining bolts, creating a cascading failure.[6]

Following the disaster, investigators inspected other similarly supported ceiling panels and found that 161 out of 634 bolts—more than one in four—were pulling out from the roof. State senator Steven Baddour toured the site after the collapse and was stunned at how obvious the problem was: "You could see where the bolts had slipped. You didn't have to be an engineer. You didn't have to have an advanced degree. If they had done the most basic, cursory inspections, they would have shut down the tunnels. That's inexcusable neglect."[7]

The slipping bolts were clearly visible, though unseen. The real problem, however, was invisible.

What was the underlying cause of the slippage? The epoxy supplier makes two versions: Standard Set and Fast Set. The Fast Set epoxy is susceptible to creep. After the ceiling collapse, Modern Continental told investigators that they were "99 percent certain" they had used the Standard Set epoxy. In fact, they had used the Fast Set.[8] The tragedy is that this eminently fixable process flaw wasn't uncovered until after Milena Del Valle's death. It wasn't uncovered because no one was committed to examining the process and discovering the root cause of the slipping bolts. In an odd way, the most important bolt in this drama wasn't the one that gave way and started the fatal collapse. It was the red herring bolt, a bolt that had been replaced seven years earlier.

The ceiling collapse was just the latest mishap for a project already synonymous with failure, corruption, and mismanagement. The Big Dig tunnels were barely open in 2004 when they began leaking profusely, with water gushing so heavily that portions of the road had to be closed to traffic. As late as 2007, the tunnels were pumping out 1.9 million gallons a month—more than fifty times the acceptable volume. Corruption contributed to soaring costs, as contractors overcharged for concrete and other materials. The Big Dig's early cost estimates of $2.6 billion had ballooned to $14.6 billion. During the 1990s, public officials overseeing the Big Dig intentionally misled the public about cost overruns, earning a reprimand from the Securities and Exchange Commission. During the sentencing of a company convicted of bilking the Big Dig, Federal District Court judge Mark L. Wolf took the opportunity to criticize public oversight of the project from the bench: "When a public works project soars from $3 billion to $15 billion, it breeds a sense in the community—in this case, the country—that government is incompetent."[9] The project exhibited widespread, repeated failures, which suggests that there was a systemic failure to execute unrelated to a single contractor or lone public official.

It was the death of Milena Del Valle that truly brought home the impact of poor execution. At the memorial service for Del Valle, Rev. Cesar de Paz addressed grieving friends and relatives—and gave special notice to the public officials in attendance, which included the attorney general and the head of the turnpike authority: "We should pray for the authorities, so that God will give them the wisdom, so that God will give them the intelligence, so that this will never be repeated, what happened to our sister, Milena."[10]

The final twist in this sad story would offer little solace to Milena's family. The ceiling panels had been installed to provide a ventilation passage. But because of a nearby opening, ventilation wasn't a problem. Following the deadly ceiling collapse, the concrete tiles were never replaced. The concrete ceiling in that section of the tunnel had been utterly unnecessary in the first place.[11]

Getting Past the Blame Game

It is easy to look at the engineers on the Big Dig and shake our heads in disbelief. How could they overlook the obvious signs of recurring failure? Why didn't they look at their process? How could they be so blind?

In a larger sense, however, the same sort of persistent government failures are being misdiagnosed all around us today. As we will see, the public sector is struggling to achieve success on large, important undertakings. But like the Big Dig engineers, we haven't committed ourselves to answering the most important question of all: *Why? Why is government failing on the important stuff so often?*

As with the Big Dig, the easy answer is, "Someone messed up." But workers weren't to blame for the slipping bolts. The underlying cause of the problem was systemic—the process was flawed. In the same way, the process by which government tackles large undertakings is broken, but instead of fixing the process we devote extensive energy to a national "blamestorming" contest.

Consider the response to Hurricane Katrina. Without a doubt, the rescue effort was a public debacle of monumental proportions, a poster child for public failure, and the long-term recovery effort hasn't been much better. An obvious question: what caused this failure?

With a screw-up of this magnitude, the natural human instinct is to ask: "What nincompoop is in charge of this goat rodeo?" Blame soon landed on one or more of the people in leadership positions—New Orleans mayor Ray Nagin, Louisiana governor Kathleen Blanco, President Bush, or, a popular choice, Michael D. Brown, the director of the Federal Emergency Management Agency (FEMA). No doubt individual failings were on display, helpfully pointed out by members of the other party. But were the rescue and recovery failures purely a matter of individual errors? Could there be a less obvious reason contributing to the inadequate government response?

How about this: the flawed response was largely a systemic failure. The main problem was the process, not the people. Our democratic system of checks and balances purposely distributes authority among various levels of government. Unlike subsidiary divisions of a corporation, mayors do not report to governors, and governors do not report to the president.

Local, state, and federal authorities exercise independent authority over resources that are critical in responding to a disaster.[12] Breakdowns between levels of government—between the various *independent* yet *interdependent* components of the response system—greatly contributed to the catastrophe. Scholars who have studied the Katrina response, including Professor Donald F. Kettl of the University of Maryland, note that the response system relies on coordinated action by various units of government, but doesn't include effective mechanisms for such coordination. The disaster response system was a disaster because it wasn't a system.[13] As the city was overcome by both water and lawlessness, the response by government was undermined by the division of responsibility. Mayor Nagin controlled city workers, such as fire and police; Governor Blanco controlled state agencies and the National Guard; and Michael Brown, the head of FEMA, controlled federal resources. This separation of power meant no single person was in charge. The diffuse distribution of authority is built into the design of democratic government, but in the case of Katrina, the fractured response of government proved disastrous.

This wasn't just a people problem. It was also a process problem. As with the Big Dig, however, the easy answer of human error supplanted a more nuanced appreciation of underlying systemic failure. The media plays a valuable watchdog role in a democracy, bringing us stories about government's bad guys: the inept managers, venal politicians, lazy government workers, and sleazy contractors. The media and its consumers also appreciate the tangible, easy-to-understand nature of these characters. You can see these villains, take their picture playing golf during work hours, make fun of their hair. When the FBI releases a photograph of a Massachusetts state senator allegedly stuffing a cash bribe into her bra— well, that sells newspapers. The truth is that inept and corrupt characters do exist to some extent, but, like the red herring bolt, they distract us from looking for the underlying *systemic* reasons for our shortcomings.

The business world has been through this already.

In the 1940s, W. Edwards Deming, a pioneer of Total Quality Management (TQM), went against the conventional wisdom of that time when he taught manufacturing companies that "the worker is not the problem." For Deming, understanding the system was critical to fixing the source of errors. A system is an invisible network of interdependent components that must work together to achieve a desired goal—the various steps on an assembly line, for example, or the various activities needed to put a man on the moon. Part of Deming's genius was to stop blaming the poor slob working on the assembly line for the defect found at the end of the line. Instead, Deming argued that leaders should examine a business process as a unified whole. Outcomes are generated by people working within a system. Successful companies, such as Toyota, are fanatical about improving the systems through which they create value— they call it the "Toyota Production System" for a reason. They know that the only way to generate great results with average workers is to have great systems, and the more complex and interrelated the firm's processes, the more important systems thinking becomes.

A hundred years ago, cutting-edge corporate practice was the assembly line. Today, work flows cross both company lines and international boundaries, with practices such as outsourcing, just-in-time inventory, and supply chain management. People are still critically important, but the process of creating value for a customer is more complex and interrelated than ever before. Tools such as Six Sigma, business process reengineering, and systems thinking have been developed to deal with this increased process complexity.

Government and its work are more complicated than in the past as well. One hundred years ago, the cutting-edge innovation was the bureaucracy. The bureaucratic model of government served rather well for a long time, but as tasks and technology changed, so did the systems government used to do its work. As public officials are discovering, approaches such as public-private partnerships and governing by network are far more complicated, from a systems perspective, than traditional bureaucratic operations. Our understanding of these increasingly complex arrangements hasn't kept pace with the reality of modern governance.

Consider the government health programs of Medicare, Medicaid, and SCHIP, which provide health services to the elderly, the poor, and children, respectively. By manipulating a complicated set of market levers, a group of just 4,500 federal employees shapes a health care system in which more than *a million workers*—in hospitals, insurance companies, state agencies, and so forth—provide care to 74 million beneficiaries.[14] The opportunity for systemic failure is huge. Indeed, Government

Accountability Office audits of Medicare routinely find billions in erroneous overpayments and other systemic flaws.[15] But the invisible systems through which government executes these policies is poorly understood by policy makers and utterly incomprehensible to the general public. Instead, when it comes to big government failures, it is the shortcomings of people that receive almost all the attention.

The Journey to Success: A Map

This book arose from a question: what happens when you look at large government undertakings from a process perspective?

At first blush, the question seems impractical. Government, after all, is engaged in a dizzying variety of undertakings, from building roads to putting a man on the moon; from waging a war on drugs, to waging a war on poverty, to waging actual war. It performs these tasks through both traditional bureaucracies and increasingly complicated networks of public, private, and nonprofit providers. Does it even make sense to generalize about such diverse undertakings?

Absolutely. After all, books on management can provide insight, whether your business is making cars, selling soap, or running a hotel. Wildly diverse competitive enterprises share common elements—whatever business you are in, you'll need to know how to manage people, satisfy customers, and market your offering. The specific challenges of running a law firm may be very different from operating a hospital or managing a restaurant, but certain valuable insights can find application in any competitive market. All successful businesses are adept at both strategy (what is offered, at what price, through what channel) and execution (product development, production, marketing, and delivery of the offering). Indeed, hundreds of worthwhile business books explore every aspect of both corporate strategy and execution.

In researching the process of getting big things done in a democracy, we examined more than seventy-five major public initiatives—both great successes and monumental failures. We looked at everything from the success of the acid rain program to the struggles of immigration reform; from the federal wars on poverty and inflation to actual wars in Iraq and

Vietnam; from London's effort to reduce traffic to New Orleans's attempt at education reform. (See Appendix A, or you can visit our book Web site at www.deloitte.com/us/manonthemoon for more details on the seventy-five post–World War II case studies we analyzed, including international examples.) We looked for patterns and sought to identify, despite the differences, the universal characteristics of large public undertakings. We found that from large infrastructure projects such as Boston's Big Dig to human services initiatives like welfare reform, nearly all such initiatives follow a predictable path, a series of steps that we call, somewhat optimistically, the *journey to success.*

Tolstoy once observed that every happy family is happy in the same way, while each unhappy family is unhappy in its own particular way. So it is with public undertakings. There are lots of ways an initiative can end in disaster, but to have a happy ending, the following *must* occur:

- The undertaking must start with a good *idea.*

- The idea must be given specifics, often in the form of legislation, that become an implementable *design.*

- The design must win approval, as when a bill becomes a law, signaling a *moment of democratic commitment.*

- There must be competent *implementation.*

- The initiative must generate desired *results.*

In addition, to be successful *in the long run*, a large public undertaking requires one more step:

- Over time, both what is being done and how it is being done must be subjected to *reevaluation.*

These observations led to the creation of a high-level process map of this universal journey, shown in figure I-1. (Note that in the figure and in the following text, we call the moment of democratic commitment "Stargate" because it instantly takes the process from the political universe to the bureaucratic universe. Our apologies to nongeeks, but "Stargate" sounds better than "moment of democratic commitment." For now, just think of it as the moment when a bill becomes a law.)

FIGURE I-1

The universal journey to success

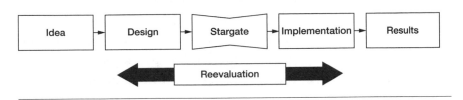

With the help of more than seventy graduate students of public policy, we used this map to help guide our inquiry and discovered that simply visualizing the execution process as a continuous flow made it much easier to identify the root causes of a particular project's success or failure. Witnessing the power of the map put to use in analyzing dozens of undertakings convinced us that this simple tool can significantly enhance our ability to comprehend large public projects.

Let's look at one of the most admired public undertakings in modern history: the Marshall Plan. The seed of an idea was planted in June 1947, when Secretary of State George Marshall mentioned in his commencement remarks at Harvard that he thought the United States should send aid to European nations seeking to rebuild after World War II. In his speech he offered no specifics. Instead, he simply pointed out that American aid could provide much-needed political stability to a decimated continent tottering on the brink of collapse. At this point the Marshall Plan wasn't a plan at all, only an idea—but one that was received favorably in the United States and seized upon by the nations of Europe like a life preserver tossed to a drowning man.[16]

Based on Marshall's idea, Congress and the Truman administration worked to shape the idea into legislation, even inviting input from European nations. Over a ten-month period, a legislative blueprint for how to distribute aid, to whom, and how much took shape.

In April 1948, legislation giving Europe aid for five years was passed by Congress. The Economic Cooperation Act was signed into law by President Truman the next day. Democratic approval to launch had been granted.

The law established a new bureaucracy, the Economic Cooperation Administration (ECA). Leaders were appointed, staff hired, and the distribution of aid begun. The Marshall Plan was implemented.

The Marshall Plan generated results, contributing not only to Europe's economic recovery but also fostering enormous international goodwill. Though critics of the plan question how much impact it had on European recovery, it is still one of the most highly regarded programs in United States history.

In 1953, with Europe's recovery well established and the Korean War consuming significant funds, Congress essentially terminated the Marshall Plan.

A high-level process map of the Marshall Plan would look something like figure I-2.

A process engineer would want to look not only at what got done under the Marshall Plan, but also *by whom*. This view is shown in figure I-3.

With rare exceptions, the map from idea to results is a universally applicable model. Some readers might object to including the ideation, policy design, and legislative debate phases in a map that is ostensibly concerned with the execution of an initiative. Many people see policy design and program implementation as entirely separate activities, and that is part of the problem. Trying to solve the problems of implementation after the law, structure, and blueprint of an undertaking are already decided is too late. Such a mindset is the cause of many failures of large undertakings. Successful execution begins at the idea phase, not during implementation. The map helps to visualize execution as a continuous process.

Having a map of a public undertaking won't ensure success any more than having a map of Mount Everest will ensure you'll make it to the top.

FIGURE I-2

Marshall Plan process map view 1

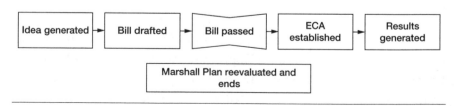

FIGURE I-3

Marshall Plan process map view 2

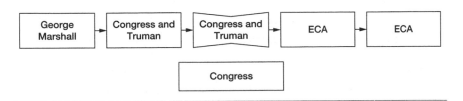

A map can help, but skill is needed every step along the way. After all, it wasn't the map itself, but the execution of each step along the journey that made the Marshall Plan a great accomplishment. Without execution, the Marshall Plan would have been just another forgotten flourish in a speech. But thanks to skillful execution, the Marshall Plan actually accomplished what it set out to do. It changed the world.

What the map does is provide a framing tool for visualizing the journey from idea to results, enabling those engaged in public undertakings to prepare for the rigors of the journey. Combined with the insights from the examples in this book, the map can help those who travel along this treacherous terrain to know what sort of challenges they can expect along the way.

The Seven Deadly Traps

If every public effort were as successful as the Marshall Plan, this book wouldn't be necessary. What our analysis showed is that the potential for failure lurks at every phase along the journey to success. In researching hundreds of large undertakings, we identified seven recurring pitfalls, traps that can bedevil any significant change effort in the public sector. Unfortunately, these traps do not announce themselves with trumpets blaring. The most dangerous aspects of the journey come from the hidden snares embedded in the terrain of the public sector.

The Tolstoy Trap. It was Leo Tolstoy who popularized the notion that we see only what we are looking for, often while staying blind to what is really in front of us. Our preexisting mental maps prompt us all—liberals and conservatives, businessmen and bureaucrats—to discover in the world exactly what we expect to find. The Tolstoy syndrome causes enormous problems in execution. *The Tolstoy Trap most often occurs at the idea phase.*

The Design-Free Design Trap. Many large public failures are rooted in a failure of policy design. Why? Many legislators and other public officials don't see the legislative process as a design process. Most policy ideas go straight from the idea stage to drafting of legislation without ever going through the exacting design process and business case analysis that occurs for nearly every good or service launched in the private sector. Overcoming this trap requires a fundamentally different mindset, one based on designing policy for implementation first and foremost and passage through the legislature second. *The Design-Free Design Trap most often occurs at the design phase.*

The Stargate Trap. This trap, which refers to the democratic commitment point, separates the "political" universe of policy development from the "bureaucratic" universe of implementation. The trap is the distortion effect created by this unique phase—the most unpredictable stage of the journey. The risk is that your idea never makes it through the Stargate or is so distorted that the initiative will never achieve the intended results. The challenge is to get through with your integrity intact, your idea recognizable, and a design that can actually be implemented. *The Stargate Trap occurs only at the Stargate phase and is particularly challenging in the public sector.*

The Overconfidence Trap. Despite what you may hear from many politicians, failure is always an option. Those who fall into the Overconfidence Trap dismiss those who advise caution, consider only the best-case scenario, and plan with unrealistic budgets and impossible time lines. The best way to avoid the Overconfidence Trap is to take the possibility of failure seriously—and take precautions to avoid it. *The Overconfidence Trap can occur anywhere but most often arises during the implementation phase.*

The Sisyphus Trap. Like the mythical Sisyphus, those in government face a daunting uphill fight. The Sisyphus Trap is the distinctive interaction between the uniquely challenging public sector operating system and the people who work in government. Though understanding the systems of government is critical to success, we also need to understand the people rolling the boulder up the hill, particularly how their behaviors are shaped by the culture in which they toil. *The Sisyphus Trap can arise anywhere, but problems most commonly arise at the results phase.*

The Complacency Trap. In our modern world, conditions change fast, but democracy changes slowly. The result is that programs need regular reevaluation. In some cases *what* is being done no longer makes sense. In other cases, *how* it is being done no longer makes sense. Too often, the way things are becomes a barrier to needed changes, particularly in the way the public sector deals with risk. *The Complacency Trap occurs in the reevaluation phase.*

The Silo Trap. Each of the traps described so far roughly corresponds to a phase of the journey to success. The Silo Trap, in contrast, is the failure to fit all the pieces together. Countless public undertakings underperform because participants fail to see the end-to-end process of reaching a result as a set of interdependent steps, and they behave accordingly. *The Silo Trap arises throughout the journey from idea to results.*

These seven deadly traps can make the journey to success in the public sector feel like an Indiana Jones movie, as Indy bravely travels the globe in search of the Golden Idol of the Chachapoyan Temple. (Forgive the hokey comparison.) Though public officials, like Indiana Jones, might have a map to help them know where to go, that doesn't mean they won't have challenges along the way. The Golden Idol will doubtless be guarded by booby traps and snares, and Indy's greatest gift is his ability to expect the unexpected. He is at once both a romantic and a cynic, enabling him to retain his idealism while avoiding overconfidence. If it ever looks like he can just walk up and grab the idol, he pauses, wondering where the poison darts might come from or what huge rock is going to drop on his head. The corpses of earlier idol seekers that litter his path heighten his appreciation for the difficulties of the journey.

This book is intended to assist those who are seeking the elusive treasure of public sector results. We approach this task with great humility.

With over forty years of combined experience in and around the public sector, we know that government is too large and too complex to yield its secrets easily. Between us, we have worked for the federal government, run four agencies in two different states, and served as a local elected official—and have the scars to prove it. We have seen the good, the bad, and the ugly, and we have known both success and disappointment. We have great appreciation for those who serve in the public sector, and a great appreciation for how challenging—and frustrating—working in government can be. We don't claim to have all the answers, but the stories in the book are intended to illuminate these hidden traps and offer some strategies for overcoming them.

The Delicious Cause of Cholera in London

The traps are hidden. The system is invisible. You can't touch a process. It's often hard to detect the factors that make executing a large initiative in the public sector so difficult, and often so deadly.

What you can't see can indeed hurt you. In the mid-1800s, public officials in London were confronted with a deadly outbreak of cholera.[17] At the time, London was filled with the noxious odors of human and animal waste, as well as the fumes from various primitive manufacturing facilities scattered throughout the city. The dominant theory at the time linked cholera to these malodorous fumes. The "miasma theory" held that diseases such as cholera and the Black Death were caused by a noxious form of "bad air." This theory makes a certain amount of intuitive sense—bad-smelling things can indeed make you sick. The pattern of those contracting cholera, however, didn't match the theory. It wasn't until Dr. John Snow and others made a systematic analysis of who was getting the disease that a competing theory was developed. Snow literally mapped out the address of every cholera victim, which allowed him to discover a pattern. He came to believe that cholera was caused by drinking from a public water pump on Broad Street. This theory initially seemed absurd to public officials—the water from the Broad Street pump was clear and delicious, regarded by many as the best-tasting water in London. As evidence accumulated, however, Dr. Snow convinced officials to shut down the pump. Excavation subsequently revealed that the well's wall had been breached, allowing raw human sewage to contaminate the water. It took an overwhelming accumulation of additional evidence for officials to abandon their miasma theory, but Snow's insistence on a hidden cause proved correct. Only when the correct underlying cause had been discovered could public officials take the appropriate steps to combat the deadly disease. Cleaning up the water supply was the answer, not cleaning up the smell.

The bacteria that cause cholera are odorless, colorless, and invisible to the naked eye, but they are real and they are deadly. Today, the systemic causes of public failures—and even of many successes—cannot be seen. Like cholera bacteria, these systemic forces are known only by their effects. People aren't inclined to believe in things they can't see, touch, or smell. But you do believe in gravity, don't you?

Dr. Snow solved the cholera problem by relying on data and evidence. He openly challenged the prevailing theory of the time, demonstrating it was only that, a theory. It was his systemic study of where London households got their drinking water that enabled him to uncover both the cause and the cure for the cholera epidemic. Snow in his method could be considered an early practitioner of forensic science, long before this problem-solving method was popularized by crime shows such as *CSI*, *Law & Order*, and *Cold Case*.

In conducting our research for this book, we've adopted a similar line of attack to unearth the hidden pitfalls that plague public projects as well as discover the success factors of great achievements. Eschewing a partisan or ideological line, we've tried instead to approach our task like detectives or forensic scientists. We asked questions that forced us to probe beneath the surface: Why was the acid rain emissions trading program such a success while similar approaches have so often disappointed? How did the mayor of London gain support for a controversial transportation plan, and how did he manage its successful implementation? What did California's legislature miss when it *unanimously* passed a restructuring of the electricity market that quickly proved disastrous? What enabled NASA to successfully manage complex networks of contractors, while contracting arrangements on the Big Dig and in Iraq proved problematic?

This book will enhance your understanding of the journey to success, and being aware of the seven deadly traps should be a big help in any large public undertaking. But don't expect miracles. There are no guarantees, no magic formulas, no sure-fire recipes for success. Large government undertakings are hard, and a healthy respect for the challenges along the road is essential. This book will make your journey to success a little easier by showing how difficult it is. As the Zen master says, "If you meet the Buddha on the road, kill him." That is, anyone offering all the answers in a neat package isn't telling you the truth.

We begin by looking at something invisible: an idea.

CHAPTER 1

The Tolstoy Trap

You'll See It When You Believe It

Idea → Design → Stargate → Implementation → Results
(←——————— Reevaluation ———————→)

CHAPTER GUIDE

- The Idea of an Idea
- Dick Nixon: Tire Rationer, Inflation Fighter
- Whip Inflation Now
- The Tolstoy Syndrome
- Health Care Reform in Massachusetts: The Meeting of the Minds
- Pearls of Wisdom from the Cyber Mob
- The Opposite of an Idea
- Politics, Economics, and the Copenhagen Consensus

A man may die, nations may rise and fall, but an idea lives on.

—JOHN F. KENNEDY

I DEAS MATTER. In ways profound and prosaic, for better or for worse, an idea made into law makes an impact.

What is an idea? The term merits some thought. In the policy world, an idea can refer to an intention ("we should help the homeless"), an action ("we should give every homeless person $500 a month"), or an understanding about how an action will achieve an intention ("if we give homeless people $500 a month, they'll be able to obtain shelter"). In common discourse, these meanings are often conflated, but they are quite different. You could argue that the "idea" laid out for helping the homeless is a mistake based on its intention ("the government shouldn't help the homeless"), on its implementability ("the government won't be able to find the homeless"), or its instrumentality, that is, how well the action will achieve its intention ("giving the homeless $500 each month won't help them since most recipients will spend it on drugs or alcohol").[1]

The debate over what government ought to do and at what level is thus both a philosophical question and a pragmatic one. A philosophical objection to a policy requires no facts, only beliefs. This observation in no way belittles philosophy. If you object to the idea of treating people of different races differently, or in fact believe that we are all members of a single human race, then you don't have to consider how well government could implement Jim Crow laws or whether they would achieve their vile goal. You can oppose Jim Crow laws on principle.

This chapter isn't about philosophy, however. Our goal is not to advance a particular set of policy ideas or promote a particular political agenda.

Instead, this book looks at ideas from a process perspective, focusing on the practical question of whether an idea is implementable and efficacious. From a process perspective, it is these second-order ideas, ideas about how government works and how the world works, that determine whether a policy idea put into practice will be successful or not. An examination of this nature does depend on facts.

Unfortunately, "facts" do not speak for themselves. Too often, evidence that doesn't fit our preconceived notions about the world is ignored. The Tolstoy syndrome is the biggest trap at this phase of the journey, and it can blind us to the inconvenient facts right in front of us.

In the next few pages, you'll read about America's losing battle against inflation in the 1970s. Everyone agreed on the need to fix the problem, and dramatic federal actions were taken—but inflation only got worse. The failure wasn't due to some bureaucratic implementation snafu. Rather, the fundamental ideas about what caused inflation and what government could do about it were mistaken, and the process in place to test these ideas was nonexistent. As a result, those at the highest levels of government expended incredible effort, yet ended up causing more harm than good. The story of the war on inflation demonstrates the importance of a robust ideation process to the success of large undertakings.

Dick Nixon: Tire Rationer, Inflation Fighter

Upon taking office in 1969, President Richard Nixon inherited from his predecessor the war in Vietnam and the War on Poverty. He soon found himself embroiled in a third war, a war on inflation. This battle would be fought not with guns or programs, but through the realm of ideas.

For most of the 1960s, inflation had been low, usually less than 2 percent a year. In the late 1960s, however, inflation briefly climbed above 6 percent, and into 1970 and 1971 persisted at between 4 and 6 percent—higher than the early 1960s but a far cry from runaway inflation. Nonetheless, at the time inflation was viewed with great alarm, and there was great demand for government to "do something" about it. What Congress decided to do was put the problem on the president's plate. In 1970, Congress passed the Economic Stabilization Act, which gave President Nixon extraordinary powers, including the authority to stabilize wages, prices, rents, interest rates, and dividends, as well as civil and criminal enforcement powers.[2] The only thing Congress didn't give Nixon was a cape and a pair of tights, which definitely would have been a bad idea. In retrospect, it was probably a mistake to grant any single individual that much control over the economy, let alone a man known as Tricky Dick.

The Economic Stabilization Act didn't require Nixon to actually do anything. It merely granted the president vast, probably unconstitutional authority. How and if he used these powers was up to him. During the 1968 campaign, Nixon had criticized the idea of wage and price controls, saying they "can never be administered equitably and are not compatible with a free economy."[3]

Ironically, Nixon was one of the few Americans with firsthand experience implementing price controls. During World War II, before joining the navy, Nixon had served as an attorney in the tire division of the Office of Price Administration.[4] In 1983, Nixon reflected on his thrilling experience as a tire-rationing bureaucrat:

> It seemed to me that, as I was in government and saw what they did, that it was very important not to have government run things . . . I mean, the way they seemed to really delight in turning down some poor guy at a service station and so forth when he'd write in about his tires that he needed for his ration . . . It gave me a very good feeling about why government should be limited to what is necessary and what it really can do and not be expanded.[5]

President Nixon initially resisted the temptation to use his powers. As time passed, demands for him to use his expanded authority grew stronger. Resisting temptation, unfortunately, wasn't Nixon's strong suit, and in August 1971 he took the dramatic step of announcing a ninety-day freeze on wages and prices—an unprecedented measure for America during peacetime.

And so, on August 15, 1971, the Cost of Living Council was born. To ensure success, Nixon tapped two promising young conservatives to lead this historic initiative. Donald Rumsfeld, age thirty-nine, would head up the Cost of Living Council. His right-hand man was a thirty-year-old congressional staffer named Dick Cheney. The Cost of Living Council oversaw a host of bureaucratic price control agencies, including the Price

Commission, the Pay Board, the Committee on Interest and Dividends, and the advisory committees on rent, state and local government, and the health services industry. This was a major government foray into every nook and cranny of the economy.

Public response to the initiative was generally favorable. Finally, someone was doing something about inflation. Would it work?

Rumsfeld himself had his doubts. He placed a copy of the Economic Stabilization Act on the floor next to his desk, and every time one of the various boards issued a new regulation, he placed it on top of the law. "Before too long it started working its way up to the ceiling," said Rumsfeld, "as a reminder for everybody for the potential damage we were doing."[6]

In the early days, there was good news: inflation was going down. In December 1971, just a few months after the Cost of Living Council was established, Nixon rushed in to claim credit, saying: "Already their work has produced heartening results. The Consumer Price Index was increasing at an annual rate of a little more than 4 percent during the six months prior to August, but since August it has been cut dramatically to an annual rate of less than 2 percent."[7] President Nixon's claim rested on the unstated logical fallacy known as *post hoc ergo propter hoc* (Latin for "after this, therefore because of this"). Since inflation went down *after* the Cost of Living Council was established, Nixon breezily asserted that inflation went down *because* of the Cost of Living Council.

All politicians like to claim credit when anything good happens, but President Nixon's premature basking in the success of his wage and price controls is simply unpardonable. Within months, inflation was again rising at an alarming rate. Nixon's original ninety-day wage and price freeze morphed into a three-year bureaucratic journey into madness. Rumsfeld's stack of regulations kept getting higher, and so did inflation. Figure 1-1 shows the trajectory of inflation and the impotence of the Cost of Living Council. When Nixon resigned in August of 1974 because of the Watergate scandal, inflation was around 10 percent. The Nixon wage and price program is now universally viewed as an utter fiasco. What went wrong?

The problem wasn't the law's intent. Everyone agrees that holding down inflation is a worthwhile goal. The problem wasn't poor implementation by the bureaucracy—it wasn't as if the boards and commissions

FIGURE 1-1

CPI inflation rate

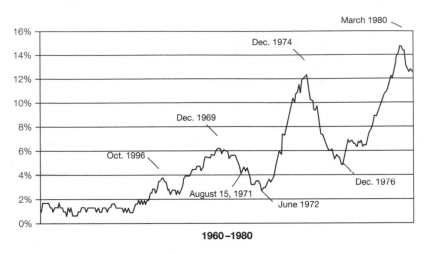

1960–1980

Source: Bureau of Labor Statistics.

didn't set prices at the correct level, or failed to issue regulations fast enough. No, the very idea upon which the law rested was faulty.

On the surface, the idea of wage and price controls seems reasonable. If you want to stop inflation, you need to keep prices from increasing. So why not outlaw price hikes? The idea was flawed in two ways. First, as Nixon knew firsthand and Rumsfeld learned, it is extremely difficult for government to *enforce* wage and price controls. Attempting to track all the wages, prices, and rents for every transaction in a free economy is hardly realistic, which means that enforcement is uneven at best. The idea is thus not especially implementable.

More importantly, however, wage and price controls aren't efficacious. The idea is based on a mistaken belief that inflation is primarily a psychological phenomenon. Upon signing an extension of the wage and price law, Nixon argued that soon "we will see the end of the inflationary psychology that developed in the 1960s, achieve lasting price stability, end controls, and return to reliance on free market forces."[8] But that's not what causes inflation. While expectations play a role, by the early 1970s a wealth of data showed that inflation occurs when government increases the money supply. This idea is known as monetarism, and the idea's primary proponent was economist Milton Friedman. According to Friedman: "Inflation is always and everywhere a monetary phenomenon."[9]

According to Friedman, inflation is neither a psychological phenomenon nor the result of weak character; rather, inflation is a natural consequence of an increase in the money supply, as individuals respond to market signals conveyed through price. In other words, rising prices aren't the cause of inflation; rising prices are a symptom of the inflation of the money supply.[10] Friedman had more than just a theory. He had data, too.[11] But it would be several more years before Friedman's theory would receive a real-world test drive. Meanwhile, the wage and price control idea did not survive its test in the real world.

Whip Inflation Now

Wage and price controls did not control inflation, and when they ended around the time of Nixon's resignation, inflation was hovering around 10 percent. President Gerald Ford, thrust into office by events, would now have to face this daunting economic challenge. Sadly, like Nixon before him, he decided that the cure to inflation was a change in attitude.

In October of 1974, two months after taking office, President Ford gave a nationally televised speech before a joint session of Congress. This was an important speech, coming on the heels of the Watergate scandal. It was Ford's chance to lead the nation as commander in chief in the war on inflation. He used this historic opportunity to urge citizens of the nation to don "WIN" buttons, short for "Whip Inflation Now."

Ford's speech is worth reviewing because it highlights the importance of the hidden, underlying factors that influence behavior. At the beginning of his remarks, Ford makes a critical error:

> *I will not take your time today with the discussion of the origins of inflation . . .*[12]

Why not? Without a clear understanding of what causes inflation, won't it be difficult to evaluate ideas for fixing it? Ford continued:

> *During the meetings on inflation, I listened carefully to many valuable suggestions . . . I have evaluated literally hundreds of ideas, day and night.*

Without a theory as to what caused inflation, Ford simply chose, seemingly at random, a laundry list of cures. In his address, Ford asked Congress and the American people for a bizarre hodgepodge of compulsory and voluntary nostrums, including asking farmers to grow more food, asking everyone to drive 5 percent fewer miles, and asking financial author Sylvia Porter to organize a nationwide volunteer mobilization effort from the White House, "enlisting" citizens willing to wear "WIN" buttons. These ideas, while worthless in combating inflation, had the benefit of being mostly harmless. Ford's next idea, however, was far from harmless. In a move that would forever enshrine the administration in economics textbooks as an example of what not to do, Ford promised to pump more money into an inflationary economy:

> *I have personally been assured by the chairman of the independent Federal Reserve Board that the supply of money and credit will expand sufficiently to meet the needs of our economy and that in no event will a credit crunch occur. The prime lending rate is going down.*

Lacking any understanding as to what was causing inflation, Ford didn't know that this "solution" would be like pouring gasoline on an inflationary fire. The promise of easy money triggered the spontaneous applause of Congress. Ford concluded his momentous speech before the joint session of Congress by noting, "I stand on a spot hallowed by history." He continued:

> *Many presidents have come here many times to solicit, to scold, to flatter, to exhort the Congress to support them in their leadership. Once in a great while, presidents have stood here and truly inspired the most skeptical and the most sophisticated audience of their co-equal partners in government. Perhaps once or twice in a generation is there such a joint session. I don't expect this one to be.*

Like wage and price controls, "WIN" buttons didn't help in curbing inflation, and increasing the money supply made inflation worse. By December 1974, inflation had risen to 12 percent with no relief in sight.

Ford's speech revealed a fundamental misunderstanding about how the world worked. The war on inflation was ultimately a war of ideas, and like Nixon before him, Ford had gone unarmed into battle. He was not alone. Various economic advisers, media pundits, and politicians disagreed about what caused inflation. A national "blamestorming" session attached the blame to the usual suspects—Big Labor, Big Oil, corporate greed, and Wall Street speculators. As is often the case, however, the hidden influence of unseen forces was more important than the visible "culprits." Both Nixon and Ford based their remedies about inflation on the flawed notion that inflation is a psychological phenomenon.

As the 1970s trundled on under the burden of high inflation and high unemployment, Milton Friedman, barely five feet tall, stalked the halls of Capitol Hill like a Yoda with data, hounding policy makers with his argument for monetarism. When Friedman won the Nobel Prize in economics in 1976, it didn't make him any taller, but it greatly enhanced his stature and made it more difficult to overlook the diminutive economist—and his ideas. Slowly, Friedman's argument for monetarism gained currency. At the tail end of the 1970s, Federal Reserve chairman Paul Volcker decided to give Friedman's ideas a chance. The results were not instantaneous, but within a few years inflation was under control. With the idea of monetarism guiding the Federal Reserve, America enjoyed a stable currency, which helped fuel a two-decade run of economic prosperity. Ideas have consequences.

You will notice that the name of Milton Friedman pops up several times in this book. Though often out of the public eye, intellectuals such as Friedman frequently play a key role in shaping policy ideas. John Locke, Adam Smith, and Karl Marx aren't weighing in on issues today, but their beliefs are still informing judgments about the way the world works. John Maynard Keynes, John Kenneth Galbraith, Daniel Patrick Moynihan, Arthur Schlesinger, Friedrich Hayek, and other deep thinkers have all had significant influence on policy by influencing the intellectual climate of their times—and ours. These invisible influencers can be more influential than the politicians who are center stage, acting on their ideas. Far more people have heard of John Kennedy and Richard Nixon than John Maynard Keynes and Milton Friedman. Upon further review, however, the quality of our political ideas may be every bit as important as the quality of our political leaders.

The lessons from the war on inflation apply to a more recent undertaking of government: the economic bailout. Both the $700 billion

Troubled Asset Relief Program (TARP) under President George W. Bush (coincidentally titled the Economic Stabilization Act of 2008) and the $787 billion economic stimulus package under President Barack Obama are based on ideas about the impact these programs will have on the finance sector, the automotive sector, and the economy in general. The lessons of the Great Depression and the ideas of John Maynard Keynes are actively being debated, but the lessons of wage and price controls ought not be forgotten. Then, as now, an urgent problem confronted the nation. Then, as now, Congress granted the president broad authority to deal with it. Then, as now, there was a lack of clarity and consensus around the root cause of the problem. (In January 2009, the Congressional Oversight Panel for TARP asked the Treasury Department to provide an "analysis of the origin of the credit crisis"—after Treasury had already spent $340 billion on a cure.[13]) This is not to say that these more current efforts are doomed, only that the debates surrounding the ideas on which they are based are terribly important, not with respect to intent, but in terms of their implementability and instrumentality. Gerald Ford, after all, was guided by some of the smartest economists of his time. Flawed ideas he adopted from certain economists, however, led to results that were exactly the opposite of those intended. According to Robert J. Samuelson, author of *The Great Inflation and Its Aftermath*: "America's most protracted peacetime inflation was the unintended side effect of policies designed to reduce unemployment and eliminate the business cycle. It was a product of the power of ideas . . . At its base, double-digit inflation was their [economists] doing, a product of their bad ideas."[14]

How could so many have missed the substantial evidence regarding the real cause of inflation? In part because they fell into the most dangerous trap of the idea phase of the journey to results: the Tolstoy Syndrome.

The Tolstoy Syndrome

> *The simplest thing cannot be made clear to the most intelligent man if he is firmly persuaded that he knows already, without a shadow of doubt, what is laid before him.*

—LEO TOLSTOY[15]

Nixon and Ford ignored the inconvenient facts that Milton Friedman placed before them, preferring to believe that wage and price controls or lapel buttons could curb inflation. Managers on the Big Dig ignored inconvenient evidence of a recurring problem with the bolts, preferring to believe sloppy work was the problem. Public health officials in London were so invested in the miasma theory they had a hard time believing that the delicious water from the Broad Street pump was killing people, even when confronted with the facts.

These examples all represent a condition referred to by psychologists as "confirmation bias." It's the cognitive practice of seeking and acknowledging only those facts that confirm an individual's worldview, and of ignoring and dismissing evidence that conflicts with that worldview. The phenomenon of seeing only what you're looking for is also popularly known as the Tolstoy syndrome, named for Count Leo Tolstoy. Tolstoy noted how hard it is for people to accept the most obvious truth if doing so would oblige them "to admit the falsity of conclusions which they have proudly taught to others, and which they have woven, thread by thread, into the fabrics of their life."[16]

Comedian Stephen Colbert captured this phenomenon in 2006 when he roasted President George W. Bush at the White House Correspondents' Dinner with a stinging mock tribute: "The greatest thing about this man is he's steady. You know where he stands. He believes the same thing Wednesday that he believed on Monday—*no matter what happened Tuesday.*"

Facts are digested through each individual's cognitive filter. Consider an instance in which tainted peanuts or toys with high levels of lead make it past government inspectors and onto the shelves, where they then harm consumers. Free market advocates see this and say: "Aha! Look at the failure of government regulatory agencies! And look at how the marketplace economically punishes these companies! Markets work, government doesn't." At the same time, proponents of tighter regulation say: "Aha! Look at the failure of the market! We need a more robust regulatory system to protect us from the predatory practices of profiteers! Government works, markets don't." The same event is seen as confirming two totally opposite theories, because proponents on each side focus only on those aspects of the event that confirm their worldview. It turns out that when

we look at the world, we tend to see what is inside of us. This phenomenon isn't limited to public officials—it happens to all of us. It is the idea
behind the Rorschach test, for example, in which psychiatric patients are
shown an inkblot pattern and asked to describe what they see. As one patient said upon being shown an inkblot, "Look, doc, I didn't come here
to look at dirty pictures." The response reveals more about the patient
than the inkblot.

Too often, policy makers begin with a theory, and then seek the facts
that support the theory while discounting any evidence that does not support that theory. It's the opposite of the scientific method, which requires
looking at all the data, not just some of it. Good scientists approach the
daunting challenge of understanding the universe with great humility.
Theories must be held loosely, to be readily discarded when contradicted
by evidence. When the observable facts fail to support a hypothesis, the
theory gets changed, not the facts.

Most voters also avoid evidence that doesn't fit their beliefs. During
the 2004 presidential race, a team from Emory University led by Professor Drew Westen hooked thirty men up to a brain scan machine and
asked them to assess a number of statements by George W. Bush and John
Kerry. The statements were selected to show each candidate contradicting
themselves. The Republicans were highly critical of Kerry, the Democrats equally so of Bush, and each group let the inconsistencies from their
own candidate slide. No surprise there.

More interesting was the fact that the scans showed that the part of the
brain most associated with reasoning *wasn't even active* when judging the
candidates' statements. Instead, the most active regions of the brain were
those involved in processing emotions and moral judgments. The brain
scans showed that the subjects in the study focused on evidence that made
them emotionally at ease. Dr. Westen summarized the findings:

> *Essentially, it appears as if partisans twirl the cognitive kaleidoscope until
> they get the conclusions they want, and then they get massively reinforced
> for it, with the elimination of negative emotional states and activation of
> positive ones . . . The result is that partisan beliefs are calcified and the per-
> son can learn very little new data.*[17]

It turns out that humans are hard-wired to avoid inconvenient facts.
This result won't shock anyone who has followed national politics over

the past decade or two. For those who don't like having their worldview disturbed—which psychologists tell us is *everybody*—the media make it easy to "massively reinforce" what one already believes. Democrats and liberals have their own television networks (CNN), radio networks (Air America, NPR), Web sites (Huffington Post and Daily Kos), newspapers, and blogs. Likewise, Republicans and conservatives can tune in to their own networks (Fox), radio talk shows (Rush Limbaugh, Laura Ingraham), Web sites (Drudge Report), newspapers, and blogs. It's easier and more comfortable to listen to people who agree with you than to have to sort through competing evidence in an attempt to determine what is really going on—and to acknowledge the very real limitations of those you have identified as "your team."

That's not good news for democracy, which depends on the populace to guide the action of government. When evaluating policy ideas, the Tolstoy syndrome becomes the Tolstoy Trap, and it can cause enormous problems in execution. That's because which policies we choose to pursue are based on ideas about how the world works, and execution depends on the quality of these ideas. The quality of our ideas is diminished when we close off debate with those who disagree with us, when we ignore evidence that challenges our preconceived notions.

Health Care Reform in Massachusetts: The Meeting of the Minds

Both Nixon and Ford pointed out that the wage and price controls of World War II didn't work terribly well. These wartime measures also created a remarkable unintended consequence. During the war, companies couldn't attract talented employees with higher wages, so they began to offer health care benefits as a way to circumvent the rules. The IRS was initially unaware of these benefits and thus didn't tax them, giving companies an even greater incentive to offer benefits rather than wages. The practice became enshrined through tradition, which is partly why most people today purchase health insurance through their employer. Taken on its face, this is a bizarre practice. You don't buy your car or your car insurance through your employer. Do you want your employer having the intimate details of your medical history? Do you want to have to change your doctor when you change jobs? Any politician who wants to reform the existing health care system must contend with these odd practices that stem from the unintended consequences of World War II wage and price controls.[18]

In the fall of 2004, Governor Mitt Romney wanted to address the health care issue, but he had a problem. The November elections had left the Republican governor with just twenty-four Republicans out of a two-hundred-member legislature—two fewer than he started with, leaving him, in his own words, "feeling like a cattle rancher at a vegetarian convention." To make matters worse, speculation had already begun that Romney wouldn't be running for reelection in 2006, marking him as a lame duck. With two years left in office, Romney wanted to make a mark, to create a change of which he could be proud, and if it happened to enhance his national profile, well, that would be okay too. Any reform, however, would need to go through the overwhelmingly Democratic legislature. The journey to success hardly looked promising for Romney.

Some time earlier, Romney had asked his secretary of health and human services to suggest a reform that would address the problem of the uninsured. The secretary convened a group of his senior staff, but when they presented their suggestions for reform, Governor Romney wasn't satisfied. Their recommendations did nothing to alter the institutional, bureaucratic focus that prevailed in programs such as Medicaid, which serves the poor. The health care bureaucracy was locked into the existing framework of hospitals, insurers, and state rate-setting agencies. The reforms suggested by the subject matter experts within the agency were too incremental, and weren't in keeping with Romney's guiding principle of giving greater choice and greater responsibility to individual consumers.

Romney turned the reform effort over to a small policy team and located it within the governor's suite, just steps away from his office. That ruffled some feathers. It also jump-started the effort. Rather than a group steeped in the state's health care culture, this team was composed of "private sector types" from Romney's investment banking circle: Tim Murphy, Kelt Kindick, and Brian Wheelan from J.P. Morgan, Bain & Company, and Harvard Business School, respectively. They brought a different skill set, a different language, and a different perspective to the problem. Shiny wingtips, Ferragamo ties, and PowerPoint decks were the new order of the day. The new policy group didn't have much institutional knowledge, but they were familiar with examining organizational structures and looking at value streams, and were used to dealing with complicated finances.

"Leaders coming into government from the private sector have to appreciate that one thing government does quite well is to collect data. There's tons of it," says Tim Murphy, who would eventually become Romney's secretary of health and human services. "The key is being able to translate that data into usable information. To do that you need to have people who are experienced with analytics, people who understand systems, and who can offer suggestions around process changes. Those skills tend to come from certain training grounds—management consulting, investment banking, operations managers."[19]

Romney's team used these skills to analyze the market: Who was providing what sort of products? How did each industry player make its money? Which consumers were using emergency rooms, and why? They found a vast amount of underanalyzed data buried in various reports. For example, a state agency had done a major survey of the state's uninsured population and come up with a total number of uninsured residents: 460,000. The agency had also gathered reams of additional socioeconomic information regarding age, marital status, language, medical condition, and so forth. Instead of just accepting the top-line number, the team approached it as a business analyst would any consumer population: they did market segmentation. It turned out that the population of 460,000 represented vastly different demographic segments, ranging from healthy young workers who simply didn't bother buying insurance, to the indigent and mentally ill who qualified for Medicaid but had never bothered applying, to the working poor and illegal aliens.

The policy team had the luxury of focusing on the problem exclusively, with no other day-to-day management responsibilities. This gave them the chance to review not only all the data from within Massachusetts, but also to study the literature on health care reform from academics and think tanks. They even looked at the political history of previous reform efforts, including the failed "Hillarycare" effort of the early 1990s. They were determined to learn from prior failures—including their own. Before tackling the health care issue, Romney's policy team had worked on a school construction program. The group had looked at the relevant data, formulated a policy, and then sent it over to the legislature—where it landed with a dull thud. It seems that lawmakers wanted to be involved in the process. This time, the team would reach out early and often, approaching the health care reform effort with an open mind and an open process, while still adhering to Governor Romney's guiding principles.

After compiling a set of eye-opening data, Murphy and the health policy SWAT team set up dozens of meetings with all the key players in the health care arena: advocacy groups, insurers, hospitals, doctor groups, and legislators. Many were prepared to be hostile to Romney and his team. Instead of coming in with a plan, however, the team came in to share information and to listen. Romney's team presented its data and then probed for a response: Does this sound right to you? Are we missing any key factors in our analysis? What are your biggest concerns?

Early on, before there was a firm policy design, the team tested the idea of market-based reform in the same way Secretary of State George Marshall had floated the idea of aid to Europe—no specifics, just a general concept to gauge response. Market-based reform wasn't always in the playbook of the interest groups. Nonetheless, the response showed that these interest groups were willing to accept the approach if it had certain features. They were willing to work with political leaders from the "other team" in part because they were afraid that if they didn't, nothing would be achieved. "Nobody ever complains about being invited to a meeting at the governor's office," says Murphy. Particularly in the face of ideological differences, proactively reaching out, sharing information, and asking intelligent questions helps break down preconceived notions. Sharing promotes trust.

"Don't be afraid of information that conflicts with your preconceived notions," advises Murphy. "Also, don't be afraid of those people who are likely to disagree with you. Be open to alternative ways of defining your problem and developing various approaches." In other words, take steps to avoid the Tolstoy syndrome. Murphy says:

We purposely put ourselves in the firing line with people who viewed us with great skepticism. We had to gain credibility with them early on. We wanted them to have confidence that we understood their business, and that we weren't married to any particular solution. We wanted them to have a personal relationship and an open line of communication with us, to make them comfortable. "After every meeting, we'd debrief. What did we learn that we didn't know before? What adjustments can we make to accommodate this group's concerns? After a while, you start to gain confidence that the plan you are formulating is robust, that it makes sense."

Romney's team sought to develop the idea collaboratively, not collectively. Too often, collective decision making is a recipe for gridlock, epitomized by the much-derided "blue-ribbon task force" composed of fifty different interest groups. "A meeting with fifty people never allows individuals to be intellectually honest, and that's essential to developing a sound approach," says Murphy. Collaborative decision making, in contrast, means developing an idea by involving those who have a stake in the outcome. It does not require reaching consensus—which is a good thing, since very few transformative changes can be arrived at through consensus. Change is difficult. Individuals in impacted groups often have a lot riding on the status quo. Ultimately, significant change will yield winners and losers. But a collaborative approach gives interested parties a way to gain adjustments that make sense.

After Romney's policy team had vetted all the information and developed an idea in concept, they briefed the governor. Was he comfortable with the approach that was emerging? Yes. Soon thereafter, the governor began giving a series of speeches, not pronouncing "Here's my health care solution," but rather, "Here's what we are finding on health care, and here's what the legislature and I need to be thinking about." There was no grand unveiling of "Governor Romney's plan." Rather, Romney was preparing the ground, educating the press, and putting the issue on the agenda of lawmakers. If Romney wasn't ready to share in the success of reform, there wouldn't be any success to share.

Without question, the ideas being discussed represented a radical departure from previous practices anywhere in the United States. For the first time in American history, a state would require people to obtain health insurance. The state would fully cover the indigent and subsidize low-wage workers, but virtually every resident of Massachusetts would have to get insured or face stiff tax consequences. (The mandate existed in part to ensure that individuals couldn't game the system by signing up for insurance only after becoming sick.) The state also established a health care "connector" to enable unaffiliated individuals to purchase at group rates. This wasn't a warm cup of tea. This was strong medicine.

The legislature was coming around. In addition to the policy team's inclusive approach, it turns out lawmakers had 385 million reasons to consider Romney's idea. Medicaid is a federal-state program, and Massachusetts was operating under a special waiver that was set to expire, meaning $385 million in federal funds would disappear unless a new approach could be developed. This was the "burning platform" that would provide the political pressure for radical change. As the waiver deadline loomed, Governor Romney and Senator Ted Kennedy jointly asked the federal government to extend the waiver for one year. There is agreement on the basic idea, they said, but we need time to hammer out the details. Tommy Thompson, then secretary of health and human services, agreed to the extension.

Romney's market-based "idea" for health care reform now entered the design phase. The legislation Romney proposed to the legislature did not survive intact. When the legislature sent back a new version, Romney vetoed two sections, including a tax on businesses, but his vetoes were overridden. The resulting legislation was not the ideologically pure vision of any single person, including the governor, but it did conform to Romney's desire for greater individual choice and greater individual responsibility. Romney and his Democratic counterparts in the legislature, notably House speaker Sal DiMasi and Senate president Robert Travaglini, chose to behave as principled pragmatists, accepting compromise in exchange for accomplishment.

Romney signed the legislation in a grand ceremony at Boston's Faneuil Hall, where revolutionary firebrands had once exhorted Bostonians to shatter the status quo of a different sort. Romney was flanked by a slew of Democrats, including Ted Kennedy, on the same stage where the two had squared off in debate during a Senate race twelve years earlier. When Romney scratched his signature on the parchment, an idea had become reality. If Romney had to share center stage with old foes, at least he had a reason for being on stage in the first place.

Is it a good idea? Will it work? It may take years to answer those questions. Some object to the reform in principle, either because it fails to deliver "free" health care to everyone or because it forces people to buy something they may not want. Most people, however, are willing to see how it plays out before rendering a verdict. The truth is, no one knows for certain how individuals, health insurers, and businesses will behave under the new rules. Success or failure hinges on how unpredictable humans will behave under new circumstances, as well as how capably a new state bureaucracy implements the reforms. One thing is certain. This idea-turned-into-reality will provide a learning opportunity, a chance for others to see how Massachusetts's mandates will perform in the proving fire of real-life experiences. This idea is getting a test run in the real world because Romney and his policy team beat the Tolstoy syndrome, inviting those with differing views to help nurture an idea.

Pearls of Wisdom from the Cyber Mob

What if Starbucks used ice cubes made of coffee in their iced coffee drinks? That way, as you got toward the bottom and the ice melted, the drink wouldn't get all watered down. Don't you think that would be a good idea? Wouldn't you like to tell Starbucks about it?

You don't have to. A Web site run by Starbucks inviting customer input has already come up with the coffee ice cube idea, and more than two thousand customers have "voted" for it as something they'd like to see happen. Some bloggers on the site have identified some implementation challenges—the fact that the ice comes from an ice machine, not little plastic trays, for example. "There are too many drinks to have different ice cubes for," notes "Eclectek," an anonymous blogger who no doubt has spent some time as a barista. By tapping into the passion of their customers and employees, Starbucks not only has a source of new ideas, but a way to gauge these new ideas through online voting. Who knew that people wanted a coffee-based energy drink? People did. They told Starbucks, and now Starbucks sells a tasty blend of coffee, B-vitamins, guarana, and ginseng in a snazzy fifteen-ounce can.

Welcome to Web 2.0, the online networking world that enhances creativity and interactivity between users (of almost anything) and providers (of almost everything). Web 2.0 takes advantage of the low cost of Internet technologies, including blogs, wikis, discussion groups, and voting tools, to capture the "wisdom of the crowds" and bring "small d" democracy to the marketplace.[20] Historically it would have required costly test marketing and focus groups to hear what people wanted. Now, the voice of the people can be heard in cyberspace, and the people are saying, "Make me a coffee-based energy drink. With guarana."

In the public sector, one of the early pioneers in this movement to tap into the wisdom of crowds is the U.S. Transportation Security Agency. "We are interested in your innovative technology and security ideas, products and services," reads TSA's Web site, "Evolution of Security." The site captures and, in a moderated format, posts complaints from travelers. Not only does it provide managers a source of ideas for improvement, it also creates a form of frontier justice through which various airports and regions can be compared, albeit imprecisely. Frequent flyers weigh in on which airports do security right and complain about the ones that don't.

In its initial years, TSA earned a reputation for what could charitably be described as inflexibility. ("Pardon me, Sister, could you please get out of your wheelchair and step behind the curtain for me?") Not privy to the security concerns behind the regulations, the average traveler perceived many of TSA's procedures as nonsensical, providing fodder for late-night comedians. TSA wanted to change that reputation.

Through Web 2.0, TSA discovered that America's road warriors have some pretty good ideas. One blogger, a business traveler frustrated after being stuck behind a mom frantically trying to herd several toddlers through a metal detector, offered an idea. Ski slopes have different trails for experts and beginners. Why not airline security lines? TSA liked the idea and decided to test it. A few months later, several airports rolled out designated "Black Diamond" lanes for "expert travelers," as well as lanes for "casual travelers" and travelers with special needs. People can self-select the line that best fits their profile. "You have to see it to believe it," says Kip Hawley, TSA's former administrator. "It has improved the flow and calm at the checkpoints."[21] The expert lanes move about thirty to forty percent faster than the average lanes, improving the overall throughput. Says Lee Kair, TSA's federal security director in Orlando: "People can go through with the least amount of aggravation."[22]

Through the "Evolution of Security" Web site, airline passengers have an opportunity to dialogue with bloggers from TSA—not PR flacks but real people with full-time jobs on the front lines of airport security; people like TSA blogger Jay, a former high school football coach who is now a federal security director. "The blog is intended to bridge the gap with people who have legitimate issues with the TSA," Jay blogged. "There's no doubt some people have had a bad experience with the TSA. Our job is to fix what's broken, but hey let's face it—security is a tough business. There's an old saying, 'Security is a great thing . . . until it applies to me.' "[23] The Evolution of Security site offers TSA employees a chance to educate the public, to explain why taking your shoes off may not be as silly as it seems.

The public also has a chance to educate the TSA, even if that education is sometimes a bit harsh. "Passengers are going to insult you whether they have the blog or not, so you might as well learn from what they are saying and get some constructive comments," says Stephen Goldsmith, a professor at Harvard's Kennedy School of Government.[24] This kind of raw, unfiltered information from customers and employees is both the most difficult feedback to accept and the most illuminating.

Beating the Tolstoy syndrome is all about confronting information that makes you uncomfortable, and Web 2.0 is a great way to make yourself uncomfortable.

TSA didn't stop there with its use of Web 2.0. The TSA has forty-three thousand workers on the front line. They have ideas about how both they and TSA headquarters could do their work better. TSA created an internal Web site called "Idea Factory" that uses a wiki platform to allow TSA management to tap into that pool of wisdom. The Idea Factory has become kind of a supersized brainstorming session where TSA's leadership can put out questions to the organization: "How can we improve morale?" "How can we improve the check-in process?" "What should our new uniforms look like?" The Idea Factory allows leadership to get unfiltered, unsolicited ideas from the front lines. No doubt some of these ideas make TSA management a tad uncomfortable. It's worth it. Six months after launching the Idea Factory, more than twenty TSA policies had been changed in response to employee suggestions.

While these mechanisms generally provide incremental improvement, the cumulative effect of this technology creates a revolutionary shift in the relationship between citizens and government, between government and its work force, and between various government agencies. It enables government to "reboot the public square" and engage different communities— both physical and virtual—in solving tough problems. Explains Valerie Lemmie, the board chair of the National Academy of Public Administration:

> *We unwittingly pushed citizens out of the public square. We did this not out of spite or meanness or because of any lack of confidence in citizens, but rather because we honestly believed we could and should fix their problems. Our generation of public servants strongly believed and still believes that government should work for the people, but we did not really understand that we also needed to work with the people. The truth is today's challenges are too big for government to solve alone. It is time to re-engage citizens in the work of government to solve the "wicked" problems of our times.*[25]

A popular song warns that we've been "looking for love in all the wrong places." Have we been looking for ideas in all the wrong places, too?

The Opposite of an Idea

Imagine you are Indiana Jones. You are looking for the fabled "Great Gem of an Idea," and you find yourself in a room with two exit doors. One is marked "Idea" and the other is marked "The Opposite of an Idea." Which door do you choose?

Looking behind familiar doors for new ideas is the very trap we want to avoid. On the journey from idea to results, "The Opposite of an Idea" is a result. So, if you are looking for a great idea, don't look for an idea. Instead, look for a great result, and behind it you will undoubtedly find the great idea you seek.

That's the concept behind the X PRIZE, a groundbreaking, privately funded initiative that seeks to discover great ideas by rewarding great results. The first X PRIZE of $10 million was awarded in 2004 to the first team to launch a spacecraft capable of carrying three people to a height 100 kilometers above the earth's surface, twice within two weeks. Some twenty-six teams from seven nations combined to invest more than $100 million in pursuit of the $10 million prize, helping to jump-start the private space flight industry.[26] Current X PRIZES include $10 million for a 100-miles-per-gallon car, and a $30 million prize for the first privately funded team who can land a robot on the moon, collect some dirt, and return to Earth. Rather than investing in promising ideas, the X PRIZE pays off for successful results.

Private prize money spurring rapid innovation is not new. In 1919, hotelier Raymond Orteig offered a prize of $25,000 for the first team to fly a plane nonstop from New York to Paris. This prize encouraged a number of groups to compete, leading to research and development expenses far in excess of the prize money. Charles Lindbergh famously won the competition by landing the *Spirit of St. Louis* in Paris on May 21, 1927. (Just two weeks later, even before Lindbergh had collected his prize money, another unlucky team managed to fly not one but *two* people from New York to Germany, but nobody remembers those guys.[27]) Lindbergh's success helped spur massive interest in aviation. As the X PRIZE folks are quick to point out, Lindbergh's single-pilot, single-engine approach was scoffed at—until it worked.

The federal government spends a lot of money on research, more than $137 billion a year, both through federal research facilities such as the National Institutes of Health and through support of university research.[28] Paying for research, however, can be a very inefficient way for government to get what it really wants: results.

Until recently, government has been the only way to bring serious sums of money to bear on serious problems. Not so today. The mission of the X PRIZE Foundation is "to bring about radical breakthroughs for the benefit of humanity." A bold goal for a private charity, but with heavy hitters including Google cofounders Sergey Brin and Larry Page, the X PRIZE can bring significant resources to bear on their mission. Similarly, the Bill and Melinda Gates Foundation, with an endowment of $37 billion, can sponsor initiatives more often associated with the public sector, such as tackling AIDS in Africa, world hunger, and reform of America's urban education system.

Consider what Vivek Kundra, then the chief technology officer of Washington, D.C., did in 2008 with a program called "Apps for Democracy." Frustrated with the costly and failure-prone software-procurement process, Kundra literally put data in the hands of the people. After making millions of public records accessible on the D.C. Web site, Kundra held a contest and invited anybody to solve any problem they wanted solved. The best programs, as judged by a panel, would be eligible for prize money totaling $50,000. Anyone could compete—companies, schools, teenagers living in their mother's basement. The only rule was that the application had to have an open source license—meaning that anyone would have access to the design code in full.

The results were astounding. For $50,000, the district got over $2 million worth of new, useful software applications in just thirty days. The new tools included everything from "BanksNearMeRightNow," which takes GPS information from your mobile phone and tells you where the closest banks are, to iLive.at, which takes any address in the district and provides a raft of valuable information on everything from crime rates to the nearest post office to neighborhood demographics.

In addition to the benefit of these new applications, the contest showcased a new way of thinking about public data, and about the relationship between government and its citizens.

"All interesting developments today are occurring at the intersection of disciplines—math and philosophy, for example, or crime and public health," says Kundra. "So we wanted to allow creative people out there to take our raw data and create usable information in a context that makes sense to them."[29]

Being open to new sources of thinking is critical for a variety of reasons, not the least of which is that experts often get things very wrong. Being deeply steeped in knowledge about the way things are had made it difficult for the health care experts working for Governor Romney to envision radical change—it took newcomers to the problem to accomplish that. University of California, Berkeley psychologist Philip Tetlock asked 284 people who made a living commenting on political or economic trends, commonly known as "pundits," to make predictions about a series of future events.[30] The result: these experts performed worse than random chance. Even more surprisingly, the more famous the pundit, the less accurate the predictions. "The dominant danger [for pundits] remains hubris, the vice of closed-mindedness, of dismissing dissonant possibilities too quickly," writes Tetlock. They become "prisoners of their preconceptions."[31]

The CIA and larger intelligence community have learned this the hard way. Their experts have struggled to foresee dramatic changes, such as the fall of the Berlin Wall. Explains Mike Wertheimer, assistant deputy director and chief technology officer of the Office of the Director of National Intelligence for Analysis:

> *Ask three groups of people to predict an event—say, "what is going to happen to Cuba after Castro dies?" First ask the Cuban experts—the people who have studied this problem forever. Then ask really smart people with no Cuba experience. Then just take a random sampling of people. Who does the best job of prediction? The answer is smart people with no experience, followed by the average person, and in last place are the experts. Why? The experts are anchored to the past. Their thinking about tomorrow is determined by everything that preceded it. And as a result they never predict change . . .When smart people just look at the data, they are more creative.*[32]

Today, even the most unlikely individuals can create dramatic changes that rival governments' efforts to deal with intractable issues. The microcredit revolution is a good example. For decades, the governments of advanced nations have been sending aid to the developing world in an effort to foster economic growth. The result of all that aid has been disappointing, at times even counterproductive. Then an obscure professor with a small idea stood conventional banking wisdom on its head.

In 1976, Muhammad Yunus founded Grameen Bank and began offering women tiny loans to enable them to establish themselves in self-employment—a small loan to buy raw materials to sew into salable clothing, for example, or other humble enterprises. The bank requires no paperwork and no collateral, and extends credit only to the poorest of borrowers. There is, in fact, no legal instrument between bank and borrower. Loan amounts are very small, often less than $100. As an idea, this must have sounded ridiculous, either in terms of making a profit or in terms of boosting the economy. In the rural villages of the third world, however, this idea proved to be wildly successful. Today, the Grameen

Bank has loaned $5 billion to more than 5 million families in rural Bangladesh. In 2006, Yunus and the Grameen Bank shared the Nobel Peace Prize "for their efforts to create economic and social development from below." The idea of microcredit has become a major force for economic development in the poorest regions of the world.

There are too many big challenges out there. Finding and nurturing good policy ideas should no longer be considered the job of the public sector alone.

Politics, Economics, and the Copenhagen Consensus

Economics teaches that want is infinite, while resources are limited. In this particular, the dismal science appears to be correct. Experience confirms an enduring mismatch between what we would like to do and what we can afford. Politicians are inundated by advocates seeking funds for early childhood education, the homeless, the environment, cancer research—you name it. In every instance, the argument is framed as, "This is something worth investing in." Rarely is the case made that "this is a more worthwhile investment than these other proposals." The reality is that many worthwhile causes are in competition, yet rarely are they compared against one another. The result is that political influence trumps sound judgment as the best-organized groups get their funding regardless of merit.

Recognizing this incongruity, in 2002 Danish economist Bjørn Lomborg, who hails from the left-of-center part of the political spectrum, brought together a group of distinguished economists, many of them Nobel laureates, to the Consensus Center at the Copenhagen Business School to apply a cost-benefit analysis to various approaches to world problems. The question addressed by the gathering was this: Given $75 billion to spend over four years, what public investments would do the most good for the most people? The approach taken by economists to this question proved to be eye-opening, and as a result the Copenhagen Consensus Center is now a think tank that studies the best ways for governments and philanthropists to spend aid and development money.

The idea is simple, yet often neglected; when financial resources are limited,
it is necessary to prioritize the effort. Every day, policymakers and business

leaders at all levels prioritize by investing in one project instead of another.
However, instead of being based on facts, science, and calculations, many
vital decisions are based on political motives or even the possibility of media
coverage.

The Copenhagen Consensus approach improves knowledge and gives
an overview of research and facts within a given problem, which means that
the prioritization is based on evidence.[33]

The priorities that tend to make it to the top of the list typically aren't
the marquee causes that capture celebrity endorsements. In 2008, the center's top ten priorities included mundane-sounding ideas like fortifying
children's diets with salt and iron and a school-based deworming program.
While these ideas might not be very sexy, the economists found that they
had very high payoffs. For example, just $60 million spent on providing vi-
tamin A and zinc supplements for those two years of age and under in sub-
Saharan Africa and south Asia would generate annual economic benefits
(from lower mortality and improved health) of more than $1 billion.[34] Ex-
plains Lomborg, "Focusing first on costs and benefits means that we can
reconsider the merits of policies that have gone out of fashion," such as pu-
rifying drinking water and fighting tuberculosis. In contrast, though concern for global warming is a hot issue, the Consensus Center economists
determined that spending money curbing or mitigating emissions wasn't a
good investment—the likely benefits didn't justify the costs.[35] A better payoff would come from spending money helping people adapt to the impacts
of warming. This unsolicited input from economists can help politicians as
they sort out which ideas to pursue and which to forgo—as long as they
are willing to listen. Explains Lomborg:

The essential thing is that this is a process that doesn't just make it easier
for you to confirm your preconceived notions, but it gives you an opportunity
to see what some of the best experts on all these issues come up with . . . [It
is] not about what's fashionable. It's not just about what looks good on TV.
It's about making sure we reveal lots of hidden, reclusive, not very publicized
issues that we should be listening to.[36]

Overcoming the Tolstoy syndrome is all about listening. If we think
we know the answer, we close off avenues of exploration. We ignore

evidence that conflicts with our theories. We don't invite people with different skill sets to apply their unique combination of knowledge, wisdom, and experience to work with us. Beating the Tolstoy syndrome means breaking across all kinds of boundaries: professional, psychological, organizational. It means economists weighing in on world hunger, management consultants reforming health care, and a university professor revolutionizing economic development in the third world. It means letting your customers design your products, letting frontline workers set your policies, and letting the private sector help solve public problems. It means the federal government allowing a state to experiment, it means Republicans working with Democrats, and it means someone having the courage to tell the president that lapel buttons are *not* going to whip inflation, not now, not ever.

In sum, beating Tolstoy syndrome is no ski ride down the bunny slope. It's the only way to successfully get through the idea phase, however, so you can tackle the next challenge on your journey: the design phase.

FIELD GUIDE: IDEA PHASE

The challenge in the idea stage is to break free of bias and invite new voices into the idea generation and selection process.

Biggest Danger

The Tolstoy Syndrome. Also known as confirmation bias, it means looking only at evidence that confirms your view of the world.

Guiding Principles

Fight confirmation bias. Embrace the ethos of the scientific method. Don't ignore data that contradicts your preconceived notions. Actively test your idea with skeptics. Be data driven, and eschew policy making by ideology.

Find the right, *diverse* people: Look to other fields and disciplines. Subject matter experts should be joined with systems thinkers and other smart people with diverse interests—artists, scientists, and engineers. If your problem is in transportation, ask, How can I involve nontransportation people in my problem? An *interdisciplinary* team might include management consultants, investment bankers, and anthropologists.

Expand the idea pool. The technologies of Web 2.0 make it easier than ever to tap into the potential of large numbers of "experts"—the customers and workers closest to the problem.

Reach across boundaries. There are no such things as Republican ideas or Democratic ideas. An idea doesn't care if it came from an economist, a public manager, or a politician.

Find areas of agreement. Can't agree on a solution? Bring opponents together to agree on data. Make sure you understand the concerns of others. Listen. Role play and articulate the views of others until they know you understand their position. Shift from position bargaining to interest bargaining. Have stakeholders illustrate their view of what stands in the way of the solution. This will help to surface some of the assumptions and preconceptions people bring with them.

Tools and Techniques

Transform data to information. Find skilled professionals who know how to move up the cognitive food chain—from data to information, from information to knowledge, from knowledge to wisdom.

Construct an idea-generating environment. Create opportunities to encourage wild ideas, sketches, and novel scenarios. An approach such as Deloitte Consulting LLP's "Deep Dive," for example (search for "Deep Dive" on www.deloitte.com), is a group facilitation technique that combines brainstorming, prototyping, and role playing to help generate solutions for specific challenges.[37] Design firm IDEO also thoughtfully structures ways to foster ideation. (You'll learn more about the firm in the next chapter; you can also visit www.ideo.com.)

Look for the opposite of an idea. Find someone getting the results you want, and then work backward. Prototype and let "end users" surprise you. Visit the X PRIZE Foundation (www.xprize.org).

Assertive inquiry. A technique for breaking people out of their pre-existing mental models. Participants are encouraged to adopt the worldview of others (at least temporarily) in an effort to discover insights that would have been missed. Explains author Roger Martin: "Its aim is to learn about the salient data and causal maps baked into another person's model, then use the insight gained to fashion a creative resolution of the conflict between that person's model and your own." (Read: *The Opposable Mind* by Roger L. Martin.)

Web 2.0. Seek ideas from customers, staff, and citizens using Web 2.0 technologies. Let the best ideas rise to the top through organization-wide voting and then have leadership select the best of the lot. Use the wisdom of the crowds as a way of testing your predispositions. (Read *Wikinomics* by Don Tapscott and Anthony Williams and *The Wisdom of Crowds* by James Surowiecki.)

Get ideas from partners. Give the problem to someone else to solve. Let your network of partners, both governmental and nongovernmental, help to develop new solutions to old problems. (Read "Connect and Develop: Inside Procter & Gamble's New Model for Innovation," by Larry Huston and Nabil Sakkab, in the March 2006 *Harvard Business Review*, and visit www.pgconnectdevelop.com.)

Get out of your office. Change the physical space. Talk to users. If you're working on recycling policy, go visit a smelter. Talk to the truck driver who delivers scrap metal. Read chapter 1 of Tom Kelley's book *The Ten Faces of Innovation*. The chapter argues that good design requires more people to think and act like anthropologists.

Use mash-ups. Combine ideas from unrelated fields to create new solutions—free-market environmentalism, for example, to promote acid rain reduction. Another mash-up is Virtual Alabama, which merged Google Earth 3-D visualization tools with emergency response data to create a state-of-the-art disaster response system (www.virtual.alabama.gov).

Still another example: applying the process mapping tool of the manufacturing assembly line to public policy—as this book does.

Resources (Books, Web Sites, and Other Cool Stuff)

For further reading, we recommend *Big Think Strategy: How to Leverage Bold Ideas and Leave Small Thinking Behind* by Bernd H. Schmitt; *How to Get Ideas* by Jack Foster; *The Public Innovator's Playbook* by William D. Eggers and Shalabh Singh; and *Solutions for the World's Biggest Problems* by Bjørn Lomborg. *How We Decide* by Jonah Lehrer is a terrific book on the science of decision making that includes an interesting discussion on confirmation bias. For ideas worth spreading, millions of people a month from all around the world visit www.Ted.com, which features wide-ranging talks from the world's most fascinating thinkers and doers on ideas that could change the way we live.

CHAPTER 2

The Design–Free Design Trap

Blueprint Bootcamp

Idea → **Design** → Stargate → Implementation → Results
(⟵——————— Reevaluation ———————⟶)

CHAPTER GUIDE

- Don Shula and Medicare Reform
- Choice Overload
- The Design-Free Design Trap
- California's Electricity Belly Flop
- A Blueprint for Disaster
- Failing the Enron Test
- How Legislation Gets Written Today
- The Discipline of Design
- Designing for the Real World
- Ready, Fire, Aim
- Design for Execution

Do not worry if you have built your castles in the air. They are where they should be. Now put the foundations under them.

—HENRY DAVID THOREAU

D ON SHULA DOES not usually shop at Walmart. But just after midnight on November 15, 2005, the NFL coaching legend made history at the Walmart store in Hallandale, Florida, becoming the first senior in America to sign up for the new Medicare prescription drug benefit.

It should have been a great day for America's seniors. It was, after all, the first day they could sign up for the new program. The Bush administration had gone to great lengths to pass the bill, which was meant to ease the pain of paying for prescription medications. Instead, the new law was sending seniors to their pill boxes seeking relief.

"This whole program is so complicated that I've stayed awake thinking, 'How can a brain come up with anything like this?'" lamented a seventy-nine-year-old retired business manager. Americans do not normally lie awake pondering the design of a federal program. But the Medicare prescription drug program was something special.

"I have a PhD, and it's too complicated to suit me," said a seventy-three-year-old retired chemist. "Confusion, frustration abound as drug program gets under way," blared a headline echoed by newspapers from coast to coast. Plan officials knew they had a problem. "Many of the seniors I speak with are dazed and confused," said a Medicare counselor, whose job it was to help seniors choose the best plan.[1]

Sending the nation's elderly voters into apoplexy was not what the administration of George W. Bush or members of Congress had intended. The bill was supposed to be a huge boon for seniors. But the design of the program created so many complicated choices that—at least initially—it failed to do justice to the very people it was intended to benefit. The number of plans the typical senior had to sort through depended on where he or she lived. In Colorado, retirees faced a choice of fifty-five plans from twenty-four companies. Residents of Pennsylvania selected from sixty-six plans. Copays, deductibles, generics, and a complex little feature known as the "donut hole" made it impossible even for experts to understand the choices being offered. The problem wasn't the intent, or the implementation. The problem was the program's design.

In theory, the choice-based model made sense. People like choice. Your local supermarket probably carries about two dozen kinds of mustard, and no one is upset about that. In fact, some shoppers would be angry if mustard were stocked in only one flavor. Competition also holds down prices. But introduce too many complex options all at once and you wind up with choice overload.

In the case of the Medicare drug benefit, the problem of too many choices was compounded by three factors. First, consumers were being presented with a new product. Imagine being confronted with the wall of mustards at the local grocery store when you have never purchased mustard before. Sorting through all the brands, flavors, and prices would take a while. Second, the target population—senior citizens—is particularly averse to confusing menu options. Third, this was not a $3 jar of mustard. This was an important decision that could affect seniors' health and their finances.

When governments design markets for the provision of public services, whether for schools, housing, or health care, they create massive markets that spring into existence overnight. In contrast to organically shaped markets, established reputations don't exist. Consumers lack tools to assist them in making meaningful choices in a world of many options. Consider high school seniors shopping for colleges. Over time, the market has developed not only a diverse offering of schools, but also a variety of tools that can help with the choice. High school guidance counselors are aware of colleges' reputations and are skilled at matching the strengths and weaknesses of schools and students. Magazines, handbooks, and Web sites compare colleges on everything from the quality of the physics faculty to the quality of the intramural sports program. Rankings also exist, touting, for example, the fifty best engineering schools. Such sorting mechanisms arise naturally over time in response to a market need, in this case the need for information. *Consumer Reports, Car and Driver* magazine, the *New York Review of Books*—all cultivate their own reputation as providing a reliable source of information about the choices facing consumers. In artificially created markets such as the Medicare prescription drug benefit, there are no established sorting mechanisms, at least not in the beginning.

In rural Baxter Springs, Kansas, the chief pharmacist at Wolkar Drugs, Brian Caswell, had dozens of customers ask him to choose a plan on their behalf. He declined, citing federal regulations. "The program is so poorly designed and is creating so much confusion that it's having a negative effect on most beneficiaries," said Caswell. "It's making people cynical about the whole process—the new program, the government's help."[2]

"The bill's designers probably didn't have a clear picture of seniors' mental models of prescriptions," explains Peter Coughlin of the industrial design firm IDEO. "Just some decent human factors work, whether it was demographics, psychographics, or different user scenarios around how people deal with medication or insurance, would have gone a long way to making it less complicated." Unfortunately, today this kind of analysis is not even on the radar screen of most policy makers. Like too many policies, the prescription drug benefit fell victim to what we call the Design-Free Design Trap.

Design-Free Design

Most large initiatives take shape through the legislative process. The Design-Free Design Trap occurs because the work of drafting a bill that launches a major initiative isn't generally treated like the design process it truly is. Instead of a sound, executable design, the goal of the legislative process is often producing a bill that can pass, that can be sold to constituents back home. Laws often aren't subject to the sort of exacting scrutiny they deserve. Too frequently, the result is legislation that shows fundamental flaws when put to the test in the real world. The bill gets passed, but the design is unworkable.

A good design is essential in many undertakings. Imagine you want to build your dream house. You begin with an idea: you want a three-bedroom home with an open floor plan, an office, and, being environmentally conscious, the capacity for solar power. You share this idea with your spouse and family and they have some suggestions, too. As the idea evolves, you engage an architect to start sketching possible layouts. At some point you have a finished design, a blueprint to give a builder to turn your idea into reality. To be effective, a design must do more than look good on paper or appeal to your eco-friendly sensibilities. A good design must be buildable. If the blueprint calls for eighty thousand pounds of solar panels on the roof, but the walls can support only fifty thousand pounds, your new home will collapse. Your dreams will be crushed along with the Prius hybrid in the garage.

There is no exact point at which a project moves from the idea phase to the design phase. An idea, however, can be stated in broad, inspirational terms: "an eco-friendly house," for example, or "a government of the people, by the people, for the people." In contrast, a design involves laying out the technical aspects of execution, whether it's the layout of the plumbing and wiring found on a construction blueprint or the delineation of the roles of the three branches of government found in the Constitution.

There is no inherent problem with the idea of an eco-friendly house. Nor can the builder who faithfully followed the blueprints be faulted for the collapse. No, somewhere in the design phase, a structural engineer should have reviewed the load-bearing requirements and realized that the walls weren't up to the task. In fact, construction law recognizes the hazards of faulty design, and building codes exist to ensure that basic requirements are met. Your dream house would never have been granted a construction permit because your local building department would have rejected the blueprints for being structurally unsound.

The political process generally lacks this sort of design scrutiny.

A bad design will always undermine a good idea. The design flaws may not make themselves known until the policy is implemented, but the failure is rooted in the design nonetheless.

When such a failure occurs, however, the public just might blame the builder rather than the designer, since the builder is the guy at the work site standing next to the pile of rubble. Just ask Gray Davis, the former governor of California, who was kicked out of office in the middle of his term when a redesign of California's electricity market that he had no part in designing collapsed while he was in office.

California's Electricity Belly Flop

The curious task of economics is to demonstrate to men how little they really know about what they imagine they can design."

—ECONOMIST FRIEDRICH VON HAYEK, IN *THE FATAL CONCEIT*

In the late 1990s, California dramatically restructured its electricity market, introducing an entirely new mechanism to generate, transmit, and deliver electricity to customers. Within just a few years, this initiative would cost Governor Gray Davis his job, cost consumers upwards of $40 billion, and literally plunge the state into darkness.[3] Longtime industry stalwart Pacific Gas & Electric (PG&E) was driven into bankruptcy, and millions—maybe billions—of dollars poured into the pockets of an unscrupulous company called Enron. After promising to reduce electricity costs by 25 percent or more, the new scheme saw electricity prices shoot through the roof, from around $30 to upwards of a staggering $1,000 to $1,500 per megawatt hour.

This monumental belly flop is 100 percent attributable to poor design. Coincidentally, that's the exact same percentage of California lawmakers who voted for the restructuring law. In 1996, this faulty blueprint was passed *unanimously* by the 120 members of the California legislature, a remarkable feat in a state with a 60–40 mix of Democratic and Republican legislators who generally can't agree on anything. Everybody loved this bill. An amazing seventy legislators were listed as coauthors.

The new law was billed as "deregulation." The goal was to make the monopolistic electricity industry more efficient through competition. The idea of deregulation, after all, had proven effective in the 1970s in the trucking and airline industries.

The existing model certainly was imperfect. As in most states, electricity in California featured two types of monopoly providers: municipal utilities and three large, investor-owned utilities—Pacific Gas & Electric, Southern California Edison, and San Diego Gas & Electric. The state's Public Utilities Commission set prices on the basis of costs plus a profit margin. The state's electricity prices were 35 percent higher than the national average, and businesses were leaving California for greener pastures.[4] Theoretically, legislators reasoned, competition should drive efficiency and result in lower electricity costs. As in Thoreau's quote, policy makers had their dream, their castle in the air. Now, all they had to do was craft a law that would put a foundation under their idea and bring the efficiency gains of competition to the industry.

There are two critical things to understand about California's electricity deregulation. First, it wasn't really deregulation at all. Second, the legislative and executive branches had no idea how the artificial electricity "market" they created would actually work. That lack of understanding was reflected, unanimously, in AB 1890, the electricity restructuring law.

If electricity were a typical good, government wouldn't need to design a market at all. Cars, ice cream, dry cleaning—nobody has to design a market for these goods. Most markets arise spontaneously as independent producers and consumers pursue their own self interests.

Electricity isn't typical. The alternating current that flows into our homes is invisible, cannot be stored, and travels at the speed of light. (The electrons don't travel at the speed of light, but the electricity does—go figure that one out.) More importantly from an economic standpoint, electricity runs through wires, and it has long been considered prohibitively expensive for multiple providers to each build a transmission system to every possible customer's house. Hence, electricity has been treated as a "natural monopoly" both by economists and by government. (The same is true of water.) Before deregulation, California's big three investor-owned electric utilities were privately operated, publicly regulated monopolies. The idea behind deregulation was that competition among producers would spur innovation and reduce prices for consumers. But since there was only one transmission grid, and one set of wires going to customers, how would electricity producers compete for customers? How would the new market actually work?

It would be complicated. In fact, the new "pseudomarket" design enacted into law was very, very complicated. California's approach called for a single, state-run entity to assume operation of the transmission grid. California utilities were ordered to sell their power-generating plants and then were barred from locking in wholesale prices through long-term contracts. Instead the state would "coordinate" the wholesale purchase and sale of all electrical power through a centralized auction called the California Power Exchange, which was supposed to match up supply and demand twenty-four hours in advance. This was not a normal auction. It was as if everyone in town called the grocery store the day before they wanted their groceries, and the price of milk and bread fluctuated based on the number of orders. In short, instead of simply monitoring the costs of a few large utilities, state electricity regulators would be overseeing a massive transmission grid and coordinating a complex, daily, multimillion-dollar auction. It was just like a real market, only different.

Moreover, rather than allowing retail prices to float freely, as in a real market, the new law mandated a rate freeze followed by rate cuts for consumers. That's a pretty cool law. Like the laws that dictated the weather in Camelot, this bill was going to control the forces of nature. "California bureaucrats weren't just capping rates," writes author James Walsh in *The $10 Billion Jolt*. "They were commanding that the market move in the direction they bade at the times that suited them."[5] Legislators can write laws, but they can't change the laws of physics or repeal the law of supply and demand.

The only aspect of the new system that even faintly resembled a competitive market was that California consumers could begin to choose their electricity company, but even that choice was fraudulent. After all, why would anyone bother to switch? Electricity is a commodity—my kilowatt is identical to your kilowatt. Not surprisingly, few Californians bothered to switch. Most were simply baffled when they were given a choice about which they didn't care a jolt. It was the opposite problem of the market designed in the Medicare prescription drug program, where consumers were overloaded with an array of services.

Design Meets Reality; Reality Wins

The "deregulated" markets were phased in starting in 1998. In May of 2000, a tipping point occurred: the wholesale price of electricity on the open market surpassed what California retailers were allowed, by law, to charge. The price increase was driven by several factors: a very hot summer, high demand from a booming "dot-com" economy, and spikes in the price of natural gas, which may or may not have been exacerbated on purpose by energy companies that operated in both the natural gas and electricity markets (companies such as Enron).[6] Unlike a real market, retail prices were not allowed to fluctuate, meaning California retailers like Southern California Edison were paying 50 cents or more per kilowatt hour while the price they could charge customers was capped, by law, at 6.7 cents. Once that critical price inversion occurred, disaster was inevitable.[7]

On June 14, 2000, design met reality, and reality won. It was the hottest day on record in much of the San Francisco Bay region, as the temperature hit 109 degrees in San Jose.[8] Workers hosed down the tracks of the city's storied cable cars to keep them from swelling. In Solano County, pavement buckled on Interstate 80, backing up traffic for miles. Electrical demand climbed with the mercury as air conditioners cranked at full blast. The power infrastructure finally hit its limit. To avert a systemwide crash, Pacific Gas & Electric was forced to deploy a tactic that would come to define the California electricity crisis and eventually bring down a governor—the rolling blackout.

The blackouts were said to roll because they moved across the landscape like an alien fog with an itinerary, darkening certain neighborhoods for a while, then moving along to cover others. At noon on June 14, 2000, PG&E started cutting back power to commercial and industrial customers. When PG&E stopped the rotating power cuts, about ninety-seven thousand customers had seen their buildings go dark for about an hour and a half at a time.[9]

This was just a taste of what was to come. About six months later, in January 2001, the state-run grid operator ordered rolling blackouts across the northern and central parts of the state, affecting several hundred thousand people. Students took final exams in the dark at George Washington High School in San Francisco.[10] On consecutive days in 2001, statewide rolling blackouts affected another 1.5 million customers. In an ironic twist, many high-tech firms relied on gas-powered backup generators to stay in business.[11] Silicon Valley, the most technically advanced slice of real estate on the planet, was being powered by gas generators bought at Home Depot.

The blackouts weren't major catastrophes. Hurricanes and winter storms often cut power to hundreds of thousands, and sometimes millions, of customers for days at a time. These were different. They were planned. Unlike a hurricane, the blackouts were a man-made disaster. Like residents of a third world country, Californians lived with the constant worry that they would happen again and again. The thirty-eight blackout days pointed out that something was terribly wrong with California's electricity delivery system.

Delivery wasn't the only thing going wrong. Responding to appeals from the utilities, the state public utility commission allowed residential electricity rates to increase. "Our electric bill was $600 a month, and we didn't have air conditioning," reported a typical Bay Area resident. Meanwhile, the price for wholesale electricity continued to shoot through the roof, allowing some companies to make big profits. At the same time, from the moment that wholesale prices on the market exceeded the legally allowable retail prices, the big-three utilities found themselves inescapably losing money. In April 2001, PG&E declared bankruptcy.[12] The state stepped in, and in the first five months of 2001, California drained $7.6 billion out of the state treasury buying electricity.[13] By 2003, Governor Gray Davis was removed from office by a popular recall, only the second time in American history voters had taken such a drastic measure. Ironically, it was his predecessor, Governor Pete Wilson, who signed the bill into law in 1998, essentially handing Davis a blueprint for disaster.

Various criticisms have been leveled at the main players who participated in the implementation of this law, including Governor Davis, the California Public Utilities Commission, and the Federal Energy Regulatory Commission (FERC). Most of these criticisms center on how they did (or didn't) respond to the unfolding problems that emerged during implementation. No one disputes that the design contained flaws that surfaced only when the new program was implemented. Never tested, never prototyped, the new design failed at scale. Where was the fatal flaw hidden?

Fat Boy, Ricochet, and Death Star

The flaw was buried in the complexity. As noted, the power exchange market run by the state was complicated, depending as it did on companies booking in advance how much power they would need. Guess who figured out this complex system? The private companies, such as Enron, who now had big roles in this odd new world. They pored over the complex rules looking for loopholes, and they found them. As Ken Lay, Enron's CEO, put it to an advisor of Governor Davis: "Well, Dave, old buddy, let me tell you. It doesn't matter what kooky rules you Californians put in place. I got a lot of really smart people down here gonna figure out a way to make money anyway."[14]

After the fact, federal investigators were able to untangle dozens of schemes used by Enron to manipulate wholesale prices and inflate profits in the California electricity market. Investigators found internal Enron memos that described these complicated gambits, which went under cute nicknames such as "Big Foot," "Ricochet," and "Death Star." Under one strategy, nicknamed "Fat Boy," Enron bought power in California, where mandated caps kept prices low, and sold it at higher prices in other states. In another scheme, known as "Ricochet," Enron shipped power generated in California to other states and then resold it back into California. This tactic, known as megawatt laundering, allowed Enron to avoid price controls and generate huge profits by doing virtually nothing.[15]

Tapes of Enron traders confirmed the paranoid public's worst fears. One recording caught two Enron employees talking about a megawatt-laundering scam:

> *Employee 1:* "Regulatory's all in a big concern about is we're wheeling power out of California. He [an Enron trader] just steals money from California to the tune of a million . . . "
>
> *Employee 2:* "Can you rephrase that?"
>
> *Employee 1:* "Okay, he *arbitrages* the California market to the tune of a million bucks or two a day."
>
> *Both employees:* [*Laughter.*][16]

Enron was not the only culprit. "Every company traded according to the rules that California put out there," says one former Enron trader.[17] The problem was that the rules of the game didn't make sense. In the topsy-turvy world of the California Power Exchange, it was possible to boost profits by *not* generating electricity. Less electricity meant a shortage, which meant that the price for available power went through the roof. One tape caught an Enron trader instructing engineers at a power-generating facility to create a fictitious technical problem and take the plant offline at a particular time the next day. How would regulators know if "the switch on the induction steam valve" had really failed or not? In fact, many generating plants, not just Enron's, were taken down at strategic times for various reasons. In June 2002, California state officials accused certain power companies of keeping 30 to 50 percent of their capacity, and sometimes more, off the market in order to drive up prices and profits. "When governments design markets badly, they will work badly; you get what you incent," says Branko Terzic, a FERC member in the early 1990s.[18]

It is easy to be critical of these companies. Enron is an easy target, and its corporate culture certainly crossed the line in its pursuit of profit. Affixing the blame on "greed," however, misses the point. Greed, which may also be described as economic self-interest, is a rather common human trait, something a well-designed system ought to be able to withstand. The real problem here was *unconstrained* greed. Enron traders were working in a system that richly rewarded bad behavior. If fast-food restaurants could boost profits by shutting down their grills during lunch, they'd probably do it. Real markets don't reward that kind of abusive behavior, however. One lesson from California is that a policy design needs to withstand actual human behavior, including the unsavory.

Gaming an artificial system comes as naturally to humans as breathing. In 1987, the IRS started requiring any filer taking a deduction for a dependent to report the child's social security number. On April 15, 1987, 7 million children disappeared. (Don't bother checking your milk carton.) In 1989, the IRS started requiring any filer taking a deduction for paid child care to list the social security number of the care provider—and on April 15, 1989, 2.6 million babysitters disappeared.[19] (It is comforting to imagine these missing babysitters in some sort of *Twilight Zone* parallel universe, forever taking care of the 7 million missing children.) People aren't angels. From a policy perspective, it is easier to change the system than to change human nature.

Caution: Legislators at Work

This section is about how lawmakers in Sacramento actually went about drafting AB 1890, and this is where the story gets scary. That's because the legislative process that created California's blueprint for disaster was—in a word—exemplary. The bill drafting process was thorough, thoughtful, open, and deliberate; a bipartisan effort by well-meaning lawmakers to do something they truly believed would benefit California. There were no smoke-filled rooms, rushed debates, or corrupt officials. This was about as good as lawmaking gets, and the fact that it produced such an awful law— unanimously—should terrify anyone who cares about public policy.

The California legislature consistently took great pains to design a good bill. Delegations were sent to Argentina and England to study best practices from their recently deregulated markets. Legislators heard over a hundred hours of testimony. (In contrast, California's legislature approved the Global Warming Solutions Act of 2006 without any hearings at all.) Leading the bill-shaping effort was state senator Steve Peace, a market-oriented Democrat from San Diego with a reputation as a policy wonk. Peace was highly respected on both sides of the aisle for his intellect and willingness to delve into the details of complex legislation. (Outside the legislature, Peace is a producer of low-budget films, including the campy B-movie *Attack of the Killer Tomatoes*, so this wasn't the first disaster he'd been associated with.) Peace brought together representatives from the utility companies, the state regulatory commission, lobbyists, and other assorted stakeholders. His marathon sessions lasted for hours in the midst of the scorching Sacramento summer, quickly becoming known as "The Steve Peace Death March."

So what was the problem? Once the idea of deregulation, with its promise of lower energy costs, was accepted in principle, lawmakers saw their primary task as crafting a piece of legislation that made everyone happy. The legislators failed to recognize that they were engaged in the process of designing a system that had to hold up under real-world conditions. Lawmakers weren't thinking beyond the bill's passage. They had no idea they were designing a system that, in order to produce positive results, would have to be "Enron-proof."

Busy legislators were only too happy to leave the details to Peace and the phalanx of industry lobbyists. "People were grateful to Peace and [former Sen. Diane] Martinez for taking it on," said Debra Bowen, D–Los Angeles, past chair of the Senate energy committee. "Historically, utilities were a pretty boring topic."[20] Most members of the California legislature, even the seventy "coauthors" of the bill, had only a vague understanding of the details. This is quite understandable. Restructuring the power grid, paying for "stranded costs," establishing a power exchange—these issues were so mind-numbingly complex that only industry experts were equipped to comprehend them.

The final bill ended up being a hodgepodge of unconnected parts, each one satisfying the demands of a key industry player. It was as if the blueprint of your dream home was created with input from every member of the family, each person making sure it had all the cool features he or she wanted, but never reviewed for structural integrity to make sure all the parts worked together. "The ability to get a unanimous vote resulted in many flaws . . . none fatal in and of themselves, but together, [they eventually] proved disastrous," explained Jan Smutny-Jones, the executive director of the Independent Energy Producers Association.

After the implosion, it was easy to see the design flaws. "It deregulated the wholesale market . . . but not the retail market," said Governor Davis. Former federal energy secretary Bill Richardson said, "The deregulation plan was botched . . . the rules of the game were created badly."[21] These observations came after the fact, as did former Governor Wilson's admission that he knowingly signed a flawed bill. "I will not pretend to you that [the legislation] was a perfect, free-market mechanism. It wasn't . . . I knew that at the time. I signed it knowing that. I thought whatever flaws would emerge . . . would be addressed by our successors."[22]

Another lesson from California is that lawmakers involved in transformational change need to actively seek out critics. If none can be found, dissenting voices need to be created for the very purpose of exposing possible design flaws.

Does that sound crazy? Careful organizations do this all the time. Our legal system provides a defense attorney to argue on behalf of the accused while at the same time paying for the district attorney to mount a prosecution. Historically, before someone became a saint, the Catholic Church would appoint an official as *advocatus diaboli*, or "devil's advocate," to bring forth reasons why that person should not be canonized. This sort of "design review by adversary" helps prevent mistakes. Smart companies, before investing in a new product design, will assign a team to conduct what is known as a failure mode and effects analysis (FMEA). The FMEA team is charged with answering the questions, "How is this new product going to fail?" and "When it fails, what are the consequences likely to be?" The very nature of the question requires the FMEA team to assume the new idea will flop, enabling them to creatively envision the disastrous scenarios that could lead to failure. Isn't it smarter to hire someone to poke your design looking for the weak points rather than wait for an Enron to find them for you?

"Details of the design did not take into account strategic behavior that firms would engage in," explained Berkeley professor Severin Borenstein, who has written extensively on this topic.[23] The market designers never imagined companies purposely shutting down plants during times of peak demand. Lawmakers were operating under assumptions developed from their experience working in a regulated environment. It "didn't occur to them that stakeholders would be profit-maximizing in a deregulated system," said Borenstein.

There was also the problem of wildly overoptimistic economic assumptions. Only one possible scenario was envisioned: electricity prices would go down. Dan Howle, then chief of staff for Senator Peace, recalled the drafting process. "At one point," he said, "there was a discussion of what would happen if the wholesale price went up. Someone said if rates ever got to 10 cents a kilowatt-hour, this whole thing would fall apart . . . There was a lot of laughter and a response of, 'That'll never happen.'"[24] The legislators thought they could predict future energy trends and wrote their bill accordingly.[25] Big mistake. Nothing is harder to predict than the future. It is best to plan for the worst-case scenario.

Flawed Design = Implementation Nightmare

The underlying factors that created the badly flawed California electricity deregulation bill are not an anomaly. The weaknesses of the drafting process—the overoptimistic assumptions, the lack of planning for alternative scenarios, the failure to submit the design to rigorous scrutiny—are repeated every day in city halls, in state capitals, and in Washington, D.C. Lawmakers' primary concern is drafting legislation that will pass, so bills almost never go through the exacting *design* scrutiny typical of nearly every new product launched in the private sector. The legislators and staffers who design system overhauls for vast segments of the economy—such as health care, education, or electricity in California—typically lack the systems thinking background of the consultant, the process engineer, or the financial analyst.

If only the public policy world had someplace it could submit policy design blueprints for review. Our surveys of senior public officials with both the federal Senior Executive Service (SES) and the National Academy of Public Administration (NAPA) confirmed the suspicion that many public policy failures are rooted in a failure of policy design. (See appendixes B and C.) Fewer than one-third of America's senior federal executives believed the federal government to be effective at designing public policy. Meanwhile, fully one-third of NAPA fellows told us Washington is outright poor at policy design. What accounts for this? One culprit is the disconnect that exists between policy designers and implementers. Fully 45 percent of federal executives say that policy is rarely designed by those with relevant experience. The dramatic disconnect between policy designers and policy implementers is perhaps the most broken part of the journey to success. In our survey of senior federal executives, no other topic elicited the vehement responses we received from our questions about policy design. The comments were scathing:

"Policy design at the federal level is pathetic."

"Many people on the Hill have little practical frontline experience in the areas they are responsible for."

"There is quite a gap in communication and understanding between a committee drafting legislation and the federal or state agency responsible for the implementation."

"Policy design is dictated top down for ideological/partisan reasons, rather than worked through from experienced professionals upwards."

"Policy design too often is done without consideration of implementation challenges."

"Policy makers rarely provide realistic, or any, benchmarks for implementation."

Whether you agree or disagree with these sentiments, remember that they come from the most senior executives in the federal government, many of whom have worked in government for decades. The frustration in their responses shows their passion—we need to listen to these voices.

Taking the Design Phase Seriously

The client was a hospital seeking to improve the patient experience. A consultant might approach such a problem in several ways, such as measuring customer waiting times or conducting a patient survey. When the design firm IDEO was hired to improve the patient experience, the IDEO team strapped a camera onto the head of an employee, put him on a gurney, and filmed a hospital visit from the patient's perspective. The resulting video is painfully humorous, as the poor "patient" is wheeled around on a gurney by a series of invisible strangers, with various heads occasionally popping into view to explain the next painful thing that is going to befall the supine victim. The journey features scary beeps from big machines, long stretches looking up at fluorescent lights, and interminable periods of tense, solitary waiting. The film captures the disorienting and dehumanizing experience of a real patient better than any PowerPoint presentation could. Doctors, nurses, and hospital administrators who viewed the film soon introduced a number of small but important empathic practices, such as attaching a small mirror to the gurney so the patient can see the person wheeling them about.

In the private sector, the design process is a field of expertise in and of itself. Companies seeking to launch something new often call on the specialized skills of a company like IDEO, which concentrates on taking clients through the design process. IDEO specializes in human-centered industrial design, that is, designs that center around real human behavior rather than the aesthetic sensibilities of the designer.

Peter Coughlin is a typical IDEO employee, if there is such a thing. Armed with a BA in English and a PhD in applied linguistics, Coughlin is an expert in human factors, meaning he specializes in how humans interact with technology. Coughlin and his team help organizations seeking to design a major, transformational change by taking them through "the

IDEO way," the firm's five-step process for driving innovation: Observe, understand, envision, evaluate and refine, and implement.[26]

The genius of the IDEO approach is that it simultaneously does two seemingly contradictory things: it encourages wild experimentation and mitigates risk at every stage of the design process. How does IDEO reconcile these two seemingly irreconcilable objectives? By encouraging "fast failure" through rapid prototyping. IDEO prototypes everything. The prototypes are developed quickly, often with the crudest materials—cardboard, plywood, glue, colored paper, old machine parts, whatever's handy. For a new service approach, IDEO might role-play through a hastily staged improvisation, perhaps even trying out these very rough prototype approaches on a few real customers. According to IDEO, rapid experimentation with quick, inexpensive prototypes helps uncover the pros and cons of an idea in a more tangible, real-world way than any market survey ever could. "Every prototype that we put in the field takes at least a ninety-degree turn in a different direction than we had initially envisioned," Coughlin explained. "The main reason problems happen at scale is that they haven't gone through this process of early prototyping." (For those of you who skipped the section on California electricity deregulation, "failing at scale" is a bad thing.) The prototyping process allows an organization to take chunks of its overall vision and try them out in a much lower-risk way than going to the market with a half-baked idea. "It costs you a lot less to go and talk to senior[s] about their insurance navigation challenges than it does to create a big new solution and then ask a hundred seniors after the fact whether they like it," Coughlin said.[27]

IDEO's key insight is that managing risk needs to start well before implementation, at the idea and design stages. It's a way of doing a "premortem," explained Tim Brown, the CEO of IDEO. "You're giving yourself a chance to uncover problems and fix them in real time as the strategy unfolds."[28] For California, war-gaming a prototype of the deregulated electricity market ahead of time would have helped the designers to get in the mindset of cocky, aggressive energy traders—called "extreme users" in IDEO parlance—whose modus operandi was to exploit any and all flaws in the legislation for their own benefit.

This kind of role playing and scenario planning has long been a mainstay of military strategists and is also used in the corporate sector. Shell

Oil's renowned Global Scenarios, used for over three decades, have helped the company explore different potential business environments. "The scenarios," explains Shell CEO Jeroen van der Veer, "provide insights on the kinds of strategy different groups may adopt in different strategic contexts."[29] Deliberately eliciting imaginative thinking about various scenarios would have forced California's bill drafters to test their extremely optimistic assumptions: What happens if wholesale electricity prices rise? How might extreme weather affect supply and demand? What if power plants intentionally withhold power during peak time? Asking such questions ahead of time might have ferreted out the policy's flaws during the design phase, before testing the law on California's 36 million citizen guinea pigs.

On March 31, 2009, nine years after California's first energy auction went bust, the state launched another daily electricity auction. This time the approach was very different. State officials spent eighteen months doing market simulations, playing out every possible scenario and working out all the bugs. It will be some time before the results of that effort are known.

Prototyping and scenario planning can take you only so far. Reality testing is the ultimate proof of concept. That is why private companies invest so heavily in testing their new launches with real consumers before placing a big bet. Hollywood, for example, might film and test three different endings to discover audience tastes. Consumer product companies like Procter & Gamble conduct extensive focus group testing and regional rollouts before investing in a nationwide launch. Software companies release beta versions to select customers so that "bugs" are found by these picky users before the official release.

Following the blackouts in California, Loretta Lynch, the president of the California Public Utilities Commission, was asked if she thought the idea of deregulating electricity could work if California used a different market structure. Her response emphasizes the value of experiential data:

> *I grew up in Missouri and I say, "Show me." Show me the right way to do it. Don't just theorize about it. Show me the path. If you can show me how it's been done in other places successfully . . . well, then I would be interested in seeing that model.*[30]

Ready, Fire, Aim

Hunting a deer is not easy. Deer are quick, have a sense of smell a thousand times more sensitive than humans, and have a 300-degree field of vision. Hunters who manage to spot a buck must take very careful aim, for a misfire will send the buck off in an instant. Hunters who hear gunfire in the woods have a saying: "One shot, one deer. Two shots, no deer." You get only one shot to get it right.

Shooting down enemy aircraft is not easy, either. During World War II, hand-operated anti-aircraft guns were pitted against fast-moving fighter planes. The best approach was the exact opposite of deer hunting. Rather than taking careful aim, anti-aircraft guns spit out bullets with a steady "rat-tat-tat," including in their ammunition belt periodic "tracer" bullets that contain a pyrotechnic charge, allowing them to be seen by the naked eye in flight. These tracers enable gunners to adjust their aim real-time. The proper protocol is "ready, fire, aim," a twist on the traditional order.

Our apologies for the violent metaphors. They are useful, however, to help illustrate that different public policy circumstances call for radically different design approaches. In some cases you will get only one chance to get it right, as with the sweeping changes to California's electricity market. In other cases, the best hope of success comes from multiple rapidly launched efforts that can then be used to provide feedback about how the design really performs in practice. Just as IDEO learns from every rough prototype, policy experts can learn from the real-world experience of small programs. Fail fast, fail small, and try again.

The "ready, fire, aim" approach works best when you know your end goal but are unsure of the best way to get there. A clear goal is more important than a clear plan, and the value of obtaining feedback from interacting with the real world is more critical than the occasional misfire. In the case of the welfare reform of 1996, the federal government had the luxury of seeing innovative approaches in Wisconsin, Oregon, and elsewhere demonstrate that the design being considered could work in the real world. "We had a lot of evidence about what would work," explained Ron Haskins, the senior congressional staffer who wrote the legislation. "Many states had demonstration programs before we wrote the bill. We just rode the wave."[31]

States were free to experiment, and thus they served as laboratories of democracy, testing a theory against reality. This is the thinking behind the many "pilot projects" that are launched by Congress and state legislatures. Unfortunately, in too many cases pilot projects serve as little more than sops to special interests or a way to gain the support of a key legislator rather than as a serious exploration into a new policy model. Results, good or bad, are generally ignored. These pilot projects, even the successful ones, almost always fail to lead to widespread reforms because they aren't viewed as part of a design process. Rather, they have become a tool of political appeasement to win passage of a bill.

There is no set of hard and fast rules that can guide policy makers in determining whether to invest in a carefully vetted design or to experiment with something and see what happens. Obviously, if the cost of failure is high, or the course of action is irreversible, then you want to have a more robust design before trying something new. You need to be wary of getting bogged down in "analysis paralysis," however. Between "ready, aim, fire" and "ready, fire, aim" falls a wide spectrum of policy situations in which some combination of these approaches is most appropriate. You can think of this as "ready, fast aim, fire, repeat." It's essentially the IDEO model—an approach that relies on a heavy dose of scenario analysis, prototyping and testing before the final design is put into practice on a wide scale.

So far, we've emphasized those instances in which policy design takes place during the legislative process, and indeed that is how most large policy initiatives take shape. But in addition to new laws, major undertakings can come from the courts, or from the more direct route of executive action, when a president, governor, or mayor launches a major undertaking under his or her existing authority. In these instances, a sound policy approach is essential, but experimentation is often easier in the absence of a legislative blueprint. In fact, the very nature of legislative deliberation sometimes creates overly detailed policy blueprints that don't allow for the sort of flexible, real-time adjustments that often turn out to be necessary.

Consider education reform. The federal "No Child Left Behind" (NCLB) law, signed into law in 2002, was a bipartisan effort led by President Bush and Senator Ted Kennedy. The NCLB law was advertised as a way to improve education through tougher accountability standards, requiring states not only to introduce testing but also to make progress toward attaining student proficiency. We doubt that many legislators read or fully understood the law's 670 pages of dense legalese, which covered a host of educational concerns in excruciating detail. In addition to student testing and teacher quality, the law covered "Ready to Learn Television," "Internet Safety," "Teaching of Traditional American History," and "Teacher Liability Protection." The bill was a hodgepodge of unconnected parts. The law passed with the support of more than 90 percent of Congress.

By the time it came up for reauthorization five years later, it was hard to find anyone who still liked the law.

The essence of No Child Left Behind was accountability, based on student test scores. But the system of incentives and penalties established in the law created powerful motivation for schools, districts, and states to manipulate test results. The fine print within the law contained loopholes that made it perfectly legal for local officials to change the rules in the middle of the game so they could create the appearance of progress even when no real progress was taking place. In one state, education officials lowered the passing score on the eighth-grade math test, which meant that a lot more kids passed, which meant they were "making progress" as defined by the NCLB. Lowering the standards probably wasn't what Congress had intended, but good intentions didn't translate into law. Other states found other creative ways to fudge results. "Are some kids being left behind? You bet. Are some people gaming the system?" admitted then secretary of education Margaret Spellings, "You bet."[32]

It turns out that Enron traders and some local education officials had something in common. Both were ready to take advantage of loopholes in the system. Instead of teaching America's school children better, the law ended up teaching local education officials how to jump through complex funding hoops. The law featured carefully worded definitions, impenetrable funding formulas, and, in contrast to welfare reform, numerous other attempts to tightly control the actions of local educators. The controls haven't worked, as local officials have found creative ways around them. The NCLB hasn't been disastrous in the same way that California's electricity deregulation was, but it has been an expensive disappointment. In essence, NCLB took careful aim at education reform and missed.

Contrast this with New York mayor Michael Bloomberg, who took a "Ready, fast aim, fire, repeat" approach as part of his efforts to radically improve New York City's underperforming school system. Mayor Bloomberg used privately funded partnerships with businesses and foundations to prototype a number of cutting-edge reforms, many of which had been bottled up within the education bureaucracy for years. By going outside the school system for funding, Bloomberg was able to get innovations moving quickly, such as the Empowerment Schools program, in which schools work under performance agreements, committing to high levels of student achievement in exchange for greater local autonomy. Another approach now being tried in New York City on a limited basis is giving students cash incentives for academic achievements. A child might get $5 for completing an exam and more cash depending on how many answers she gets right. Another group of students is getting free cellular phones whose minutes can be recharged only through more studying.[33]

Will New York's educational experiments work? No one knows for certain, but these small-scale trials give educators an opportunity to test something new quickly, get feedback, and either make adjustments or drop the effort entirely. As IDEO's design gurus emphasize, you often gain unexpected insights even from failed prototype experiments. In addition, small-scale failures are always preferable to failing at scale. As bad as the California electricity restructuring turned out, aren't you glad it wasn't a national program? Wouldn't it have been better to try out a No Child Left Behind accountability system in a state or two, to see how it would actually play out in the nation?

Design for Execution

The temptation is to assign blame for the design problem to "foolish legislators." This would be a mistake. Legislators and their staff are placed in an impossible position. The full complexity of even a single program area is often beyond the grasp of anyone, and legislators are asked to pass laws on health care, energy, the environment, and a whole host of other areas. No, the problem is a process, a system, that sees the design process take place in a vacuum, largely disconnected from the implementation process.

Can the design phase be improved? Yes, but only with a serious commitment by political leaders to do so. Currently, the sort of exacting design process necessary to the success of large undertakings is virtually nonexistent in the public sector. The first step is simply to recognize that the problem exists. Here, there is some reason for hope. During the 1980s, corporate America was getting its clock cleaned by overseas competition, particularly the Japanese. A concerted effort to improve quality through initiatives such as Total Quality Management and Six Sigma went a long way to restoring competitive balance. A similar revolution in efficiency came with such approaches as business process reengineering and value chain management. These disciplines force leaders to see the entire production process as an integrated whole, to break down functional silos, and to promote alignment among all the participants in the process. The distribution of authority in democratic government makes this particularly challenging, but the consequence of doing nothing makes it a challenge worth facing. We either adapt our democratic processes to improve how we approach large undertakings, or we resign ourselves to the bleak future of continued disappointment.

In our survey of senior executives, one response contained an idea that may be worth pursuing: "Policy makers should conduct an 'implementation feasibility analysis' during the policy design stage, and modify the design based on the result of that analysis." Just as the Congressional Budget Office now weighs in with an objective assessment of the cost of proposed legislation, perhaps an independent review board can assess the "implementability" of a new policy. (This is tricky—legislators may be loath to relinquish any of their authority to any external design review board.) Just as a building department reviews the design of a house before deciding whether to issue a permit, lawmakers might uncover at least some of the design flaws if they had to submit large and complex initiatives to the scrutiny of a feasibility analysis conducted by implementation-savvy experts. Requiring policy proposals to include more robust and vetted business cases would also help.

For some readers, this chapter may be the most challenging to imagine new approaches being taken seriously. As one observer put it, "It seems to me that when the two clash, politics is always going to trump design." If you believe that "politics" is limited to political self-interest, then this objection has validity. "Politics" of this sort does work against sound design. But if you believe that the political realm still includes a willingness to put important public outcomes ahead of narrow political gain, then the ideas in this chapter, if taken seriously, can improve a part of the process desperately in need of repair. The changes needed are not merely procedural, but attitudinal.

FIELD GUIDE: DESIGN FOR EXECUTION

The challenge in the design stage is to treat it as a design process, not a bill-drafting exercise. It is difficult, but work to bring designers and implementers together.

Biggest Danger

The Design-Free Design Trap. Bill drafting is substituted for design. As a consequence, policy ideas go straight from the idea stage through the legislature, without being subjected to the exacting design process that occurs in the private sector.

Guiding Principles

Think design, not legislation. Too often, those drafting a bill are thinking only about what they can get passed. You should also be thinking about implementation and recognize that your "bill" is really a blueprint for the bureaucracy.

Involve implementers. Good implementation cannot save a poor design. Policy implementers who faithfully execute a flawed design will end up next to a pile of rubble. By the time the bill is passed, the bureaucrats who will have to actually implement your bill should be your new best friends.

Don't confuse good intentions with good design. No one cares about how high-minded your design is if it doesn't work in the real world. No Child Left Behind sounds nice, but it failed to produce the anticipated results. Use a variety of design techniques to obtain information about how your idea will work in practice.

Probe for design weaknesses. Assign someone to shoot holes in the design at an early stage. If someone isn't looking for the weaknesses during the design phase, rest assured people will be finding weaknesses in your policy after it is launched—with far more serious consequences. (Think Enron.) Design review makes sense at the building department, and it makes sense at the legislature.

Tools and Techniques

Failure mode and effects analysis (FMEA). Charge a team with answering the question, "How is this going to fail?" Have someone other than the designers poke holes and search for flaws.

Prototype if possible. Fail fast and fail small. Test and retest your design through multiple small-scale trials with real users. Use the real-world unanticipated feedback from prototyping to adjust your design in real time.

Put on your scammer hat. Role-play how those affected by your new system might exploit potential design flaws to their benefit. Scammers can come from anywhere. New rules will generate new behaviors. Try to imagine how certain unscrupulous individuals within the affected population might try to exploit the new system for their benefit.

Develop a robust business case. Formal articulation of the intended goals, intended benefits, and expected costs of any initiative can help focus the design process and bill drafting. It also helps limit scope creep.

Do some "preengineering." Show how the new system you have designed will work—or not work—in the real world, through flow charting. Use process mapping to uncover duplication, overlap, and needless complexity in design. (It's just like reengineering except it is done during design.)

Change the psychic terrain. If you do all of your designing within the political stew of a legislature—with the associated lobbyists, partisan politics, and horse trading—your design is likely to reflect political imperatives, not design imperatives.

Stakeholder consultation. Consult with a diverse range of stakeholders during the design phase. Don't just talk to the usual suspects who perennially line up on either side of the issue.

Apply a design skill review. Do you have anyone who has ever conducted a failure mode and effects analysis? Engaged in a product manufacturability review? Been trained in Six Sigma, statistics, or design for execution? If the answers are no, then you need to figure out how to bring such skills into the policy design and bill-drafting process—whether by borrowing, recruiting, or contracting for them.

Resources (Books, Web Sites, and Other Cool Stuff)

For further reading we recommend Daniel Patrick Moynihan, *Maximum Feasible Misunderstanding: Community Action in the War on Poverty*—a fascinating look at how the inclusion of a single phrase, "maximum feasible participation," created an implementation nightmare for a major federal program. This book also dispels the notion that our execution difficulties are anything new, and shows the interplay of politics in the design and implementation phases of a major undertaking.

Improving Program Design is a useful workbook from the National Performance Review (http://govinfo.library.unt.edu/npr/library/reports/pddc.html).

A great resource on design thinking is IDEO, a leading industrial design firm (www.ideo.com). Read *The Ten Faces of Innovation* and *The Art of Innovation: Lessons in Creativity from IDEO, America's Leading Design Firm* by IDEO's Tom Kelley. Obtain a copy of IDEO's "Methods Decks," a collection of fifty-one cards representing diverse design methods used by IDEO (www.ideo.com/work/item/method-cards). Another resource on design thinking is Stanford University's Institute of Design (www.dschool.stanford.edu/).

CHAPTER 3

The Stargate Trap

The Space Between Possibility and Reality

Idea → Design → **Stargate** → Implementation → Results
(←————————— Reevaluation ————————→)

CHAPTER GUIDE

- The Stargate Trap
- Boston's Busing Nightmare: Seventy-seven Days to Disaster
- The Secret Recipe for Change
- Reducing Acid Rain: Breaking the Impasse
- Japan's Number One Elvis Fan Goes Postal
- The Distortion Effects of the Stargate Trap
- Tom Davis and the Culture of the Beltway
- Lessons from the Gulf of Tonkin
- The Marshall Plan: A Better Way

Politics is the art of the possible.

—ATTRIBUTED TO OTTO VON BISMARCK

I F YOU HAVEN'T SEEN *Legally Blonde 2*, don't bother. It's nowhere near as good as the original. Plus, we're about to ruin the ending for you.

At the end of *Legally Blonde 2*, Reese Witherspoon's character, all pretty in pink, gives a speech before Congress, passionately calling for a new law outlawing animal testing in the cosmetics industry. To gain popular support, she's wielded her considerable charm—the bill is distributed to members with a pink cover—and even organized a "Million Dog March" in Washington, led by her Chihuahua, Bruiser. These heroic efforts are needed because evil corporations that oppose the bill wield considerable influence with certain politicians, including a not-so-nice Sally Field, who plays a once idealistic but now jaded member of Congress. At last, when "Bruiser's Bill" is voted into law, there are cheers, tears, and high fives all around. It's a magical movie moment—in a lightweight, romantic-comedy sort of way.

Democracy moves slowly. Thus, any sort of action has something of the nature of the dramatic about it. The passage of a law is a special moment, a moment at which democratic possibility becomes reality. In an instant the world is changed. The vast power of the state will now be working to ensure that, in this case, no Chihuahuas will be harmed in the making of your mascara.

By design, our constitutional system of checks and balances puts up hurdles against change. The hurdles facing major changes are even higher.

In the journey from idea to results, there is a moment at which the democratic process commits to an action, transforming the possible into the real. We call this moment of democratic commitment the "Stargate."

For those unfamiliar with the term, *Stargate* is the name of a sci-fi movie and long-running television series. The Stargate is the show's main prop, a big circular ring that creates a wormhole in space (hey, it's sci-fi) such that when you walk through the Stargate, you instantly travel from one part of the universe to another. By taking a single step, you wind up in a strange new world, where the people are different, the customs are different, and a new set of bad guys is waiting to mess with you. Walking through the Stargate represents a serious commitment, because you can't just turn around and walk back. Getting through isn't easy, since the Stargate may be guarded by unsavory aliens, or it may be closed altogether.

The analogy should be clear. Everything prior to the Stargate occurs in the political universe, while beyond it lays the bureaucratic universe. Just as with the intergalactic Stargate, democratic commitment is usually instantaneous and irreversible. It's not easy to get through, either.

The closest thing to the Stargate in the private sector is a vote of the board of directors. Though there are similarities between the two, there are also big differences. A corporate CEO doesn't need the approval of the board for most business decisions, and the board isn't split along party lines. In contrast, almost every major democratic initiative must go through the Stargate, and it is right in front of the Stargate that some of democracy's most unsavory characters hang out—the unscrupulous lobbyists, influence peddlers, and bad-apple politicians looking to extract a toll. It is also where many of our nation's leading statesmen and stateswomen, from Henry Clay to Daniel Webster to Margaret Chase Smith, have made their names advancing good laws and blocking bad ones. In government, you cannot navigate the journey from idea to results without going through the Stargate.

The "Stargate Trap" refers to the distortion effect of this unique phase. A lot of good policy fails to become reality because it can't get through the political Stargate, and some pretty bad stuff gets baked into otherwise sound bills in order to win passage. The challenge is to get a policy through with your integrity unscathed, with your idea intact, and with a design that actually can be implemented. Moreover, as we'll see next, how something gets through the Stargate can have a big impact on implementation.

Boston's Busing Nightmare: Seventy-seven Days to Disaster

There are three primary ways in which policy can make it through the Stargate, corresponding to the three branches of government. The most common is to have a piece of legislation voted into law, either by the legislature or through a direct referendum of voters. The executive branch can initiate major changes as well, sometimes with an executive order, as when President Truman desegregated the military or when President Kennedy allowed the formation of unions for federal employees.

The judicial branch can also initiate major undertakings. Court decisions can require the executive branch to engage in massive and complex undertakings under the oversight of a judge—essentially putting the judge in the role of chief operating officer for a particular project. Federal judge A. David Mazzone, for example, ordered the cleanup of Boston Harbor in 1985 after finding Massachusetts in "flagrant" violation of the Clean Water Act. The judge personally oversaw the cleanup, which took about ten years and cost about $4 billion. Thanks to this court-ordered cleanup, Boston today has a clean, swimmable harbor.

With judicial action of this sort, the journey from idea to results takes a detour, knocking the standard sequence out of order. Oddly enough, the court generally sends an *idea* through the Stargate and a *design* only comes afterward. In the case of the Boston Harbor cleanup, that wasn't a problem. But in another well-known Boston court case, a policy was blasted through Stargate and created disastrous consequences.

In the early 1970s, federal judge W. Arthur Garrity Jr. began hearing arguments in a lawsuit to determine whether Boston's public schools were so segregated as to be illegal. After the conclusion of a lengthy trial, Judge Garrity spent fifteen months writing a carefully argued decision. On June 21, 1974—the last day of school in Boston—Judge Garrity issued his 152-page decision, which found that "the entire school system of Boston is unconstitutionally segregated." With the rap of his gavel, Judge Garrity sent the idea of desegregation through the Stargate, decreeing what must be done, but saying nothing about how it should be accomplished.

Implementing desegregation would be a huge challenge. Unlike an infrastructure project like the Boston Harbor cleanup, forced busing was a highly charged issue that would impact families, neighborhoods, schools, and children. To ensure minimal disruption, a change of this nature would merit a thoughtful, well-designed implementation plan. Reasonable time would have to be allotted both to craft a workable design and allow officials to prepare for implementation.

That didn't happen.

Instead, just six days after declaring that Boston schools were segregated, Judge Garrity issued his order on how to fix this, declaring that the "Glenn Plan"—a plan that had been developed by a state education employee named Charles B. Glenn—would go into effect *just seventy-seven days later*—on the first day of school on September 12, 1974.[1]

Nobody liked the Glenn plan—not even Glenn. As Glenn himself described it, the plan was little more than a set of hastily devised bus routes: "We simply took a big map and started moving across the city in a big arc from northwest to southeast, dividing it into districts so that each school would include the right proportion of black and white kids. When we got to the end of the arc, we were left with South Boston and Roxbury. We didn't have any choice but to mix those two neighborhoods."[2] Those two neighborhoods were Boston's most volatile ghettos, poor white South Boston and poor black Roxbury, and mixing them created a toxic cocktail. (It's fair to say that the Glenn plan had fallen victim to the Design-Free Design Trap.) To the amazement of those in attendance, the judge breezily announced from the bench: "I saw the [Glenn] plan for the first time late yesterday afternoon."[3]

Judge Garrity had spent fifteen months crafting a closely reasoned, carefully worded 152-page legal decision. He spent less than a day reviewing the implementation plan, and he gave officials on the other side of Stargate less than a vacation-filled summer to prepare for the launch of the poorly designed plan. Parents, public safety officials, bus drivers, teachers, principals: nobody was ready for the logistical challenges that would hit on the first day of school.

The results were predictably awful. When school opened in September 1974, violence engulfed the city. Buses were stoned. Schools were occupied in protest. Hundreds of riot police guarded buses and police roamed school hallways. Teachers were asked to teach in the midst of bedlam.

On Sunday, September 15, 1974, Boston mayor Kevin White learned of plans for what he had reason to believe would be a violent protest the following day. He alerted President Gerald Ford to the possible need for federal troops and was coordinating with the local head of the FBI. The mayor's office then called Judge Garrity at his home in Wellesley, a wealthy suburb, so that the mayor could apprise the judge of the situation and ask for an order prohibiting the march. Judge Garrity refused to take the mayor's call; the judge's wife told White's aide that the judge felt it was "inappropriate." Mayor White was furious. "That stupid son of a bitch," White fumed, "he issues his damn order, then retires to his suburban estate and refuses to talk with the only guy who can make it work."[4]

The disconnect was absolute. The universes on either side of Stargate couldn't even talk over the telephone.

As months went by and circumstances failed to improve, Judge Garrity was drawn into every detail of school operations. In 1975, he altered the busing plans. Through some four hundred court orders, Garrity became involved in every aspect of school administration, from removing a high school principal to ordering the purchase of twelve MacGregor basketballs.[5] Garrity finally relinquished authority over the schools in September 1985—an eleven-year span during which Boston had eight different superintendents. A federal judge, instead of elected officials, was essentially running a major urban school district.

The results of the desegregation program were devastating to the city, the schools, and the students. During Garrity's eleven-year oversight, Boston's public school enrollment dropped from 93,000 to 57,000, while the proportion of white students shrank from 65 percent of total enrollment to 28 percent.[6] As a rule, anybody who could afford to get out did so.

No doubt the intent of desegregation was noble. The situation prior to Boston's court-ordered busing entailed intolerable inequities. But was this really the best government could do?

Judge Garrity's ruling may have been good law, but it turned out to be awful public policy, at least as executed, which is the only thing that mattered to students and parents. As we saw in chapter 2 when discussing the Design-Free Design Trap, getting a policy through Stargate doesn't equate to success. School desegregation was going to be a wrenching change no matter how it occurred. The manner in which the idea of desegregation was sent through the Stargate, however, and the ill-conceived design that came with it, undermined any chance for successful implementation. Moreover, the utter disconnect between the policy designers and policy implementers exacerbated already daunting execution challenges.

The Secret Recipe for Change

The entire journey from ideas to results is fraught with danger. Ideas are like seeds. In the biblical parable of the sower, some seeds land on rocky soil. Others are eaten by birds, and some sprout only to be choked by thorns. Only through a fortuitous combination of sun, soil, and water will a seed grow into a plant and bear fruit. In the policy realm, similar pitfalls await most ideas, and a similar happy coincidence of factors must be in place for the seed of an idea to take root and bear fruit in the political world.

Political scientist John W. Kingdon describes the conditions that must be in place for the seed of an idea to become reality in his 1984 book *Agendas, Alternatives, and Public Policies*.[7] Kingdon argues that three separate policy factors must converge. First, there must be a crisis, or at least a general perception of a problem in need of attention. It helps if this problem can be captured in some measurable change in a well-known indicator (unemployment rate, inflation rate, etc.) or if there is a catastrophic event that calls for action. Second, the idea must be under discussion as a potential solution to the problem. That is, some number of academics, specialists within the bureaucracy, associations, and think tanks must see the idea as a viable alternative. Kingdon refers to the pool of ideas in play as a "policy primordial soup," in which ideas float around until the right combination of circumstances arise. Third, there must be a political window of opportunity, a receptiveness among politicians to be open to bold alternatives to established practice. Kingdon stresses the importance of "coupling," the magic moment when these three separate factors—a problem, an idea, and a political moment—come together. Important players in this process are the "policy entrepreneurs," who attempt to create the circumstances under which this magic might happen. Just as a suitor might bring together his date, a couch, and a Barry White CD in the hopes of creating some magic, these policy entrepreneurs purposely try to create the conditions under which major political change can occur.

Policy entrepreneurs aren't shy about taking advantage of misfortune to get their policy agenda through the Stargate. Following the fatal collapse of a bridge in 2007, *USA Today* reported that "the disaster on Minnesota's busiest bridge—which carries 141,000 cars a day—raised hopes of more money for infrastructure in general." The article noted that the American Society of Civil Engineers was estimating the government would need to spend $1.6 trillion over five years to put its infrastructure, including bridges, in good condition. "Unfortunately, it takes a catastrophe to get us busy on some things," said Sam Maggard, head of the Bridge Inspection Program at New Mexico State University.[8]

A policy entrepreneur might also promote crisis by means of data. In hopes of spurring reform, the 1983 federal report "A Nation at Risk" consciously used alarming language as well as powerful data to declare a crisis in American education.[9] Not much came of it. That's because a crisis alone often isn't sufficient to make reform possible. When ideological differences run deep, it may require a novel approach to break the gridlock that prevents a policy change from making it through the Stargate.

Reducing Acid Rain: Breaking the Impasse

Acid rain was the environmental mega-issue of the 1980s. Caused when industrial smokestacks spew forth airborne nitrogen and sulfur, which then mixes with rain and falls back to earth, acid rain was known to kill fish, render lakes sterile, and drive species to extinction; only later was it learned that its vastly more important impacts were on human health through acidified particulates.[10] Crafting policy was particularly thorny because pollution created in one place often drifted hundreds of miles before returning to earth to do its damage. Canada claimed that most of the damage to its seven hundred thousand impacted lakes was caused by pollution that had drifted over the border from sources in the United States.[11]

Despite all the tangible evidence, efforts to reduce sulfur dioxide emissions went nowhere in the 1980s. Members of Congress introduced more than seventy bills aimed at controlling acid rain. Not one of them made it through the Stargate to become law.[12] These bills were enthusiastically opposed by industry, which had the support of both the Reagan White

House and Midwestern politicians of both parties who believed that the proposed regulations would devastate coal producers and electric utilities in their states. The opponents had a point, as the remedies proposed were often heavy-handed regulations that gave little regard to the impact on business. "There was an assumption that the more it pained industry, the better for the environment, because industry was evil and the more you hurt them, the more you helped the environment," says Fred Krupp, president of the Environmental Defense Fund (EDF).[13] Founded by a small group of scientists, the EDF had been fighting on the front lines of the environmental movement since 1967, pairing science-based analysis of environmental issues with tough legal advocacy.

The EDF was a little different from most environmental groups, however. "We talked to Republicans," says Krupp. "It sounds humorous in retrospect, but the idea that we had talked to them meant that a measure to censure EDF was actually debated at the national meeting of the Clean Air Coalition."[14]

By 1988, precious little in the way of constructive dialogue was taking place. Everyone acknowledged the damage that acid rain was doing, but nothing was being done about it.

Into this logjam stepped two senators: H. John Heinz III, a moderate Republican from the coal-producing state of Pennsylvania, and Timothy E. Wirth, a liberal Democrat from Colorado with strong environmental leanings. Heinz and Wirth represented the two sides of the acid rain debate: East versus West, Republican versus Democrat, high-sulfur state versus low-sulfur state. "Jack represented one world; I represented the other," says Wirth.[15]

Politically, Heinz and Wirth should have been on opposite sides of the acid rain issue. They probably would have been except for a curious set of personal circumstances that linked them. The two senators had been close friends since attending high school together at Phillips Exeter Academy. Their families socialized together, and they shared a passion for the environment. Perhaps most important, both of their wives, Teresa Heinz and Wren Wirth, served on the Board of Trustees of the Environmental Defense Fund.

One spring evening in 1988 over coffee at the Palm Court in New York's Plaza Hotel, the two couples, along with EDF attorney David

Roe, were lamenting how the environment wasn't even on the radar screen in the presidential campaign. To remedy this they hatched the idea of Project 88, an initiative to introduce into the campaign debate new ideas on the environment.[16] Roe suggested the senators talk to a young economist named Robert Stavins, who had worked at EDF on market approaches to environmental problems and was now finishing up his PhD at Harvard. Within a week, the two couples helped raise $100,000 to get Project 88 off the ground and signed up Stavins as the research director, a position he assumed while beginning what was to be a long career as a professor at Harvard's Kennedy School of Government.[17]

To have any impact on the candidates in the 1988 election, Stavins knew they would have to release a report quickly. A newlywed at the time, Stavins promptly cancelled his hiking trip out West with his new bride and, in a real show of commitment, this dedicated baseball fan sacrificed a summer of watching his beloved Red Sox to Project 88. To produce a quality report quickly, he enlisted the help of a number of other academics. "I was an economist, so the people I tended to reach out to were economists," recalls Stavins, whose social circle includes a lot of economists, including his forbearing wife.[18] This was critical. Stavins in essence brought new voices to a debate that had been dominated by two intractable sides—environmentalists and industry. Their deadlocked arguments were all based in the existing paradigm of a command-and-control regulatory regime, in which government determines how much industry is allowed to pollute and what technology it will use to cut emissions. By bringing in economists, Project 88 broke out of the Tolstoy Trap and found common ground where none had appeared to exist.

Stavins and Project 88 adopted as their starting point the environmentalists' stated goal of reducing acid rain by 50 percent. But Stavins and his buddies approached the problem like economists, meaning they looked at incentives, considered trade-offs, and had the nonutopian outlook famously associated with practitioners of the "dismal science." They didn't think in terms of saving the earth or zero emissions. They thought about how they might craft incentives that would encourage polluters to balance marginal cost and marginal benefit. Not surprisingly, Stavins's Project 88 proposal for dealing with acid rain broke with policy orthodoxy. Gone were the traditional regulatory proposals so despised by industry.

Project 88's approach of "tradable emission permits" (now known as "cap and trade") offered much greater flexibility. Government would dictate the overall pollution limit, but would leave it up to the market to determine how to meet those limits. In the case of acid rain, government would cap the amount of pollutants that fossil-fueled power plants could emit.[19] Energy producers could then use any methods they wanted to meet the target. Additionally, energy producers had a strong incentive to reduce emissions *below* the target level, since by doing so they could sell the excess emissions allowance to another firm—or to environmental groups seeking to "retire" the allowance.[20]

The acid rain proposal was the most important idea in Project 88. It changed the politics of the issue by offering a way to break the long-standing impasse between environmentalists and business on acid rain. "When negotiations are stuck, you have to have something new to put on the table," said Senator Wirth. "That was the magic of Project 88 and the idea of tradable permits. It gave people the chance to break out of the lockstep they were in for a long time."[21]

As a candidate for president in 1988, Vice President Bush wanted to distinguish himself from President Reagan on several high-profile issues. During the campaign, Bush pledged to cut acid rain emissions.[22] Bush's positioning on environmental issues was heavily influenced by C. Boyden Gray, his counselor and close confidante. "Boyden Gray fell in love with the idea of tradable permits," says Wirth.[23] Soon after the election, Stavins got a call from Gray seeking a meeting. The Bush White House and the environmentalists had something to discuss.

With the Bush White House getting on board, Congress now had to be convinced to go along. The flexibility of the bill made it less onerous on industry, and Heinz managed to convince some of his colleagues in the Senate Coal Caucus to support, for the first time ever, a bill that would reduce acid rain emissions. The reality was that the tradable permit program would cost some mining jobs in Pennsylvania and other high-sulfur coal states. Still, it was far preferable to any alternative on the table, so about half the caucus ended up supporting tradable permits.[24] Somewhat surprisingly, another roadblock was the environmental groups. Many hated the idea of tradable permits, calling them a license to pollute. To this charge, Senator Heinz had a clever response: "They have always had the right to pollute; now we're going to charge them for it."[25] The environmental community eventually came to terms with the bill because it delivered on their goal of reduced emissions.

The elegant simplicity of the policy design made it easier to get through Congress. "There was only one political decision," says Wirth. "Where is the cap going to be?" Once the overall limit was set, members of Congress could do their horse trading on the regional distribution of allowances without having a negative effect on the overall environmental integrity of the program. Being economists, the Project 88 authors were familiar with the Coase theorem, named for Nobel Prize winner Ronald Coase, which states that in the absence of transaction costs, trade in an externality such as pollution will lead to an economically efficient outcome regardless of the initial distribution of property rights. With the support of leaders from both parties, a law to deal with acid rain finally made it through Stargate, and there were cheers, tears, and high fives all around.

The acid rain tradable permit program became law as part of the Clean Air Act Amendments of 1990. It has been a massive success. More than 18 million permits were traded in Phase I, resulting in a net *over*compliance.[26] Not only did firms voluntarily participate in the program, but third parties also purchased and retired permits.[27] Thanks to overcompliance, the price of an allowance dropped from about $150 per ton in 1994 to as low as $65 in 1996.[28] This meant not only less pollution, but lower cost to industry. With a 40:1 benefit-to-cost ratio and 40 percent reduction in sulfur dioxide emissions, the acid rain program is considered one of the more successful environmental programs of all time.[29]

Thanks to the acid rain program, market-based incentives have become a popular environmental tool around the world. The acid rain program is the intellectual godfather of the current cap-and-trade proposal aimed at reducing carbon emissions.

Project 88 illustrates the power of the policy "mash-up": combining two ideas drawn from two different sides to break a political logjam. The acid rain program succeeded because Heinz and Wirth were willing to consider ideas from diverse sources without prejudice, without sacrificing the integrity of their principles. EDF and Stavins, the intellectual forces behind the idea, bucked the orthodoxy of environmental advocates and traditional business interests alike to create a highly original solution. By bringing in the perspective of economists, policy makers broke a logjam that held back progress on acid rain for years.

But what happens when politicians can't find a compromise that will make it through Stargate? In these cases, it's often necessary to make the case directly to the people. This is risky. It is also, however, the ultimate in democratic transformation. If you can win the hearts and minds of the people, legislators will take heed, and change will follow.

Japan's Number One Elvis Fan Goes Postal

This book is about getting big things done in a democracy. Ultimately, in a democracy the people rule. Democratic processes are designed to make it difficult to get big changes through the Stargate, but if the people support change, it will happen. Consider the story of Japanese prime minister Junichiro Koizumi's attempt to overhaul that nation's postal system.

Japanese prime ministers in the post–World War II era have tended to be cut from similar cloth: cautious, change averse, and old. Japan has been largely dominated by one party, the Liberal Democratic Party (LDP). As with America's big-city machines of old, the most important skill for a Japanese politician was the ability to dole out favors to party members while avoiding indictment. As a consequence, Japan's public sector was bloated and overfed, like a sleepwalking Sumo wrestler heading for the refrigerator with an appetite for everything but real reform.

Then in 2001, along came a politician who thoroughly broke the mold. Junichiro Koizumi, a fifty-nine-year-old politician from outside Tokyo, shocked the world when he defeated the two favored candidates of the old guard.[30] Nicknamed "Lionheart" due to his fierce spirit and wavy mane of hair flowing down to his shoulders, Japan had never seen a prime minister quite like him before.

Though center-right politically, Koizumi was anything but conservative in temperament. He campaigned on a platform that promised change. He famously pledged to "change the LDP, change Japan," even if it meant he had to "destroy the LDP" to make it happen. Koizumi had another nickname, "Henjin," meaning "the odd one out" or "maverick." Calling for "reform with no sacred cows," he framed his first election as a choice for the country: Japan could either cling to its semisocialist, big-government roots, or press ahead with reforms to upend Japan's crony-dominated political system and create a more modern, competitive economy.[31]

This maverick politician is a man of many passions, one of which is music. One singer in particular holds a special place in Koizumi's heart: Elvis Presley, with whom Koizumi shares a birthday. A member in good standing of Japan's Elvis Presley Fan Club—his brother once served as the club's vice president—Koizumi has the habit of bursting into song whenever he hears one of the King's songs. Knowing his affinity for Elvis, George W. Bush helped Koizumi fulfill a lifelong dream by giving his friend a special gift: a guided tour of Graceland hosted by Priscilla and Lisa Marie Presley. True to form, with just the slightest prodding from the American president, the Elvis-loving prime minister draped his arm around Lisa Marie and crooned "I Want You, I Need You, I Love You" in front of a throng of television cameras. Seven thousand miles away, Japan's political old guard suffered a collective heart attack.

Koizumi's other lifelong passion is—and we are not making this up—privatizing Japan's postal service.[32] By the time he became prime minister, Koizumi had spent two decades arguing for postal privatization.[33] To understand why, you need to understand that for Japan Post, delivering mail was a quaint side business. The hundred-year-old, state-owned Japanese postal monopoly consisted of three main services—mail delivery, postal savings, and postal life insurance. Between the banking and life insurance operations, these two "postal" businesses accounted for about $3 *trillion* in assets, making it the world's largest financial institution. Japan Post held more than one-quarter of all of the personal financial assets in Japan.[34] Roughly 80 percent of Japan Post's enormous assets were held in government bonds. Koizumi and others saw postal privatization as a crucial economic reform because it would free up capital for the private sector and encourage Japan's financial markets to enter the twenty-first century.[35]

In addition to reinvigorating the economy, postal privatization could dramatically alter the political landscape. For the party in power, the LDP, Japan Post has long been a great source of patronage. Japan Post amounted to a giant government piggy bank—one that could conveniently deliver pork for those in power. The LDP took care of Japan Post, and Japan Post took care of the LDP. This cozy arrangement had given rise to the "postal tribe" (*yusei zoku*), a group of politicians within the LDP.[36] Since Japan Post employed roughly one in every three government employees, it wasn't hard for the postal tribe to "get out the vote." Never mind singing with the ghost of Elvis; talk of privatizing Japan Post could really send LDP party elders into cardiac arrest.

Recalling Kingdon's recipe for transformational change, Koizumi had two of the three ingredients in place to make a run at Japan Post. There was a crisis (Japan's economic stagnation), there was an idea (postal privatization), and the only thing needed was a political openness to the change. There wasn't any of that. Nobody in power had any interest in postal privatization becoming a reality. Nobody except Koizumi and his blue suede shoes.

The Stargate was closed. So Koizumi decided to change the political climate all by himself.

First, Koizumi stacked his cabinet. He broke with tradition and put postal privatization directly on the agenda of his handpicked cabinet. Koizumi took the debate outside the reach of opponents within his party lying in wait to kill the idea.[37] Political observers came to dub this Koizumi's "cabinet to realize postal privatization."[38] It was not intended as a compliment, but Koizumi felt it was critical that his highest-level appointees were behind his key reform initiative.[39]

Koizumi's second key strategic decision was to establish a dedicated unit to drive postal privatization. Just as Mitt Romney created a health care reform SWAT team with no other day-to-day responsibilities, Koizumi created a new unit whose sole focus was planning the postal privatization initiative. Koizumi knew he couldn't rely on the bureaucrats in the Ministry of Internal Affairs and Telecommunications, many of whom were beholden to the status quo.

Koizumi's last move was critical. He waited. An impatient man by nature, Koizumi knew that a premature effort at privatization would fail, dooming all hope for reform. Though Koizumi was elected prime minister in 2001, he did not unleash his postal privatization program right away. Instead, he initiated several incremental reforms that boosted the economy (and his popularity) while simultaneously fleshing out the idea of postal privatization into an executable design.

The Death of a Reform

As soon as he was reelected, Koizumi put his cards on the table. In January 2005, Koizumi kicked off the 162nd session of the Parliament, Japan's bicameral legislature, with his bombshell. "Postal privatization is the main target," said Koizumi. "I will submit the bill which aims to privatize Japan Post in April 2007 and try to realize it."[40]

Three months later, a set of postal privatization bills was sent to the lower house. Privatization opponents, including the main opposition party (the Democratic Party of Japan, or DJP) and the LDP postal tribe, swung into action. A group called the Postal Service Association was created to oppose the bill. More than a hundred lawmakers, many of them members of the LDP postal tribe, quickly signed up. Groups opposing the bill held demonstrations around the Diet.

Koizumi made it clear that to be on his team meant you were in favor of postal privatization. He demoted two executives within the Ministry of Internal Affairs and Communications after they ignored his instruction and lobbied legislators to oppose his reforms. Challenged on their dismissals, the Koizumi camp was blunt. "[They] conspired with members of the ruling LDP who are opposed to postal privatization," explained a Koizumi aide.[41] Any cabinet member who opposed privatization was summarily dismissed by the prime minister.[42] The LDP was at war with itself.

Deliberations in the lower house stretched out for 109 hours. The final vote was a cliffhanger, with Koizumi squeaking out a narrow five-vote margin of victory in favor of privatization.[43] Thirty-seven LDP members had rebelled against Koizumi to oppose the bill and another eleven LDP members abstained from voting.[44]

The bill now moved to the upper house. Koizumi upped the political ante by threatening to dissolve the lower house and call a snap election if the upper house failed to pass the bill. With the political repercussions so high, LDP lawmakers were expected to approve privatization.[45] They did not. Koizumi's privatization plan was shot down by a vote of 125 to 108 in the upper house.[46] After four years of meticulous planning, postal privatization was dead, its battered corpse motionless in front of Japan's Stargate.

Or maybe it only looked dead.

Some of the rebel LDP lawmakers admitted that they thought Koizumi's promise to dissolve the lower house was a bluff.[47] They had misjudged the man. Koizumi followed through on his threat and dissolved the lower house on August 8, 2005. He then held a press conference where he took the issue over the heads of the politicians directly to the people:

> *Today, I dissolved the lower house. This is because the upper house rejected my plans to privatize Japan's postal service which I have targeted for structural reform. The Diet judged that postal privatization isn't necessary. I'd like to ask you [the Japanese people] whether you think postal privatization is necessary or not. In other words, this election will be a referendum on the issue of postal privatization . . . If the LDP and the New Komeito fails to retain the majority of seats, I will definitely go out of office.*[48]

Junichiro Koizumi was making the biggest of political bets. The snap election would be held September 11, 2005, only a month away.

Snap Election

Soon after his shocking announcement, Koizumi moved quickly to control the political debate. Koizumi announced that not only would he not support any LDP lawmaker who had voted against postal privatization, but he would also personally recruit candidates to run against each and every one of them. Koizumi's handpicked candidates came to be known as "the Assassins." The Assassins were not exactly your typical party regulars who had worked their way up the system and were now next in line. Instead, with his flair for the dramatic, Koizumi recruited semicelebrities—many of them young, articulate, and good looking—whose popularity would appeal to the wider Japanese public. Koizumi's slate of Assassins featured a number of high-profile female candidates, including a television celebrity chef, a former beauty queen, and a former news anchor. These were dubbed the "Female Ninjas" by the Japanese media. "It's like a virtual harem," complained one of the opposition candidates who ended up getting knocked off by one of Koizumi's recruits.[49]

One of Koizumi's female Ninjas, Kyoko Nishikawa, was asked by Koizumi to run against an LDP rebel. The incumbent had close ties to the local LDP organization, so when Nishikawa went to the district's party chief to ask for help on her campaign, she was unceremoniously turned away. "Go out and campaign on an orange crate," he told her. The comment made national news but failed to deter Nishikawa in the least. The enterprising Nishikawa got herself a wooden crate, painted it orange, and made that orange crate her symbol, standing atop it during all her campaign speeches.[50] The Ninja Nishikawa routed her opponent in the election.

Koizumi himself campaigned tirelessly, characterizing the LDP's old guard and other privatization opponents as reactionary obstructionists. The election captured the public imagination like few before it, and voter turnout was unusually high.

Once all the votes were counted, Koizumi had won an overwhelming victory. The largest opposition party, the DJP, which had steadfastly opposed postal privatization, was crushed, losing more than sixty seats in the lower house of the Diet. In addition, Koizumi's Assassins, who had run against LDP incumbents that had opposed privatization, won fifteen out of thirty-five contests, an impressive feat for political neophytes.[51]

The snap election could have been Koizumi's political Waterloo. Instead it resulted in one of the biggest party-seat gains in a single election in Japan's postwar history. Koizumi had his mandate. After decades fighting for postal privatization, he would finally see his signature policy initiative enacted into law. In the lower house of the Diet, this time 338 lawmakers voted in favor of postal privatization, with just 138 against.[52] Then, despite the fact that not a single member of the upper house changed, 134 of these lawmakers now voted in favor of privatization and just 100 against it.[53] "This is a political miracle," said Koizumi, who stepped down from office in 2006. "Once I was thrown down to the bottom of the valley, but the people have pulled me up."[54]

Koizumi's victory created massive change in both the political and economic climate in Japan. By 2007, postal privatization was proceeding apace, with plans to shift over time some 240,000 government employees to the private sector. Completing the implementation is expected to take a decade, but in this case perhaps the hardest step was getting a radical, transforming public policy through Japan's well-guarded Stargate.

The story of Japan's postal privatization shows that sometimes the only way to open a political window while maintaining the integrity of your idea is to go to the people and make your case directly. (That approach doesn't always work, of course. In chapter 6 we'll see what happened when California governor Arnold Schwarzenegger took his reform agenda to the people.) Without question, those who hold political power are savvy about holding on to that power. Like Reese Witherspoon's legally blonde reformer, Koizumi found that the inside political game was rigged against the change he sought. So he went outside the political culture, bringing his case to the people. The voice of the people expressed at the ballot box changed the political equation and opened the Stargate for massive change.

The Distortion Effects of the Stargate Trap

A gazelle has to drink. That's why crocodiles hang out at the water's edge. When a gazelle puts its head down to drink, it is vulnerable and presents an opportunity for the crocodile to get a meal. Whether you think this is a good thing or a bad thing depends on whether you are a crocodile or a gazelle.

To become reality, a bill has to get through Stargate. Opponents will go to great lengths to stop a bill before it gets through. In the final stages before coming to a vote, a bill is particularly vulnerable.

In the early 1990s, President Clinton's massive health care reform effort, spearheaded by First Lady Hillary Clinton, advanced through months of task force meetings, Congressional testimony, and bill drafting. Many observers believed that there was enough support in Congress to make it a reality. But when the Health Security Act was submitted to the House in late 1993, the long, detailed bill became a target for opponents. It was ridiculed mercilessly for months in TV ads, news shows, and talk radio. Support evaporated. The bill lay wounded just in front of the Stargate for months before being declared dead. The McCain-Kennedy immigration reform bill of 2006 met a similar fate. The measure appeared to have enough support within Congress for passage, but the compromise measure died when talk radio generated massive popular opposition to it.

How you feel about the demise of these would-be reforms depends on your opinion of them as laws. But those seeking transformational change learned from these experiences, and thus the conventional wisdom in Washington today is that the best way to get a big piece of legislation through the Stargate is to ram it through fast, so fast that legislators don't have time to read it and opponents don't have time to kill it.

That's how the Medicare Part D prescription drug reform was rammed through Congress by Republicans in 2003. In the middle of the night, the Republican leadership pushed through a bill whose lengthy text had been published only one day before, leaving little time for a public debate. Despite the push, the measure still almost perished. The bill was trailing two hours into voting (which is supposed to take about fifteen minutes), and House Republicans simply kept the vote open, as members browbeat fence-sitters in an attempt to squeeze out victory. The House Ethics Commission would later rebuke two Republican members, including House majority leader Tom DeLay, for making inappropriate offers of quid pro quo in an attempt to sway votes. The measure passed by a razor-thin margin, and within a month it came to light that the cost estimates of the program had been understated by 35 percent. Nancy Pelosi, then the Democrat minority leader, characterized the vote as an outrage. "We won it fair and square," she said, "so they stole it by hook or crook."

Democrats learned from this example as well. When they came into power, they turned around and pushed through the 2009 stimulus law with little GOP input. Republican House members were first cut out of the drafting process and then given less than twenty-four hours to read the more than one thousand pages of legalese in the bill before the vote. There seems to be bipartisan agreement that messy democratic debate and public consideration of massive initiatives are an inconvenience to be avoided.

"The argument is that if you let the bill sit out there, it becomes a piñata and will get killed" says former congressman Tom Davis. Davis, a Republican, spent fourteen years in Congress, and isn't a fan of the ram-it-through approach. The result of such a process, says Davis, is "not thoroughbred bills but three-humped camels." More often than not, undue haste results in a poorly vetted policy design process, distorted cost estimates, and a deepening rancor that poisons the political climate. "We should be worried about how a bill will work eighteen months from now, not just today, but too often we aren't," says Davis.

After seeing all this up close—and seeing it get worse, not better, during his time in Congress—Davis decided he had had enough. In 2008 he left Congress in the prime of his career, fed up with what he terms the hyperpartisan, win-at-all-costs, political trench warfare that has infected the governing process in Washington and many state capitals.[55] "When we go off-site with other members of our party, we focus on how we can win, instead of how we can solve problems," he says. "The overwhelming focus is how to stay in power or get back to power."

Davis chaired the House hearings on immigration reform in 2005. Neither side, he says, had much interest in a real exchange of ideas. His Republican colleagues figured they would be better off in the 2006 election without any bill. In the middle of a rancorous discussion about amnesty, Davis asked another member to define the term. "He said, 'It's whatever the talk radio hosts say it is,'" Davis recalls.

It's not that Davis didn't care about winning (he had, after all, headed the National Republican Campaign Committee for two campaign cycles). However, when it came to legislating, he had a very different approach: measured, bipartisan, focused on governance. "If you're solving a big problem, whether it's welfare reform or Social Security, you want every perspective at the table—not so they can veto it, but so you can get everyone involved," says Davis.[56] Davis knows this approach can work, but it takes time and effort. In his fourteen years in Congress, Davis sponsored more than a hundred bills that became law, many focused on governance issues. As a freshman legislator, Davis, who hails from neighboring Fairfax County, Virginia, partnered with Democrats to address the financial collapse of Washington, D.C.'s city government by creating the D.C. Control Board to oversee the city's finances. "That taught me right away up here—if that had been a partisan deal, it never would have gone."[57] Sadly, in today's Beltway culture such an approach seems like a quaint anachronism.

Davis and other observers will tell you that very few good things happen in front of the Stargate. The best that can be said of the Stargate Trap is that it sometimes kills bills that deserve to die. More often, the damaging distortion effects on a policy proposal are profoundly negative. Sometimes a bill sits out there and gets picked apart like a wounded animal by opponents, eventually being killed. Sometimes a bill gets loaded with so many goodies and special exceptions to gain the support needed for passage that the final bill becomes unrecognizable from the original idea. Or perhaps the bill is rammed through with little debate. None of these routes through Stargate enhance democracy. In 2009, confidence in the lawmaking process, already shaky, took another hit when a month after the 2009 stimulus bill was rushed through Congress, AIG, a company that had received billions in federal funds, handed out $160 million in bonuses to executives. Initial Congressional outrage turned to embarrassment when they realized the stimulus bill they passed without reading allowed just such bonuses.

Lessons from the Gulf of Tonkin

Speed can get something through Stargate, but that doesn't guarantee happy results. In August 1964, Congress passed the Gulf of Tonkin resolution with stunning rapidity based on a misunderstanding of what actually happened, giving President Johnson a blank check to wage war in Vietnam. How did this happen?

The official version of events at the time went like this. On August 2, 1964, the destroyer USS *Maddox* was on "routine patrol in international waters" when it was subjected to an "unprovoked attack by three [North Vietnamese] PT-type boats." The *Maddox* returned fire, inflicting damage on the attackers. Then on August 4, the *Maddox*, now accompanied by another destroyer, the USS *Turner Joy*, once again came under attack in the same waters. In response, President Johnson ordered an air strike against North Vietnam, sinking half their navy. At the same time, near midnight on August 4, Johnson addressed the nation and asked Congress to pass the Gulf of Tonkin Resolution, which authorized him, without a formal declaration of war, to use military force in Southeast Asia. On August 7, 1964, the resolution sailed through the House after just forty minutes of "debate" by a vote of 416–0. A few hours later, the vote in the Senate was 88–2, and Johnson had the support he was looking for.[58]

That was the official version of events, mind you. Documents released decades later confirm what few suspected at the time, which was that the first attack wasn't unprovoked and the second attack hadn't happened at all.

White House recordings from August 3, 1964, leave no doubt that President Johnson knew more about what was behind the North Vietnamese attack of the prior day: "There have been some covert operations in that area that we have been carrying on—blowing up some bridges and things of that kind, roads and so forth. So I imagine they wanted to put a stop to it."[59]

The second "attack" took place in heavy weather, and documents released by the National Security Agency in 2001 state: "*No attack happened that night . . . In truth, Hanoi's navy was engaged in nothing but the salvage of the two boats damaged on 2 August*."[60] The sailors on board the *Maddox* and *Turner Joy* likely misread the radar, and opened a barrage of fire on imaginary targets, believing themselves to be under attack. Johnson admitted this privately at the time. "When we got through with all the firing," Johnson told his secretary of defense, Robert S. McNamara, "we concluded maybe they hadn't fired at all."[61]

Rushed through on bad intelligence, the Gulf of Tonkin Resolution may have served Johnson's short-term political goal, but the results ultimately served neither Johnson nor the nation. Senator Wayne Morse, one of the two votes against the measure, had it right: "I believe that within the next century, future generations will look with dismay and great disappointment upon a Congress which is now about to make such a historic mistake."[62] Over time, as opposition to the war grew, the manner in which Congressional approval for the conflict had sailed through Stargate actually made successful execution more difficult.[63] There was no need for haste—Johnson had already launched his retaliatory strikes—but an unthinking stampede in Congress allowed a terribly ill-advised bill to pass with overwhelming support. The Gulf of Tonkin Resolution was quietly repealed in 1971.

Are there easy solutions to these problems? No. They are part of the political terrain. Is there a better way to get an idea through the Stargate? Yes. It's the approach Tom Davis used to break a ten-year impasse when he moved postal reform through Congress in 2006. It is the approach Senators Heinz and Wirth used to break the acid rain logjam. It is the approach used to get many of the most successful undertakings of the past fifty years through the Stargate, including one of the biggest, initially most controversial, initiatives, the Marshall Plan.

Today, the Marshall Plan is widely considered one of the great achievements of the post–World War II period. But when George Marshall first broached the idea in June 1947, it was by no means a foregone conclusion that Congress would support such an unprecedented aid package to Europe. Americans were worried about their own economy after World War II; the isolationist movement was quite powerful; and the GOP-controlled Congress had been elected on a platform of limited government, anti-interventionism, and fiscal conservatism. Howard Buffet, a Republican congressman from Nebraska, voiced a sentiment held by many Midwesterners at the time when he ridiculed the Marshall Plan as "Operation Rathole."[64]

Despite formidable challenges, the Marshall Plan passed the Congress by a large margin with strong support from the American people. How did Truman, Marshall, and other proponents do it? They didn't try to steamroll the bill through Congress but instead used a measured and respectful approach that allowed for plenty of debate, discussion, and hearings, even arranging for tours of battle-ravaged Europe for members of Congress. They established a bipartisan national council divided equally among Republicans and Democrats. They eschewed a shrill, strongly ideological hard sell. "We should not embark on the Marshall Plan program," cautioned supporter Allen Dulles (future head of the Central Intelligence Agency), "until we have counted the effort, the cost, and the sacrifice that we are disposed to put into it."[64] We would do well to remember Dulles' admonition today. His words, along with the exemplary manner in which advocates moved the Marshall Plan through the Stargate, are as relevant today as they were five decades ago.

FIELD GUIDE: THE STARGATE PHASE

The Stargate Trap isn't something you avoid; it's something you get through. For this most unpredictable phase in the journey, the challenge is to get through with your integrity intact, your idea recognizable, and a design that can actually be implemented.

Biggest Danger

The Stargate Trap. The biggest dangers are the distorting, and sometimes lethal, effects of the dangerous political terrain of the Stargate itself.

You run the risk of the idea never making it through the Stargate or being so distorted that the initiative will never achieve the intended results.

Guiding Principles

Hold on to your integrity. The Stargate is the essence of democracy—both good and bad. The best and worst of democracy are right in front of the Stargate. It is where the statesmen prevent bad ideas from going through but also where all the unsavory characters hang out: the special interests, the log rollers, the horse traders. Avoid the temptation to sacrifice your principles to get something through.

Maintain the integrity of your idea. Don't sacrifice your principles to get your idea through. There is a temptation to water down an idea to get it through Stargate, but what is gained?

Be ready to champion change. Democracy is designed to limit big change. Work through all the things that could go wrong during the legislative process. Develop strategies to counteract each scenario and be prepared to make a public case.

- **Take it to the people:** The Stargate is heavily guarded. Those in power are often beneficiaries of the status quo who will resist change. If you can win the hearts and minds of the people, legislators will take heed, and change will follow.

- **Steer the debate:** The Japanese postal reform drama was staged as a play, "Koizumi Theater." Koizumi was the producer, the director, the writer, and the star of the play. The Assassins were the heroes, a charming group of characters. The old-guard politicians were the villains. Would the good of postal privatization triumph over the evil of entrenched interests? That was up to the audience, the voters. Koizumi's exceptional sense of stagecraft helped him to control the conversation from the day he announced the snap election to the day he won a resounding victory six weeks later.

Don't rush or force an idea through Stargate before you've achieved consensus. If you go to war by executive order—that is, without a declaration or resolution—it can be infinitely harder to execute, because if things get tough, the Congress might abandon you. When Boston implemented busing through a court order, it made things infinitely harder because the executive players weren't in alignment and weren't ready to execute the plan.

Don't stifle debate. See the Stargate not just as a barrier on the way to getting something done but as a part of the democratic process. In the long run, the civil debate that takes place is critical to being able to achieve what you really want done. It is much more difficult to execute on an unpopular exercise, such as the Vietnam War, when there hasn't been a true democratic commitment.

Tools and Techniques

Articulate your deal breakers. Every dog has fleas, and every law has flaws. What principles are essential? What aspects of reform are negotiable? What are the nonnegotiables that will cause you to walk away from your own bill?

Get "sticky." Those opposed to the 2005 comprehensive immigration bill had a short, simple message that resonated with voters: we don't reward lawbreakers in America. Proponents had position papers and economic statistics. Guess who won? (For more information, read *Made to Stick*, by Chip and Dan Heath.)

Encourage public debate. From the Lincoln-Douglas debates to the less grand NAFTA debate between Al Gore and Ross Perot on *Larry King Live*, public discourse is the lifeblood of democracy.

Require a workability assessment. Require an "implementability" assessment before a bill passes from the political realm to the bureaucratic world. Are the time lines realistic? Is the funding sufficient? In Canada, departments coming forward to the cabinet with new program proposals are required to detail the implementation implications of their proposals (as opposed to simply coming forward with a new program proposal—and funding request—with only a broad implementation plan).

Resources (Books, Web Sites, and Other Cool Stuff)

Study the art of political statesmanship. Read *Profiles in Courage*, by John F. Kennedy; *Path to Power*, by Robert Caro; *Going Public*, by Samuel Kernell (profiles how Reagan pushed through his tax cuts); and *The System: The American Way of Politics at the Breaking Point*, by Haynes Johnson and David Broder.

CHAPTER **4**

The Overconfidence Trap

Fear, Risk, and the Best-Laid Plans

Idea → Design → Stargate → **Implementation** → Results
(←——————— Reevaluation ———————→)

CHAPTER GUIDE

- Mayor Livingstone Makes London Drivers Pay
- The Overconfidence Trap
- The Real Tragedy of the Commons
- War Games in London
- A Trip Up Mount Washington
- Iraq Reconstruction: Plan B
- First Impressions: The Boy with the Vase
- The Scary Secret of Successful Implementation

There ain't no horse that can't be rode, and there ain't no rider that can't be throwed.

—COWBOY SAYING

L ONDON, FEBRUARY 17, 2003, 5:30 A.M.: The sky is still dark when Ken Livingstone, the fifty-seven-year-old mayor of London, opens the door to leave his flat. Flash, flash, flash, flash. The mayor is bathed in a blinding white light.

"What's going on out there, honey?" calls out Emma, his partner and the mother of his two young children. "It looks like *Close Encounters* in here."

"I think our fine press corps is under the impression that by the end of the day I'm going to announce I am resigning from public life forever," jokes the mayor, gazing upon the media hordes gathered outside his door. "They want a picture of the historic occasion."[1]

With that he kisses Emma goodbye, steps through the throng of cameras, and walks down to the local tube station to catch his subway to city hall, just as he's done every day since becoming mayor. Today is not just another day, however. Today is the first day drivers will be charged a fee of five pounds (about eight dollars) to drive a car into downtown London. It is the most important day of Livingstone's first term as mayor. This new fee will affect more than a hundred thousand commuters each day, and if the London "congestion charging" launch goes poorly, it will likely mean this will be his only term as mayor of the city he loves so dearly. Despite his jaunty manner, Mayor Livingstone's gallows humor reveals his true inner state. The mayor is afraid.

The Overconfidence Trap

Confident, bold, and optimistic. These are the traits that voters look for in a leader. They are all wonderful characteristics. Then again, so are their complements. Yet who wants to vote for someone who is humble, cautious, and realistic? Voters tend to prefer leaders who exhibit self-confidence that borders on narcissism.

In his 1992 State of the Union address, the first President Bush told the nation: "I pride myself that I'm a prudent man." Bush's prudence had served the nation well during the Gulf War when, after driving Iraqi troops out of Kuwait, he declined to take the fight all the way to Baghdad despite the urging of many to do so. Good policy judgment didn't translate into a good image, however. President Bush, a World War II pilot, got tagged with the "wimp" label. The president's cautious nature was pilloried mercilessly by Dana Carvey of *Saturday Night Live* with his finger-wagging impersonation of the elder Bush: "Wouldn't—be—prudent." Carvey's schoolmarmish impression was deadly funny because it took a very real aspect of Bush's personality and skewered him with it. In the real world, prudence is a virtue. In politics, it can be a fatal weakness. Ten months after boasting of his prudence to the nation, Bush lost his bid for reelection with the worst showing of an incumbent president in eighty years.

Voters prefer a confident, can-do attitude. Politicians give it to them. Time and time again, the self-assured, successful men and women in position of public leadership devote insufficient attention to the details of implementation. Too often, political leaders underestimate the risks that accompany a new initiative. We call this the Overconfidence Trap, and it is the most dangerous pitfall of the implementation phase. More failures we studied fell into this trap than any other. When they're overconfident, public leaders sometimes don't take the sort of prudent steps they should to ensure successful execution.

Blame it on NASA. Perhaps putting a man on the moon created unrealistic expectations for the public sector, particularly for anyone witnessing the success of *Apollo* as a youth. In his "Last Lecture," probably the most-watched classroom lecture of all time, Professor Randy Pausch credited the moon landings with inspiring him to dream big. "I was born in 1960. When you are eight or nine years old and you look at the TV set, and men are landing on the moon—anything's possible."[2] An entire generation of young Americans had that experience. The moon landings were without a doubt inspirational, but did they teach too much of a good lesson? Don't we need some realism as well as optimism? Simply because you really want to reach a destination doesn't mean you are going to get there. If President Kennedy had challenged us to send a man to Mars within the decade, we'd have lost that challenge. Just because government put a man on the moon doesn't mean it can do something really hard, like preventing teenagers from—well, doing the stuff teenagers do.

Here is the paradox of political confidence. A political leader has to be confident enough to take on big challenges, while at the same time being cognizant of the very real possibility of failure. Somewhere between timidity and foolhardiness exists a sweet spot of self-confidence that recognizes both the possibility and the peril of tackling a big challenge. A smart mountaineer is confident he can reach the summit, but he respects the hazards of the journey.

So maybe it was a good sign that Mayor Livingstone was a little bit scared.

The Real Tragedy of the Commons

The road pricing experiment launched by Ken Livingstone in February 2003 was all about changing the incentives. When something is free, it tends to get overconsumed. Economists call this "the tragedy of the commons," referring to the problem of overgrazing on common pasture land.[3] Sharing a pasture, it turns out, gets the incentives all wrong. Every farmer has an incentive to graze an additional cow on the town common to get his beast a free lunch. There is no such thing as a free lunch, however, and economists point out that the costs are borne by everyone else in town, because now the common is a little less grassy. In theory, the result is an overgrazed commons—a tragedy, for both the farmer and the cow. As a historical point of fact, the tragedy of the commons didn't usually end in tragedy. It ended in new rules. Overgrazed fields quickly led to laws regarding the use of common lands, and in 1664, some unknown public policy guru in Northumberland, England, came up with a way to address the problem by imposing a "stint," or limit, regarding "how many sheep and beasts everie tenement may keep" on the town's common lands. In other towns, drovers were charged a fee to graze their animals, in essence introducing a congestion charge for cows and sheep.[4]

In the 1950s, Columbia University economist William Vickrey argued that "free" urban roads exhibit the same sort of overconsumption. Each additional driver gets a free ride, and the costs are borne by everyone else in the form of greater congestion, slower travel, and more pollution. (Economists call costs borne by others "externalities.") The best way to ration an overused resource, argued Vickrey, is to charge for it. Charge a fee and you can prevent "overgrazing" of a field or "overdriving" on a road. "In no other major area are pricing practices so irrational, so outdated, and so conducive to waste as in urban transportation," Vickrey wrote.[5] Charging drivers to drive in urban centers is called congestion pricing, and in 1996 Vickrey, widely regarded as the father of road congestion pricing, was awarded the Nobel Prize in Economics for his work in the area of incentives. (Somewhere beneath the Northumberland sod, the unknown policy guru was smiling.)

Economists may like the idea of congestion pricing, but politicians generally do not. Congestion pricing is a widely hailed idea that usually fails to get through the political Stargate to become reality. Congestion pricing efforts have failed to make it beyond the design phase in the Netherlands, Hong Kong, San Francisco, Seattle, and Minneapolis. In 2008, Mayor Michael Bloomberg's hope for a congestion pricing plan for New York City was crushed by the state legislature—politicians don't like introducing a fee for something that has always been "free." Among the world's urban centers, only Singapore had a road charge for its downtown center prior to the London experiment.[6] Stockholm has since joined the club.

Economists have long pointed to London as a good candidate for congestion pricing. After decades of studies and discussion, however, by the late 1990s that city appeared no closer to implementing a large-scale congestion pricing scheme. Just as the tragedy of the commons would predict, congestion in London had grown intolerable. Average vehicle speeds during the day in Central London dropped to 14 kilometers an hour, speeds slower than the horse-drawn carriages that traversed the city during the Victorian era, resulting in billions in lost productivity.[7]

Recall the three ingredients for transformational change: a crisis, an idea, and a political opportunity. In London, the crisis was acute traffic congestion. The idea of congestion charging had been in play for decades. All that was needed was a political window for change, and that came in the form of the first election ever for a mayor of London.

Possibly because it is the home to the queen and the prime minister, London has never really had a proper mayor. In late 1999, the Greater London Authority Act established the city's first directly elected mayor with true executive powers. Recognizing the traffic problem, the Greater London Authority Act also established a new transport agency, Transport for London (TfL), and gave the mayor authority over public transportation as well as the power to implement a congestion charging program.

The issue of traffic and congestion pricing figured prominently during the historic campaign to be London's first true mayor. Seeing that the new mayor would at least have the option of introducing congestion pricing prompted a nonpartisan group of transportation experts, known as Road Charging Options for London (ROCOL), to study the issue. This group of nonpartisan experts released a report during the campaign making the case for a congestion pricing scheme and outlining how to do it. In other words, rather than the "design-free design" so often associated with design by legislation, the ROCOL group was able to put together a plan with a focus on workability rather than politics. "There was a fear that they [the next mayor] might use the powers irresponsibly or naively," relates a member of the ROCOL group. "So it was felt that we should give them something to be more solid on."[8]

Ken Livingstone strikes an unlikely profile as the politician who would adopt a road-pricing policy favored by free market economists. Livingstone is unapologetically a man of the left. For decades, the man routinely referred to by the British press as "Red Ken" had been a leader of the Labour left, the left that never really gave up on socialism.

It is hard to describe just how different Livingstone is from most of today's poll-driven, blow-dried politicians. With his patched-up off-the-rack suits, searing intellect, and argumentative nature, in both appearance and bearing Livingstone could be mistaken for the sort of university professor who is constantly holding teach-ins and earnestly denouncing the dean. Livingstone delighted in antagonizing Margaret Thatcher. After learning that Lady Thatcher liked to take her tea on a terrace in the House of Parliament and gaze across the Thames, Livingstone, then on the Greater London Council, placed an anti-Thatcher billboard on the roof of the council's headquarters, which just happened to be right across the river from said terrace. As you might imagine, Thatcher was not overly fond of Red Ken. She appeared to enjoy the last laugh when she abolished the Greater London Council altogether—on April Fools' Day in 1986.

Livingstone kicked around politics and entered a three-way race for London's first-ever mayor in 2000. He campaigned on the promise to deal with the dreadful traffic in London, and he was the only one of the three top candidates to pledge to implement ROCOL's congestion pricing recommendations.[9] So how did a left-leaning politician end up embracing a policy initiative more associated with people like Milton Friedman, Margaret Thatcher's favorite economist? Livingstone is a passionate environmentalist and, while hardly a free marketer, he does have a keen understanding of economics. He recognized that road pricing could be both a way out of London's congestion nightmare and fully consistent with his environmental values: by getting some people out of their cars and into public transport, it would reduce air pollution.

Livingstone's gamble paid off. He handily won the historic election.

The stars had aligned. Road pricing was through the Stargate. Livingstone had the power and he had a plan. Now all he had to do was implement it.

Risky Business

The hazards of implementing the congestion charge were so intimidating that Mayor Livingstone's political advisers unanimously urged him not to pursue it during his first term. He ignored their advice.

Comfortable with risk, he was willing to make a bold move and willing to accept the possibility of failure. "The area where politicians are totally lost is taking risks," said Livingstone. "They want civil servants to guarantee that what they are about to do will work. Life doesn't work like that. So nothing ever gets done."

The chances of implementing congestion pricing were slim. Having been booted out of the Labour Party, Livingstone had zero support from

Prime Minister Tony Blair's Labour government, and clearly the opposition Conservative Party—Margaret Thatcher's Conservative Party—would never back the initiative of a politician long considered a mortal enemy. A bevy of other interests—from associations of motorists to small businesses—also lined up against the scheme. Londoners as a whole were pretty evenly divided on the merits of the congestion charge, with a slight majority opposed.[10] Even this was misleading, however, because the scheme's diffuse benefits and concentrated costs meant that opponents were far more vocal and organized than supporters. Although he had the legal authority to implement congestion pricing, Livingstone still had to keep political peace.

The operational challenges were no less difficult. Coming into existence at the same time as the mayor, TfL was a start-up organization. It lacked the expertise to deliver on a complex project like congestion pricing. Further complicating the situation, no road-charging scheme of anything near this scale had been tried before—ever. To have any hope of reelection, Mayor Livingstone had to successfully implement the scheme before the next mayoral election four years hence, which made for an aggressive timeline.

If that wasn't enough, there was also the issue of the physical layout of the city. London's road system is medieval, probably designed by the same guy from Northumberland who came up with the rules for cow grazing. The city's layout is so complex it takes London cab drivers years of study to learn the myriad routes through the city. This makes setting up an enforcement system more complex than in the more conventional grid system of a city such as New York.

Between the political opposition, the mixed public opinion, and the many operational challenges of implementation, all the elements were in place for a failure of epic proportions. It turns out that Mayor Livingstone had good reason to be afraid.

To have any chance of success, Livingstone knew that he'd need a strong implementation team, starting with an experienced hand to lead the effort. He found him in a lifelong transportation bureaucrat named Derek Turner.

On his first day in office, Mayor Livingstone sat down with Derek Turner at city hall. Turner knew London's roads and subways, traffic lights and street signs, better than anyone on the planet. He had been traffic director for London throughout most of the 1990s, and had helped prepare the ROCOL report on congestion pricing. His entire career had laid the groundwork for this kind of initiative. Just minutes into their first meeting, the mayor looked Derek in the eye and said: "I want you to deliver congestion charging for me." Turner readily accepted the challenge. From that point forward it became very personal to Derek Turner.

For this assignment, Mayor Livingstone wasn't looking for someone warm and fuzzy. Turner is a respected civil servant, but with a hard edge. He's focused, extraordinarily driven, and capable of working long hours at high levels of intensity. He's also abrasive, emotional, and, at times, insensitive. He can burn out some staffers and tick off others. "Derek was the only person brutal enough to drive this through the resistance, and enough of a workaholic and manic enough to do it," said Livingstone. "Everybody else would have given up."

This was a critical moment in the congestion pricing launch. In too many public projects, the political leader pretends he or she is going to personally manage the execution of the plan. Most political leaders don't have the time for such involvement. When executives do get involved in details, their contribution is rarely positive, as when President Johnson was personally selecting bombing targets during the Vietnam War. But it can also be a mistake for political leaders to distance themselves too much from a project, in effect creating separation from any future failure. In contrast, Livingstone linked himself very publicly with the congestion pricing project while also making it clear that Turner was the leader—no one else.

Turner built a team that included many who had participated in the creation of the original ROCOL plan. After assembling his core team, Turner knew he still didn't have enough in-house expertise to implement an initiative of this size and scope. "The number of people who have done something like this, on this scale, more than once in a career is negligible," explained Turner. "We needed people with experience doing large, complex projects, so we bought the expertise."[11]

Deloitte United Kingdom was selected from among several firms in a competitive procurement to manage the project, run the IT procurement, and coordinate all the moving parts—skill sets in abundance at consulting firms and in short supply in the public sector.[12] The technology firm

Capita was hired to install the actual hardware and software that would form the technical infrastructure of the system—cameras, databases, and the like. Derek had seen his share of consulting engagements fail miserably. He was determined that this project would be different. To mitigate the risk of failure, he insisted on handpicking each of the senior people who would work on the project. Then to ensure continuity of project management, something critical to success in these endeavors, he insisted that as part of the contract these individuals be committed to the project for a minimum of two years. Livingstone's tilt toward activist government didn't preclude him from taking advantage of what the private sector had to offer—he and Turner proved skillful at extracting public benefit from private providers.

Turner's team was 100 percent immersed in congestion charging for two years. "We needed a dedicated resource. The team needed to be able to concentrate on this with no distractions," Turner said. This meant walling off the congestion pricing team from the rest of the TfL organization. This special status caused some friction with the rest of the organization, earning the team the nickname "Fortress Congestion Charging." But Turner is adamant that having a singular focus was essential to successful implementation. "You can't do it right if you have a day job," says Turner.

Facing the Opposition: Divide and Rule

Mayor Livingstone and the TfL team understood that the charging scheme would engender fierce opposition—opposition that if allowed to coalesce and gather strength, could lead to the project ending before it ever got to launch day—the dreaded "nonstarter." After all, this had been the fate of congestion pricing schemes from Hong Kong to Seattle. Preventing a stillborn project became Livingstone's initial focus.

The goal was to bring enough stakeholders on board to reduce opposition to a tolerable level. In the shorthand used at TfL, the stakeholder strategy was dubbed "divide and rule." "Our challenge . . . was just to get to day one; then the 'machine' could be turned on, and the scheme could speak for itself. We didn't mind people being critical for their own members or expressing their own views, but if they all got together under an umbrella 'no' campaign [saying] 'don't turn the "machine" on,' it could be very difficult to go forward with the scheme," explained Simon Burton, one of the architects of the strategy.[13] Potential political opponents were identified and strategies formulated to neutralize their opposition. A customized approach was fashioned for each major constituency group that could potentially derail the scheme—including local councils, the business community, citizen groups, and the press.

Although Mayor Livingstone had the legal authority to introduce congestion pricing, he was required to engage in a consultation process that allowed for public input, and as a practical matter he needed the support—or at least the acquiescence—of the majority of the local councils representing London's thirty-two boroughs. More than a dozen of these councils were controlled by the Conservative Party—Red Ken's longtime nemesis—located in London's swankiest sections, including Westminster, Kensington, and Chelsea. Over the course of the consultation period, each of the Conservative-controlled councils declared its opposition to the congestion charge. The Westminster council, in fact, mounted a high-profile legal challenge against congestion pricing, which was ultimately dismissed by the High Court.

To gain the support of the councils, about £80 million was spent on traffic projects ostensibly designed to ease bottlenecks that various councils claimed would be caused by the scheme. Most of these bottlenecks failed to materialize, but the projects produced enough goodwill to keep these councils on board. These projects have been described as "impact mitigation costs," but most people see them as a form of political payola. Just as Mayor Livingstone bought the expertise of outsiders, he also in effect bought off the opposition. Change isn't cheap.

A significant percentage of the business community favored congestion pricing from the start. London First, representing three hundred of the largest corporations in London, was an ardent supporter of congestion charging.[14] Small business owners and retailers mostly opposed the scheme, fearing that people would stop coming into town. Theater owners in London's West End, for example, argued that the proposed 7:00 p.m. cut-off time for the charge was too close to curtain time and would discourage theater goers from attending shows. Employing the divide-and-rule strategy, the cut-off time was changed to 6:30 p.m. to eliminate the opposition of the West Enders.

The press was a whole different animal. London's Fleet Street press is notoriously sensational, and any slip-up, real or perceived, would be pounced on without mercy. Livingstone calls the British press "probably the worst media in any country that has a free press." Livingstone went to the extraordinary length of hiring Fishburn Hedges, a noted public relations firm, to coordinate communications a full two years before the launch. Two press agents from the public relations firm set up shop directly outside Turner's office. They organized monthly one-on-one lunches between the TfL leadership and editors of each of the major papers. They developed a simple, concrete message to help the public understand congestion pricing: "It's needed. It's workable. And it's fair." Anytime London government officials discussed the scheme, they were sure to mention at least one of these points. TfL worked to reduce hostility toward the plan among the media. The press was like London weather—unpredictable and often inconvenient. You couldn't control it, but you could take steps to reduce its impact. The way TfL handled the media showed political savvy and contributed to the success of the implementation of congestion pricing.

War Games in London

I'm quite happy to be regarded as a pessimist. But the advantage of a pessimist is that they're always prepared for whatever's going to come up, and therefore they've got plans . . . That way you don't get into this sort of frozen thing of, "Oh, my God, what are we going to do now?"

—DEREK TURNER, TRANSPORT FOR LONDON

Big public initiatives are often judged on their initial success—or failure. This particularly holds true for traffic-related projects, where the launch impacts commuters. In 1980, New York City mayor Ed Koch introduced, at significant expense, bike lanes on some Manhattan streets. The ensuing traffic snarls generated road rage, which translated into voter rage, and the project was quickly abandoned. "It was one of the worst mistakes I ever made," Koch admitted.[15] When Turner and his team flipped the switch on congestion pricing that first day, everything had to work flawlessly: the cameras, the enforcement mechanisms, the call centers, the payment systems—everything.

Every aspect of the launch had to be worked through in excruciating detail. More than seven hundred cameras, for example, were set up around the charging zone to ensure proper enforcement mechanisms. The cameras would identify the vehicles coming in and out of the zone through automatic number plate readers. Without these "captures," motorists who drove in without paying couldn't be fined. Fiber optic cables had to be installed on the cameras and then laid in the ground to transmit these captures to the databases. Each had to be tested and retested—as did every component of the infrastructure required to make this system work.[16]

The most important aspect of the "Go Live" phase was how the TfL team approached risk. Everyone involved in the effort believed the congestion charge scheme could succeed, but also believed it could fail—big time. "No one really knew for sure what was going to happen on day one," said Linda Swinburne, the operations manager for the congestion charging team. "Everyone had an idea but no one really had a clue."[17]

Every imaginable scenario that could potentially derail the launch had its own contingency plan, from technology failure to public protests to opponents tearing down street signs. "My whole focus was risk—identifying and mitigating every risk to the project," said Brian Green, the day-to-day project manager from the Deloitte side.[18] "Today the difference between successful and unsuccessful projects lies in the degree to which managers understand and mitigate risks."[19] For example, even the best-designed scheme will usually experience a surge of customer questions and complaints in its early stages. The TfL team managed this risk by building in an initial period of extra capacity at call centers. Another way they mitigated risk was by putting a moratorium on all street repair work within the congestion charge area for several months. There would be no ripped-up roads on launch day.

While managing risk is an exercise that takes place largely at the staff level, good chief executives—and Mayor Livingstone, for all his bluster, is a strong manager—tend to have an intuitive sense of how to ask the right questions to ensure their team has planned for every possible contingency. The mayor and his senior staff had a number of intense meetings with Derek and the TfL team, at which they challenged every assumption of the implementation team, asked question after question, and in some cases challenged the team's decisions. Some of these sessions got pretty heated. Derek, never one to hide his emotions, at times clearly resented this questioning of his ability to get this done. "It was a brutal process, but in something like this if you don't go through that whole process, you end up making a mistake," explained Livingstone. "If Derek's team hadn't been able to stand up to the level of scrutiny we were giving them then it most probably would have meant they weren't doing enough themselves to be certain that we were going to get this thing right when it came time to launch it."

Two weeks before the launch, TfL had its equivalent of a preseason game with the pads on. For an entire day, the core congestion charging team would be called on to address an endless stream of potential nightmare scenarios. This would resemble the sort of war games run by the military. The rules were simple: the TfL group had no idea beforehand what they would be facing. They would have to deal with problems on the fly, in real time, just like they would on launch day.

The TfL team is just sitting down with their coffee at 7:00 a.m. when the first call comes in: "The communications between the cameras and the hub have broken down." There is no way to track vehicles coming into the zone. The team quickly establishes that the breakdown was caused by a major failure within the hub site. It will take several hours to fix. In just minutes, they decide to order an immediate switchover to the disaster recovery facility. The effect will be to duplicate the whole system: two supplier fiber optics networks, multiple power supplies, and a backup image processing center. Inconvenient, but with this fix the majority of drivers will still be detected. Total time elapsed: twenty minutes.

At 8:00 a.m., a new crisis: a major traffic accident has caused a huge bottleneck on a major road bordering the charging zone. The police are diverting hundreds of cars into the zone. Many of these cars had not planned on entering the zone voluntarily and thus haven't paid the charge—and shouldn't have to. If something isn't done, they'll get hit with a fine. Fortunately, the team's prior planning had anticipated this scenario and developed business rules to address the situation. Vehicles detected entering the zone at the detour site are electronically flagged. Provided they leave the zone within a reasonable period of time, they won't be liable for the charge.

About 10:30 a.m., another crisis: "Someone has jumped off the Tower Bridge." It goes on like this all day, with calls coming in from the traffic control center. "Massive numbers of drivers are coming into the zone without paying." "The call center is overloaded." Everyone on the team is physically and mentally spent by the time the grueling day of war gaming is finally over. "After going through that, nothing was going to throw us on launch day," said Swinburne. "Being under that kind of pressure helped prepare us for the real thing."

In the days before the actual launch, the press coverage started getting nasty. The Fleet Street press tends to hunt in packs, and congestion charging had become the favored prey: "Dastardly Plot Will Ruin London," "Road to Madness," "End This Class Warfare on Motorists," and "Ken's Road to Ruin." The *Evening Standard*, London's largest circulating daily, went to war against the charge in the month before the launch, going so far as to plant an undercover journalist in the call center of Capita, the IT operations contractor for the scheme. The resulting sensationalistic article, "Congestion Chaos Exposed," appeared five days before the launch.[20] The hysterical coverage was epitomized in *The Observer*'s interview with a rabbi whose synagogue fell within the charging zone: "This building was bombed in the war, but Livingstone is going to cause more damage than the Germans."[21]

"In the final weeks leading up to the launch, Fleet Street really did gang up against the scheme. There was a lot of hardening of the coverage," recalled Luke Blair, formerly of Fishburn Hedges. "The press was convinced there'd be a godawful cock-up on day one."[22]

The TfL team had a hard time dealing with the negative press. "I could not pick up a newspaper, I could not go out with friends, without somebody being critical of congestion charging, without really knowing anything other than what they had read in the paper," TfL staffer Swinburne recalls. Ironically, the nasty press coverage ended up helping the launch. Early on, TfL had worried whether it could design a public education campaign that would reach every affected London commuter. The scary headlines from Fleet Street solved that problem.

The two weeks before the launch were devoted to details. Hundreds of signs informing drivers they were about to enter the charge zone had to go up, with one small catch: the signs were covered with plastic sheets that would all have to be removed immediately before the scheme went live. Reflecting TfL's obsessive level of planning, Kate Robinson, a twenty-something consultant, spent the weekend before the launch walking the entire route around the charge zone—twenty-six miles in all—with a pad of paper. Her assignment: to make sure nothing was going to happen along the road network without TfL knowing about it, whether it be public works scaffolding being put up or a hole about to be dug. "We didn't trust anything," said a TfL operations manager. Despite the meticulous planning, doubts remained. "No matter how much work we'd done, we couldn't really plan exactly how drivers would react once we actually switched this on. People would behave how they would behave," says Swinburne.

"It's Going to Be Bloody"

Mayor Livingstone still had a trick or two up his sleeve. In the week before the launch, he publicly warned London motorists to stay out of central London if at all possible on launch day because no one knew what would happen. "It's going to be bloody," Livingstone told Londoners. It was a brilliant, pithy phrase, designed to lower expectations and increase the likelihood of success, the political equivalent of underpromising and overdelivering.

The night before the launch, the TfL congestion charging operations team gathered for dinner at a downtown hotel. This tightly knit group, which had worked long hours together for close to two years, had a last meal together. Tomorrow, their hard work would pay off—or the team would be lining up on the Tower Bridge themselves.

By 5:30 a.m., about the time Mayor Livingstone was being bathed in the blinding white light of the television cameras, weirdly reminiscent of an alien abduction, the morning commute was just getting going, and the TfL operations team was already hard at work monitoring traffic.

At 7:30 a.m. Mayor Livingstone held a press conference to formally announce that the pricing charge was in effect. On the plasma screens in the operations center, TfL staffers could see traffic flowing freely. "It is so quiet, eerily quiet," said Swinburne. She compared the number of payments coming into the system with the number of vehicles they had projected. It was much, much lower. "People are just not coming in," she said.

At 8:00 a.m. all eyes in the traffic control center were glued to the giant monitors focused on a section of Kensington road. Opponents had picked this spot to wage what was billed as a huge protest against the scheme. Thousands of demonstrators were supposed to gather and disrupt traffic. Instead, the monitors showed a ragtag group of no more than fifty protesters milling around, holding up signs denouncing Mayor Livingstone. Maybe protesters aren't early risers. If the launch fell into chaos, it wouldn't be due to a popular uprising of enraged motorists.

About 9 a.m., London's morning rush hour is at its peak. On a typical day, the streets would be gridlocked, replete with crawling traffic, honking cars, and bottlenecks. Not today. Mayor Livingstone, Derek Turner, and the TfL team stared at the monitors. London was a ghost town. "There was not a vehicle in sight," recalls the mayor. "I thought, 'Oh my God, we've overdone it. No one is ever going to come into the city again.'"

"Where are all the cars?" asked Turner. "What have we done?" he wondered aloud to no one in particular. One uncomfortable thought rang through his head: "Have we reduced traffic so much that we won't be able to pay for the bloody scheme?"[23]

As they watched the plasma screens, someone noticed an interesting development. One of the cameras had zoomed in on an engineering company truck that had stopped in the middle of a street. A construction crew jumped out and proceeded to cordon off the area with orange traffic cones. "What's happening there?'" asked Livingstone. Everyone in the operations center watched in horror as the crew members started to unload their drilling equipment—they were about to rip up the road during rush hour. "What on earth is going on there?" yelled a TfL manager. "Get them off the road!" But no sooner had he said this than the startled road crew looked up to see a TfL helicopter hovering above them. Moments later, a TfL vehicle pulled up and ushered the crew away, possibly to the Tower of London for a beheading. Livingstone smiled. "Nothing happens on the network without us knowing about it, boss," beamed one of his operations managers.[24]

At 4:00 p.m., it was time for the press conference at Windsor House to discuss developments from the day and take questions. Derek looked out at the collected throng. "One bloody depressed lot of journalists," he thought to himself, looking at the media members who had all been poised to pen the mayor's political obituary. Though he took care not to gloat, Livingstone would relish the next day's headlines for a long time: "'C' Is for Calm"; "Congestion Charge Is a Winner as Drivers Breeze Through Rush Hour"; "Chaos, Mayhem, Dead Cyclists . . . Well, No, the Streets Are Empty." The *Economist*, a supporter of congestion charging, noted that "the biggest sound of the day was the critics of the congestion charge in retreat."[25]

Congestion charging had certainly made a great first impression. But would it produce the desired results? Would drivers change their behavior for more than a day?

Since the introduction of the congestion charge in 2003, there has been a 16 percent decline in the number of vehicles entering the charging zone.[26] This includes a one-third reduction in the number of cars, or put another way, 65,000 to 70,000 fewer cars now come into Central London each day.[27] Travel speeds have increased by more than 20 percent and average traffic delays have fallen by one-third. Bus ridership increased by 45 percent in the five years after charging, while bike riders within the zone jumped 43 percent.[28] The congestion charge also brought in nearly £137 million (almost $224 million USD) in net revenues during the 2007–2008 fiscal year.[29] London, it seems, had gotten the incentives right, reversing the tragedy of the commons.

These results helped Ken Livingstone handily win a second term as mayor in 2004. In May 2008, Livingstone lost his race for a third term as mayor largely for reasons unrelated to congestion charging. Boris Johnson, his successor, left the program in place.

A Trip Up Mount Washington

Mount Everest is the highest mountain in the world. It stands a majestic 29,029 feet in elevation. The summit can be reached only by highly capable mountaineers. Between 1990 and 2008, it claimed the lives of a hundred climbers.

Mount Washington is the highest mountain in New Hampshire. It stands a not-so-majestic 6,288 feet. The summit can be reached by any reasonably healthy twelve-year-old, or if you are feeling lazy you can just drive your car to the top. So it might surprise you to learn that between 1990 and 2008, little Mount Washington claimed thirty-three lives itself.

Why? It's not because Mount Washington is so difficult. It's because Mount Washington can unexpectedly become much more difficult than it appears. Nestled in the leafy, unimposing White Mountains, the well-worn trail up Mount Washington looks like a piece of cake from the trail-head. Overconfident hikers don't prepare as well as they should and often get a rude surprise when they emerge from the timberline at about four thousand feet. "They underestimate how difficult the White Mountains can be. They're starting from the valley, where it's 80 degrees. They're in shorts and tee shirts, and they get up high, and there's sleet. It's a really different world," says Rebecca Oreskes, a spokeswoman for the national forest.[30] In winter, would-be skiers can fall victim to avalanches as well as storms.

An overconfident hiker will fail to adequately prepare for the possible hazards of the journey, the "what-ifs." What if a storm comes in? What if I twist an ankle? What if I get lost? A prepared hiker has adequate clothing, water, food, a cell phone—just in case something unexpected occurs, like a stiff breeze blows in. That doesn't sound scary, does it? Think of it this way. Mount Washington wasn't the place to be hiking in April 1934, when it was hit with a 231-mile-per-hour gust, the highest wind velocity ever recorded on the surface of the planet. Yes, little Mount Washington is a lot tougher than it looks.

Of course, there are days when an unprepared hiker will stroll to the top of Mount Washington without incident, perhaps chuckling at the Nervous Nellies with their backpacks and safety flares. More often, you will see the unprepared emerging at the base of the trail cold and miserable, having turned back before reaching the peak. Sometimes, the unprepared require rescue. Sometimes, the Overconfidence Trap can be fatal.

Introducing congestion charging in London was a difficult, risky, and very public government initiative that succeeded. Why? *Because Livingstone, Turner, and TfL took the possibility of failure seriously.* To avoid failure, they made sure to devote adequate resources, to establish clear ownership of the project, to bring on board those who could undermine their efforts, and to use the press to set expectations. They explored every imaginable worst-case scenario and planned for it. They made a good first impression and reduced opposition. Failure in any one of these areas could doom a project. Nowhere is this more clearly illustrated than in postwar Iraq, where the Bush administration stumbled headlong into the Overconfidence Trap.

Iraq Reconstruction: Plan B

The view of postwar Iraq seemed to be that reconstruction would not be terribly difficult—like a walk up Mount Washington. As a result, top officials in the administration gave scant attention to what might happen after the "shock and awe" was over and the American-led coalition had declared victory.

On February 27, 2003, just weeks before the invasion of Iraq, Deputy Defense Secretary Paul Wolfowitz testified before Congress. "There has been a good deal of comment—some of it quite outlandish—about what our postwar requirements might be in Iraq," Wolfowitz told Congress. These estimates, he said, "such as the notion that it will take several hundred thousand U.S. troops to provide stability in post-Saddam Iraq, are wildly off the mark." Wolfowitz continued, "It's hard to conceive that it would take more forces to provide stability in post-Saddam Iraq than it would to conduct the war itself."[31]

With the benefit of hindsight, we can safely say that Wolfowitz was being overly optimistic. Attempting to rebuild a war-torn nation—a nation without a government, with no history of democracy, and consisting of warring religious factions with century-old grudges; a nation roughly the size of California with 27.5 million people, a decaying infrastructure, and a lack of basic security—well, that's a hard thing to do. Underestimating a challenge, however, is what the Overconfidence Trap is all about.

In February 2003, about six weeks before the Iraq invasion, 154 experts from the Defense and State departments, the CIA, the National Security Council, and elsewhere gathered at the National Defense University to plan for postwar operations. Incredibly, it was the first time that everyone studying the issue of post-hostility Iraq had come together. (The TfL team, in contrast, spent roughly two years preparing for the launch of congestion charging.) One of those attending the meeting was retired general Jay Garner, who had been tapped by Secretary of Defense Donald Rumsfeld just two weeks earlier to run postwar operations in Iraq.

Garner was looking to come up to speed quickly and during the meeting was impressed with Tom Warrick of the State Department. Whenever a question came up, Warrick seemed to have the answer. At lunch, Garner approached Warrick and, after a brief discussion, popped the question. "Come to work for me on Monday," said Garner. (Okay, technically that's not a question, but that's how generals ask for stuff.) Warrick agreed. Garner also brought in Meghan O'Sullivan from the State Department, and they both started working for Garner at the Pentagon.

Just a few days later, Rumsfeld pulled Garner aside following a meeting. "You've got two people working for you—Warrick and O'Sullivan—that you have to get rid of."

"I can't; they are smart, really good, knowledgeable," Garner protested. But Rumsfeld was the boss, and both were removed. (O'Sullivan would eventually see a significant role in Iraq.) According to Richard Armitage, deputy secretary of state under Colin Powell, "They didn't like Warrick and Meghan [O'Sullivan] because they were both inconvenient—you know, wanted to get facts into the equation. They were not people who stood up for the party line, that we'd be welcomed with garlands."[32]

As *Washington Post* Pentagon reporter Thomas Ricks put it:

> *[Warrick and O'Sullivan] were people who were raising difficult questions and saying, "No, you need more of this and more of that," and fundamentally, "No, this is going to be more difficult than you think." That was the one answer, I think, that was unacceptable in the Bush administration.*[33]

Enforced optimism meant that only one scenario could be discussed. We would defeat Saddam Hussein's army, be greeted as liberators, and a grateful Iraq would embrace democracy. That was the plan, and there was no Plan B.

The kind of scenario planning engaged in by the London TfL team is essential for big tasks. Scenario planning means actively imagining everything bad that could possibly occur, and then preparing for it. Extensive scenario planning occurred in planning for the *invasion* of Iraq, considering the possibility of facing biological and chemical weapons and so forth. Unfortunately, the scenario planning failed to extend beyond the moment of military victory.

As with an ascent of Mount Washington, it is the "what-if" line of questioning that uncovers the hidden hazards. What if sectarian violence breaks out? What if looting starts? The Bush administration seemed to equate raising such pessimistic possibilities with disloyalty. For the Iraq postwar planning, anyone raising concerns was viewed as being "not on the team." (Where loyalty is a concern, it may be helpful to assign someone to play the role of "devil's advocate," in essence granting immunity for a team member to play the role of Nervous Nellie.)

The lack of scenario planning for the occupation translated into a lack of preparation.

"We didn't preposition significant numbers of military police; we hadn't prepared commanders to assume responsibility for public security rapidly; and we didn't anticipate that the regime's security apparatus would disintegrate and become largely useless. I think we should have, because this is, broadly speaking, what had happened in each of the previous episodes over the last decade," says James Dobbins, a former State Department official who had participated in postconflict reconstruction in Haiti, Somalia, Kosovo, Bosnia, and Afghanistan. "But I think that the administration had chosen to look to a different set of models and a different set of experiences for inspiration, and I think that that misled them as to the difficulties they were likely to encounter."[34]

First Impressions: The Boy with the Vase

Another important lesson from the London launch is to make a good first impression. Indeed, when the American military first entered Baghdad, they were initially greeted as liberators. On April 9, 2003, in the middle of Baghdad, the Saddam statue was torn down, to the delight of Iraqi citizens.

Almost immediately, things started to unravel.

Within hours, Iraqi citizens realized the government was gone and started looting public buildings. American military personnel stood by as Iraqis ran by with computers, desks, and sofas. No one had prepared to deal with looting by civilians. Failure to stop the looting sent a message that there was no one in charge and encouraged more lawlessness. On April 11, 2003, Defense Secretary Rumsfeld held a press conference. He wanted to talk about U.S. forces being greeted as liberators by a grateful Iraqi people, but the press kept pressing him on the looting issue.

Q: Mr. Secretary, you spoke of the television pictures that went around the world earlier of Iraqis welcoming U.S. forces with open arms. But now television pictures are showing looting and other signs of lawlessness. Are you, sir, concerned that what's being reported from the region as anarchy in Baghdad and other cities might wash away the goodwill the United States has built? . . .

Rumsfeld: The images you are seeing on television you are seeing over, and over, and over, and it's the same picture of some person walking out of some building with a vase, and you see it twenty times, and you think, "My goodness, were there that many vases?" [Laughter.] Is it possible that there were that many vases in the whole country?

A bit later, the press returns to the question.

Q: Do you think that the words anarchy *and* lawlessness *are ill-chosen?*

Rumsfeld: Absolutely. I picked up a newspaper today and I couldn't believe it. I read eight headlines that talked about chaos, violence, unrest. And it just was Henny Penny—"The sky is falling." I've never seen anything like it! . . . Stuff happens! But in terms of what's going on in that country, it is a fundamental misunderstanding to see those images over, and over, and over again of some boy walking out with a vase and say, "Oh, my goodness, you didn't have a plan." That's nonsense.

Despite Rumsfeld's protestations, it wasn't just one boy walking out of "some building" with a vase being shown over and over. When Rumsfeld was holding his press conference on April 11, the National Museum of Iraq was being looted of its irreplaceable treasures of antiquity—including the five-thousand-year-old Sacred Vase of Warka. (Happily, the Sacred Vase of Warka was returned to the museum a few weeks later by three men driving a red Toyota. Unfortunately, some seventy-five hundred other artifacts are still missing.)[35] "Everyone, deep in himself, is grateful to the United States that they helped us get rid of this regime," said Donny George, the Iraqi director of the museum. "But the uncontrolled situation, that is another thing. Why was it not controlled?"[36]

It wasn't just a problem at the museum. As the coming days and weeks would show, a growing sense of lawlessness pervaded the country, encouraging anti-American sentiment. In the eyes of the Iraqi people, the

failure to provide stability had to be a matter of choice. As television journalist Charlie Rose put it, "When the United States arrived, a lot of [the
Iraqi] people were saying, 'You know, this is the country that went to the
moon, for gosh sakes, they know what to do.' "[37]

Another key to an effective launch is clear ownership. Following the
military conquest in Iraq, there was a protracted period of uncertainty regarding who, exactly, was in charge of the reconstruction of Iraq. In the
summer of 2003, Colonel Teddy Spain, the military police commander in
Baghdad, asked his commanding general a very good question: "Sir, who
the hell is in charge?" The fact that Col. Spain had to ask such a question
is an indication of the muddled nature of the chain of command in postwar Iraq.[38]

Even with the benefit of hindsight, it is difficult to definitively state
who was in charge of Iraq reconstruction at various points of time.

Army general Tommy Franks led the invasion and, since the American
military were the only people around when Baghdad fell, initially military
personnel on the ground looked to him for guidance. Franks showed little interest in post-hostility operations, however, and soon after retired. In
March 2003, Jay Garner was named director of the Office for Reconstruction and Humanitarian Assistance and sent to Baghdad. Garner may
have been in charge, but only until L. Paul Bremer arrived in Baghdad in
May 2003 to head up the Coalition Provisional Authority (CPA). Bremer
was now in charge, but it was unclear exactly what the Coalition Provisional Authority was, and there was always a vague boundary between
Bremer's authority and that of the military command.

A lack of clear ownership will often prove disastrous, particularly on a
massive, complex undertaking like creating a stable democracy from a nation devastated by war. When America faced that challenge in Japan following World War II, there was no question regarding who was in charge:
General Douglas MacArthur. General MacArthur's title was "Supreme
Commander of the Allied Powers." Not only is this a really cool title,
there simply isn't a lot of ambiguity there. (In contrast, Bremer's title was
"Coalition Provisional Authority Administrator Ambassador." What in
the world is an "Administrator Ambassador"?) MacArthur took charge
from the start and provided stable leadership in Japan for almost six years.
Bremer lasted fourteen months in Iraq. By integrating the military and

civilian leadership in the person of MacArthur, there was none of the "ownership confusion" that reigned in Iraq. The military headquarters in Iraq was located only a few miles from the CPA, but that separation contributed to countless implementation snafus.

Rebuilding a war-torn country is incomprehensibly more difficult than implementing congestion pricing in London, but the same principles apply in both cases. What comes through again and again in comparing the two experiences is that those in charge in London had one thing that those running the show in Iraq lacked: humility. Mayor Livingstone and Derek Turner knew that what they were attempting was difficult, so they prepared for it. They thought about how it might fail. They planned ahead. In contrast, the prevailing attitude on Iraq reconstruction seemed to be: this is going to be a piece of cake. In 2003 key members of the Bush administration expressed unrealistically cheery views about the difficulty of what they were undertaking—failing to contemplate that even with impeccable execution, Iraq reconstruction was going to be a massively difficult operation.

The Scary Secret of Successful Implementation

The United States entered Iraq with a leadership team of substantial experience and intelligence. They were confident that they could handle anything that came up; that in their skillful hands the resources of the United States could overcome any challenge that came their way. They were capable leaders who made the classic error of thinking that their ability would carry them to success.

Reviewing large undertakings by the public sector, one lesson becomes abundantly clear: be humble or be humbled—this is much harder than you think. Being humble means you embrace the risk of failure and take steps to avoid it. You designate a clear project owner, you strive for management continuity, you involve policy designers in the implementation, you establish a team of dedicated resources to the project, you manage expectations (down!) in the press, you devote sufficient time for planning and sufficient resources for implementation, you allow "naysayers" to have their say, and you conduct scenario planning that imagines a host of worst possible scenarios. You launch knowing that you are prepared for whatever might come your way.

On the morning of the launch, Mayor Livingstone walked out of his London flat with butterflies in his stomach, well aware that his congestion charging scheme could flop. It was that awareness—that fear—which led him and the TfL team to success. After it was over, Mayor Livingstone had this to say about his congestion charging program: "It's the only thing I ever did in public life that turned out better than I hoped it would."

FIELD GUIDE: IMPLEMENTATION PHASE

The challenge at the implementation phase is clear: make it happen, on time and on budget, and produce the desired results. A good start is critical, since you never get a second chance to make a good first impression.

Biggest Danger

The Overconfidence Trap. In the public sector, everything is harder than it seems. Overconfidence—the congenital unrealistic optimism of the political realm—makes the job harder. If you embrace the possibility of failure, you can take steps to reduce its likelihood.

Guiding Principles

Establish clear ownership. Who is the high-level political sponsor? Who is the day-to-day manager? Everybody knew that Derek Turner was in charge of congestion charging. No one knew, at any given moment, exactly who was in charge of what in postwar Iraq.

Make a great first impression. You get only one chance to make a good first impression. Day one of congestion charging in London was serene. Day one of freedom in Iraq meant looting at the National Museum.

Be realistic. Take a hard look at the resources, time, and costs needed to execute the initiative. Fight the political pressure to produce unrealistically rosy projects and time lines. Assign a dedicated team. It is unrealistic to ask people with major current responsibilities to do the job. It either won't get done or won't get done right.

Reduce opposition. Mayor Ken Livingstone bought off political opposition with road projects and small changes, like ending the charge at 6:30 at night instead of 7:00 to appease West End theater owners. In contrast, the de-Baathification order and dissolution of the Iraqi Army generated opposition—much of it armed.

Manage expectations. Livingstone set expectations low. In contrast, overly optimistic pronouncements ("Mission accomplished") from the Bush administration led to disappointment.

Embrace the risk of failure. And take steps to avoid it.

Bring a design perspective to program design. To one extent or another, those doing the implementation will have a certain amount of discretion with respect to building a program based on the legislative blueprint provided. Make sure to bring a design perspective when making implementation choices.

Tools and Techniques

Embrace the project management mindset. Gantt charts, Microsoft Project, task lists—you need people with the skills to use the tools that manage implementation. These are some of the key activities of the project management discipline:

- **Task and milestone management:** Set your goals, time lines, and key milestones/achievements.

- **Stakeholder management:** Accurately identify stakeholders and their needs, set expectations appropriately, and work to meet needs and expectations.

- **Change management:** Develop transition strategy and change management to increase program support and adoption.

- **Technical management:** Almost all implementations involve technology. Use what you need, but avoid "gee-whiz" and "bleeding edge" technologies.

- **Risk mapping:** Use this tool use to identify, evaluate, and prioritize a group of risks that could significantly influence the success of a given initiative. By plotting the significance and likelihood of the risk occurring, the map allows you to visualize risks in relation to each other, gauge their extent, and plan what type of controls should be implemented to mitigate the risks.

Set up a war room. Take a cue from many successful initiatives and set up a war room to manage your implementation. Avoid the box-checking tendency of many project management organizations. Having a war room like the congestion pricing initiative had forces you to have clear ownership.

Scenario plan. Don't just plan, scenario plan. Maybe nobody's going to jump off the Tower Bridge, and maybe a storm won't blow in on Mount Washington. But you need to be ready in case they do. Indiana Jones always expects the unexpected, so should you.

Segment your customers. Break up the universe of potential customers into manageable segments with similar characteristics. Done right, segmentation involves data-driven analysis of the customer universe, based on surveys, focus groups, and test marketing that cover almost all aspects of product delivery.

Chunk your projects. Government projects are often huge—much larger and more complex than in the private sector. Chunking initiatives into bite-sized pieces reduces risk by making challenges smaller and less complex. It also enhances organizational learning because later phases of a project can learn from the earlier ones. Some tasks, of course, just don't chunk. You can't leap a six foot chasm in a series of one foot jumps.

Resources (Books, Web Sites, and Other Cool Stuff)

For further reading, we recommend *Implementation: How Great Expectations in Washington Are Dashed in Oakland; Or, Why It's Amazing That Federal Programs Work at All*, by Aaron Wildavsky and Jeffrey Pressman. A classic in this genre, the authors delve into the complexity of real-world government implementation. We also suggest *Executing Your Strategy,* by Mark Morgan, Raymond E. Levitt, and William Malek, and *Against the Gods: The Remarkable Story of Risk*, by Peter L. Bernstein—the classic book on the history of risk and risk management. *Connecting the Dots* by Cathleen Benko and Warren McFarlan is a good resource on project management. Another good resource is the Project Management Institute (www.pmi.org). With more than 250,000 members, it is the world's largest organization of project managers.

CHAPTER 5

The Sisyphus Trap

The Rock, the Hill, and You

Idea → Design → Stargate → Implementation → **Results**

(←——————— Reevaluation ———————→)

CHAPTER GUIDE

* Mayor Riordan Turns Around LA, and Vice Versa
* The Sisyphus Trap
* Incentives Without Carrots or Sticks
* Culture Matters
* Politics and Bureaucracy: Bridging the Divide
* James Webb and Putting a Man on the Moon
* An Ever Steeper Hill
* Pretzel Logic
* Welfare Reform 1996: Beating the Double Sisyphus Trap
* Systems, People, and Results

There's a mood among us. People are worried. There has been talk of decline. Someone even said our workers are lazy and uninspired. And I thought: Really? You go tell Neil Armstrong standing on the moon. Tell the men and women who put him there.

—PRESIDENT GEORGE H. W. BUSH, STATE OF THE UNION
ADDRESS, 1992

W HEN HE DECIDED to run for mayor of Los Angeles in 1993, Richard Riordan had a long track record of business success. He had cofounded both a law firm and a highly successful private equity firm, earning him enormous wealth. He campaigned on the slogan "tough enough to turn LA around." And he would need to be: when Riordan took office, Los Angeles was a hotbed of gang violence, in tough financial straits, and home to some of the worst public schools in the nation.

Once elected, Riordan brought leading management experts into government, including business guru William Ouchi as his chief of staff. Ouchi was a professor of management at UCLA and author of the best-selling business book *Theory Z*. From the start, Riordan also put his own business expertise into practice. He required department heads to submit yearly business plans and gave them annual performance reviews—something new to LA city hall. He streamlined business permitting and is generally credited with improving city operations while holding down taxes. His budgets balanced. He added police during his first term, which helped lower crime. There were few earth-shattering achievements, less of the remarkable results that had marked his tenure in the private sector, but his administration was generally viewed as capable, honest, and reform minded. Riordan handily won reelection in 1997 with more than 60 percent of the vote—a remarkable feat for a Republican politician in predominantly Democratic Los Angeles.

Soon after his reelection, Riordan declared his intention to become "the education mayor." This was a challenging target, since Riordan had little formal authority over his city's public schools. Chicago's mayor Richard M. Daley, however, had already demonstrated how a big-city mayor could gain influence over a large, dysfunctional school district.

Riordan and management guru Ouchi thought the best way to improve the Los Angeles public schools was through "local control"—that is, giving each school greater control over its budgets and hiring, in essence cutting the ineffective central bureaucracy out of the loop. The idea was to put the principal, teachers, and parents in charge of their own school. The effort was known as LEARN—Los Angeles Educational Alliance for Restructuring Now—and for a period Ouchi served as the group's chairman. LEARN began with high hopes and many supporters, including the mayor, business leaders, and the president of the teachers' union. Though there was little open opposition, the Los Angeles Unified School Board dragged its heels, and bickering among teachers, teacher unions, and principals led to LEARN's demise. Riordan was blunt in his assessment: "LEARN failed."[1]

Frustrated, he redoubled his efforts. In the 1999 school board elections, Riordan backed a slate of reform candidates for the school board and held a fund-raiser for them at his Brentwood home that raised more than $200,000.[2] Though some of his candidates won, the new school board failed to achieve any significant results.

Riordan had other problems. In March of 1998, six pounds of cocaine went missing from an LA Police Department evidence room. Thus began one of the largest police corruption scandals in U.S. history. The corruption centered around a group of officers who worked in their off hours as "security" for Death Row Records in Rampart, an eight-square-mile stretch of gangland. The scandal ultimately uncovered corrupt police officers engaged in beatings, shootings, and the framing of innocent citizens. Close to one hundred convictions have been overturned because of wrongful arrests and miscarriage of justice, and the LA city attorney estimated that Rampart-related civil suits are likely to cost the city $125 million.[3]

Perhaps partly as a consequence of the problems with the police force, murders in Los Angeles jumped 39 percent from 1988 to 2001.[4] Riordan as mayor was no less capable a leader than he had been in the private sector. He was simply working in a different operating context—the public operating environment, where things are harder. Here's how Riordan's deputy mayor Michael Keeley described it: "Think of city government as a big bus. The bus is divided into different sections with different constituencies: labor, the city council, the mayor, interest groups and contractors. Every seat is equipped with a brake, so lots of people can stop the bus anytime. The problem is that this makes the bus almost undriveable."[5]

Riordan earnestly applied business management principles to government, only to run into the headwinds of the public operating system. He discovered what many capable private sector managers have to learn the hard way about the public sector: it is a much more difficult place to achieve big results on large undertakings.

Riordan left the mayor's office in 2001 under term limits he had championed. But that didn't stop his efforts to improve public education. After serving for a time as Governor Arnold Schwarzenegger's secretary of education, he created a nonprofit group called Pathways to Success designed to turn around failing public schools with outside management. In 2008, he offered to play a management role in turning around LA's notorious Dorsey High School, where only 1 percent of the students tested as proficient in math. "I'm offering my heart, my soul, my reputation, my pocketbook, and everything to the students at Dorsey High School," said Riordan.

District officials rejected Riordan's offer of help.[6]

Richard Riordan is a model public official, capable, experienced, and with a deep and sincere interest in making a positive difference in the lives of citizens. He did an excellent job as mayor. Despite his best efforts, however, he could not bring about a turnaround for Los Angeles or its school system. Riordan's frustrating experience shows the hazards of what we call the Sisyphus Trap.

The Sisyphus Trap: Rolling the Rock Up a Hill

Striving to find a meaning in one's life is the primary motivational force in man.

—VIKTOR FRANKL, *MAN'S SEARCH FOR MEANING*

When the Greek gods decided to punish Sisyphus for his trickery, they assigned him the task of rolling a huge boulder up a steep hill. Each time, before he could reach the top of the hill, the rock would roll back down again, forcing Sisyphus to repeat this fruitless task throughout eternity. Those who work in the public sector often feel like Sisyphus rolling and rerolling a rock up a hill.

The Sisyphus Trap is the unique set of challenges in the public sector facing the person rolling the rock up the hill. Public sector leaders fall into the Sisyphus Trap when they fail to fully comprehend the special challenges of the public sector terrain. Too often, policy makers believe that they can achieve results simply by devising the right strategy or passing the right law. They miss a critical ingredient for success because the problem of getting big things done in government isn't merely a systems problem. It isn't merely a policy problem. It's a human problem as well.

For any given task, Sisyphus has a challenge, depicted in figure 5-1.

FIGURE 5-1

Sisyphus rolling the rock up the hill

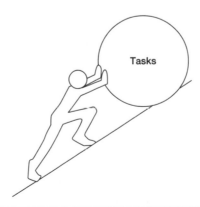

One thing is abundantly clear: nothing is as vital to success as the attitude of the living, breathing human beings charged with getting the rock up the hill. Remember that even as Sisyphus is pushing on the rock, the rock is pushing back on Sisyphus. How each individual responds to the challenges of the public sector will be different. Some, like Richard Riordan, will just keep on pushing that rock. Others, after watching the rock roll back enough times, will fall into despair and simply give up, either leaving government or throttling back on their effort. Still others, like the bad cops in Rampart, will turn their position to their own advantage, turning public service into self-service.

For a given task—say, the construction of a building—the other thing that matters is the steepness of the hill. Here, the inescapable fact is that the public sector hill is simply steeper than the private sector hill. The most frequently heard complaint of those seeking to achieve great things in government is: "It's just so damn *frustrating.*" To make a difference in government means operating within a rule-laden bureaucracy—some rules sensible, many of them not. It means working in an environment where the incentives are all wrong. It means swimming in the sometimes unsavory stew of politics. To succeed in large public undertakings, it is necessary to deeply understand the terrain that government leaders, managers, and frontline employees must contend with every day—the forces that make it so hard to push the rock up the hill.

What keeps the best people in government pushing on that rock? An understanding that the mission they are engaged in is truly, transcendently important. The desires for security, wealth, and pleasure are all strong, but nothing runs deeper than the longing to improve the world in which we live. This desire is not rational; it is human. The gods, in robbing Sisyphus of meaningful accomplishment, robbed him of his dignity. It was not the backbreaking effort that was the punishment, but the pointlessness of that effort.

Countless books explore every aspect of trying to get results in business. Very few look at the experiences of trying to get results in the public sector, particularly the motivation of those who work in government. This chapter explores how the interplay between the unique systems of the public sector and the people who work in government often makes the difference between success and failure in large undertakings.

We start by examining three invisible forces—incentives, culture, and politics—that make the "psychological terrain" of the public sector uniquely challenging.

Incentives Without Carrots or Sticks

For any organization, public or private, the key to effective performance lies in getting the incentives right, and thus in motivating employees to pursue the organization's objectives as productively as possible. This is Management 101.

—PROFESSOR TERRY MOE, STANFORD UNIVERSITY[7]

Susan works in insurance. She's a manager in a fraud prevention group, meaning she tries to catch people who submit phony claims. Her coworkers collect premiums, process unemployment claims, and pay out cash benefits. Other employees are engaged in support activities—there is an information technology group, a finance group, a human resources group, and so forth. Walk around Susan's office and you will see claims agents on the telephone, accountants working on their spreadsheets, and managers e-mailing each other *Dilbert* cartoons—just like at any insurance company.

Susan, however, doesn't work at an insurance company. Susan (a fictional name) works at the Massachusetts Division of Unemployment Assistance (DUA), an agency that one of us used to lead. If you scratch beneath the surface, you will find that despite the superficial similarities, Susan works in an environment fundamentally different from that of a private insurance company. Why? Because the incentives are different.

You won't see anyone at Susan's work talking about whether this will be a "good quarter" or not. The DUA never turns a profit, never incurs a loss. Unlike their private sector counterparts, senior managers at the DUA don't get stock options or other performance incentives. For the 90 percent of DUA's employees who are unionized and/or under civil service protection, productivity doesn't affect their compensation. Negative consequences generally result only after serious malfeasance, as opposed to merely lackluster performance.

In short, there are few negative consequences for poor performance—for workers, managers, or the organization as a whole. There are few incentives for good performance either. The DUA—whether it is run well or poorly, whether the phones are answered with a smile or a snarl, whether those who pay the premiums are happy or not—will be there next year, and the year after, and the year after that.

Susan no doubt appreciates the predictable aspect of working at the DUA, as evidenced by the fact that Susan has been working at the Massachusetts DUA for many years, in fact well before the first unemployment check was issued.

The risks and rewards of the private sector are radically different. The risks include all the vagaries of a competitive market—downsizing, outsourcing, mergers and acquisitions, technological obsolescence. Even outstanding workers may find themselves going to Susan for an unemployment check some day. On the other hand, the rewards are different. Talent, hard work, and successful risk taking can bring rewards unheard of in the public sector. Particularly for those engaged in the risky work of a start-up, employees are toiling unimaginable hours for relatively low pay along with some stake in the outcome—the possibility of the big payoff from stock options. Individual entrepreneurs start restaurants and hair salons with hopes of making it big. Some make a big splash, others a big belly flop.

Incentives (or the lack thereof) play a big role in the engagement of the workforce. Efforts to artificially replicate the incentives of the private sector—bonus programs and merit pay—have a very spotty record in the public sector. The lack of flexibility around incentives exacerbates the challenge of alignment that every organization faces. Public leaders trying to get big results must lean much more heavily on other motivators—such as a mission—than their private sector counterparts.

Incentives aren't the only factor influencing the public sector operating environment. Culture is also important.

Culture Matters

The corporate culture at a Wall Street brokerage is different from the culture at Whole Foods. The corporate culture of a Silicon Valley start-up is different from that of IBM. The only thing that all private companies share is an organizational survival imperative—all companies must be profitable to ensure long-term survival.

There is also no monolithic "public sector culture." Just as different corporations have distinct corporate cultures, so too do government agencies, and you can observe dramatic cultural differences between regions, between agencies, and sometimes even between different parts of the same organization. The city governments of Minneapolis and Chicago have very similar political structures and are engaged in very similar tasks—but how these organizations actually operate is quite different.[8] Political scientist Daniel Elazar has shown how the broader cultures of a state's population, which he categorizes as moralistic, individualistic, and traditionalistic, powerfully shape the culture of its government.[9] Such cultures in turn impact the ability of an organization to execute.

Government cultures differ widely, not only from city to city and state to state but also according to the nature of the work being performed. Table 5-1 shows some of the major functional areas in which government is involved. This table is not exhaustive and the tendencies are not uniform. It is simply a tool to help visualize the variety of activities and cultures that exist within government.

The absence of a profit motive in government puts even greater focus on mission. A strong appreciation for the importance of the mission can inspire remarkable achievement. Justice in the courts, an effective military, an honest police force—these are the essence of a free and just society, and public service to noble ends is indeed a higher ideal than the meager profit motive.

One form of the Sisyphus Trap is to ask a government organization to undertake a mission antithetical to its culture. This occurred to some extent in Iraq, when the military was put in a position of "keeping order" in a fractious nation. Combat soldiers are trained for violent, hostile situations, and the military culture reflects that. Once the military operation in Iraq was over, soldiers were asked to engage in peacekeeping, a job that is more like law enforcement. For the first few years of their mission in Iraq, military personnel had a difficult time knowing how to behave. Two kinds of mistakes were common. In some cases, military personnel failed to be wary of approaching "civilians" and were attacked by hostile ambushes. In other cases, unfortunate civilians who posed no threat were treated like armed combatants, sometimes with deadly results.

TABLE 5-1

Typology of public sector workforce cultures

Role	Enforcers	Instructors	Helpers	Processors	Builders and fixers	Housekeepers	Scientists
Function	Criminal justice and public safety	Teaching	Social services	Paperwork factory	Public works factory	Support services	Research and development
Service areas	• Police • Fire • Corrections • District attorney's office • Crime labs • Military • Environmental police • Intelligence agencies	• K-12 teachers • University professors • Job training	• Welfare • Nursing homes • Mental health • Family counseling • Foster care • Housing • Disability	• Social security • Student loans • Tax collection • Unemployment insurance	• Street repairs • Town clump • Parks • Transit • Wastewater treatment • Highways and bridges • Building construction	• IT • Human resources • Procurement • Facilities • Accounting and finance	• Space exploration • Technology research • Medical research • Data analytics • Laboratory technicians
Cultural tendencies	• Problem solvers • More male and more aggressive	• "Let's change the future" • socially responsible individuals who want to develop a better future	• "Let's make people's lives better" socially conscious, often altruistic individuals who want to alleviate people's suffering • Enjoy working in teams	• Process-oriented • Follow the rules • Detail-minded	• Engineering mentality • "Get the job done and make a respectable living"	• Keep the business running • Detail-minded • Process-oriented work life	• Highly analytical and academic • Allegiance to research area typically stronger than to organization

Recognizing the problem, the army developed a new manual with a new code of conduct. Lt. Col. John Nagel summed it up this way: "Be professional, be courteous, be prepared to kill."[10] If this sounds odd, it shouldn't. It is essentially a description of the code of conduct for police forces around the nation. Police officers, since they deal mostly with law-abiding citizens, are trained to be professional and courteous while at the same time being wary of potential dangers. Such behaviors are embedded in the law enforcement culture, as are techniques for telling the difference between an unruly drunk and a homicidal maniac. Mistakes can still occur, but at least the organizational culture and training are suited to the circumstances.

A mismatch between culture and mission can undermine transformational efforts. Similar mismatches can occur, for example, when social workers and others in the helping professions are asked to be "enforcers," in essence turning in their clients. Think twice before asking an organization to work outside its cultural comfort zone.

Just like a corporation, a public agency is simply a way that humans organize themselves to achieve a desired result. As we will see later in this chapter, culture played a powerful role both at NASA, where putting a man on the moon was more than just a job, and in Wisconsin, where a professional, reform-minded government culture helped generate great results in welfare reform.

Politics and Bureaucracy: Bridging the Divide

The successful launch of a major initiative requires the marriage of political leaders working with bureaucratic implementers. Not only does politics enter the equation, but the stark cultural divide that separates the two sides of Stargate creates a kind of organizational schizophrenia. For political leaders and bureaucratic managers, the incentives are different, the cultures are different, and, in some cases, the goals are different. The uneasy partnership between these two camps can create a barrier to coherent management.

The political world is partisan, risky, competitive, combative, image driven, ambitious, and fast paced. Outside of a small handful of advisers, political campaigns are staffed by people who can afford to spend months working for next to no money for the chance, if their candidate wins, of working in government for only slightly more money. With loyalty highly valued in the political universe—sometimes more highly than competence—the reality is that many policy initiatives will be led by young, inexperienced, highly partisan political appointees culled from the campaign.

They will be guiding the effort of career staffers, who live in a diametrically different universe, where risks are viewed askance, the outlook is long term, and the allegiance is more often to the agency than the new administration (see table 5-2 for a snapshot of these two cultures). The bureaucratic world is far more static than the political—it is not unusual for an agency to have numerous managers with twenty, thirty, or forty years of service.

The stark cultural divide that separates the two sides of Stargate creates a kind of organizational schizophrenia. This is particularly true in the case of a party changeover, when the new administration comes to office

TABLE 5-2

Characteristics of the political and bureaucrat cultures

	Political culture	Bureaucrat culture
Ego	Self-confidence that sometimes borders on narcissism. To get elected, you have to tell strangers how terrific you are.	Used to sublimating ego to political class.
Outlook	Optimism that can border on fantasy.	Realism, bordering on pessimism.
Risk tolerance	Politics attracts and rewards risk takers.	Risk averse. There is little upside to sticking your neck out.
Image consciousness	Image is critical to their success.	Image low on priority list.
Passion	Politics. Many politicians find electoral politics exhilarating and governing boring.	Governance. Many bureaucrats seem tone-deaf to politics.
Focus	Short term	Long term

having pledged to clean up, shake up, and turn around the city, state, or nation. Often, the political team wants to change things as quickly as possible, while the bureaucratic veterans patiently explain why most of the changes they seek are impossible, illegal, or simply unwise. The brash young party operatives, fresh from a victorious political campaign, view the "old dogs" of the bureaucracy with disdain, while the seasoned bureaucrats bemoan the fact that these neophytes do not know what they do not know. As one insider put it, "This is a familiar syndrome, one where twenty-six-year-old smarties spend the first critical months of a successful politician's term in office ordering around older, wiser, and more experienced career managers who know better. This hubris seems unavoidable, but it is very damaging to efforts to govern effectively."[11]

In Washington, D.C., the proliferation of political appointees means that senior executives often report to very junior staffers. "You know you have arrived when you get interviewed by the 29-year-old instead of the 22-year-old," one 57-year-old foreign service veteran told Thomas Schweich of the State Department. Another shared the story of being interviewed for the post of ambassador to a nation in Africa. "The problem was, the kid interviewing me could not pronounce the name of the country I was being interviewed for. It made for an awkward interview until he just started saying 'the country we are considering you for.' "[12]

The dissonance between the political and bureaucratic worlds can create working relationships that do not work. An example: Bill Weld became governor in Massachusetts in 1991 in part by capitalizing on dissatisfaction with government. On the campaign trail, he pilloried the "walruses" who worked in state government. When it came time to govern, these walruses, not surprisingly, never fully embraced their new governor or his lieutenants. As a result, Weld was unable to accomplish some of his key initiatives.

Another example: Craig Benson, a high-tech entrepreneur, was elected governor of New Hampshire in 2002 by promising to run the state like a multibillion-dollar corporation. He apparently believed that the main problem with state government was that smart people like him hadn't been in charge. At an inauguration day pancake breakfast, he told his audience of several hundred state workers, "I bet you that not many people in this room have been asked to bring their brains with them to work in a long time."[13] In a few short words on his first day in office, the new governor inadvertently managed to be insulting, condescending, and arrogant all at the same time. Benson's high-tech style—he held staff meetings around a stand-up desk—never meshed with the political culture. Two years later, Benson became the first Granite State governor in seventy-eight years to lose in his first reelection bid.

Some see a growing distrust between the political and bureaucratic worlds. "It started with Carter, accelerated with Reagan, and continues to this day," one longtime senior federal executive told us. "The political leadership does not trust and has trashed the career public service to the detriment of the public. Who is proud to be a civil servant these days?"[14]

Dwight Ink, a retired senior executive who served seven presidents, concurs. "The career civil service is the only vehicle through which a president can govern. Yet we continue to see instance after instance of White House staff and agency leaders not only failing to reach out to the men and women on whom their political success will largely rest but also quickly alienating them through distrust and marginalizing their roles."[15]

The senior civil service bureaucracy has been trained into a degree of passivity that diminishes the great gift they have to offer: a rich understanding of the process details that bedevil so many implementation efforts. In recent times career civil servants have often been shut out of the decision-making process, especially when it comes to the crucial policy design process. Particularly in an era of growing complexity, to dismiss this rich knowledge base is exceedingly shortsighted.

Without a doubt, the incentives, culture, and political nature of the public sector present unique challenges to successful execution of large public undertakings. It doesn't mean such accomplishments are impossible. More than anything else, success requires a leader who can navigate in both the bureaucratic and the political worlds, who understands the unique terrain of government on both sides of the Stargate. Nearly every successful initiative we studied was distinguished by the presence of a "below-the-radar leader" who led the effort. Sometimes it was a political appointee like Tim Murphy, who helped launch Romney's health care reform in Massachusetts. Sometimes it was a career bureaucrat like Derek Turner, who oversaw the London congestion pricing effort. These talented, under-the-radar leaders bridge the bureaucratic and political worlds and are often the unsung heroes of major political successes. The epitome of this sort of leader is James Webb, the man behind the moon landings.

James Webb and Putting a Man on the Moon

I'm a relatively cautious person. I think when you decide you're going to do something and put the prestige and power of the United States government behind it, you'd better doggone well be able to do it.

—JAMES WEBB, NASA ADMINISTRATOR, 1961–1968[16]

You know that in July of 1969, Neil Armstrong was the first person to walk on the moon. You've probably heard of his shipmates, Edwin Aldrin and Michael Collins. You might even know that Aldrin was nicknamed Buzz, though for an entirely different reason than your college roommate. Most people, however, have never heard of James Webb. Though he never got a ticker-tape parade, he may have been the most indispensible contributor to arguably the greatest public sector achievement in American history, leading the NASA space program through the political, administrative, and technical challenge of putting a man on the moon.

Soon after taking office, President Kennedy recruited Webb to head NASA. Webb was well suited for the job, with a powerful combination of public sector and private sector experience. He had been the director of the Bureau of the Budget for President Truman, and then served as a senior business executive at Kerr-McGee Oil Corp. Webb hadn't sought the NASA job, but when the president of the United States asks for your help, you don't turn him down.

Kennedy needed the help, because when he took office America was well behind the Soviets—and things were getting worse. In 1957, America had been shocked when the Soviets launched the world's first satellite, *Sputnik I*. In 1958, Congress created the National Aeronautic and Space Administration, or NASA, to try to catch up to the Soviet Union. The competition in space was taking place not only in the context of the Cold War, but also in the midst of an ideological contest between democracy and communism. In 1959, Vice President Richard Nixon and Soviet Premier Nikita Khrushchev had an impromptu but spirited debate in

Moscow while touring a model U.S. kitchen. Nixon and Khrushchev began bickering about washing machines and floor sweepers and moved on to rockets and missiles. Khrushchev said what every American feared might be true: "We have existed not quite forty-two years and in another seven years we will be on the same level as America. When we pass you up, in passing you by, we will wave hi to you."[17] The winner of the Nixon-Khrushchev "Kitchen Debate" would not be decided by words but by deeds. History would render the verdict, and Khrushchev had already claimed history as an ally: "Whether you like it or not, history is on our side. We will bury you."[18]

When President Kennedy took office in January of 1961, he knew space would be important for both symbolic and strategic reasons. He coaxed James Webb out of the private sector to run NASA. Events moved quickly. Three months later, on April 12, 1961, Soviet cosmonaut Yuri Gagarin became the first human to orbit Earth. "Let the capitalist countries catch up with our country!" boasted Khrushchev.[19] A few days later, on April 17, 1961, American-led forces were routed by Fidel Castro's army in the Bay of Pigs. These events lent credence to the notion that a dictatorial system, unfettered by the niceties of democracy, could actually get things done.

Less than a hundred days after his grand inaugural address, America's youthful president saw his nation beaten in space and humiliated on the beaches of Cuba within the span of a week. On April 30, 1961, *New York Times* columnist James Reston wrote of Kennedy: "He was like a young prize fighter, toying gracefully with his opponent, jabbing at will and casually waving to the crowd, when suddenly he was hit on the chin. This has hurt him badly. The magic of the first two months has vanished."[20]

Kennedy wanted to get the magic back. On May 25, 1961, before a joint session of Congress, Kennedy laid out his vision of putting a man on the moon and returning him safely to Earth before the end of the decade. Though laying out a bold challenge, Kennedy's words contained a cautionary note about how difficult a challenge this would be.

Let it be clear that I am asking the Congress and the country to accept a firm commitment to a new course of action, a course which will last for many years and carry very heavy costs: $531 million dollars in fiscal '62—an *estimated seven to nine billion dollars additional over the next five years. If we are to go only half way, or reduce our sights in the face of difficulty, in my judgment it would be better not to go at all.*

No doubt the astronauts were happy to hear that the president opposed the idea of going only halfway.

This decision demands a major national commitment of scientific and technical manpower, material and facilities, and the possibility of their diversion from other important activities where they are already thinly spread. It means a degree of dedication, organization and discipline which have not always characterized our research and development efforts. It means we cannot afford undue work stoppages, inflated costs of material or talent, wasteful interagency rivalries, or a high turnover of key personnel.[21]

It is remarkable today to read the words of an American president, during a major address to Congress, talking about the bureaucratic challenges of a major endeavor. Interagency rivalries? High turnover? Where did such notions come from?

Probably Webb. Webb played a role in crafting this part of the president's address. An earlier draft of the speech had set 1967 as the goal for a moon landing, but Webb had added what he termed an "administrative discount" to account for unforeseen contingencies. He also doubled the cost estimates developed by NASA before sending them to the president, adding his administrative realism to counter technical optimism. (Anyone who has ever remodeled a kitchen can relate.) Webb's prudence helped him avoid the Overconfidence Trap, and helped ensure that needed resources were available down the road. After all, nobody wants to go halfway to the moon.[22] Webb's conservative estimates turned out to be just about right.

Webb was a firm believer in the notion that Apollo's real achievement lay in demonstrating that a democratic system could outmanage an authoritarian state, despite the constraints. The effort to put a man on the moon cost roughly $24 billion, required the involvement of 20,000 industrial firms, 200 university labs, and 400,000 public and private workers.[23] Webb was a pioneer in the field of networked government. The astronauts used to joke that they were sitting in a rocket ship made of

20,000 parts, all of them made by the low-cost bidder.[24] How did he do it? Webb was a master at bridging the divide between the political and bureaucratic worlds. He spent a third of his time interacting with key politicians, a third of his time directing his staff, and a third of his time managing critical contracts with private sector companies and universities, private players who were essential to the space effort. Webb's infectious enthusiasm motivated all of them, from NASA employees to members of Congress. Somehow, Webb made all the parts work together.

Webb wasn't above making "political" decisions. Though Congress had agreed to fund the journey to the moon in 1961, it was a decision they revisited every year through the budget. The decision to base NASA operations in Texas and place a supporting research facility in Massachusetts clearly had the benefit of winning key members of Congress—not to mention the president and vice president—as key political allies. He also actively cultivated supporters in the press. During 1966 and early 1967, Webb averaged better than a speech a week, promoting NASA and the journey to the moon.

The journey to success experienced some bumps along the road. On January 27, 1967, a cockpit fire killed astronauts Virgil Grissom, Edward White, and Roger Chaffee at Cape Kennedy during some prelaunch testing. The political reaction was swift, and the fatal accident of 1967 became the subject of intense congressional scrutiny.[25] Webb adroitly made sure that testimony about the fire was exhaustive, because he knew the political damage that could occur in the case of a cover-up, real or perceived.

There was enormous pressure on NASA's budget as well. Whitney Young, head of the Urban League, pointed out that spending on NASA meant less for the Great Society's antipoverty programs. "It will cost thirty-five billion dollars to put two men on the moon. It would take ten billion dollars to lift every poor person in this country above the poverty line. Something is wrong somewhere," wrote Whitney.[26] In the weeks following the fire, Congress flirted with the idea of pulling out of the race to the moon.

Webb took the agency through these dark days. As the lame-duck Johnson administration was winding down, Webb decided to step down to ensure a smooth transition, to remove the political part of the equation from the leadership of the space program. In his final days at NASA, Johnson awarded Webb the Presidential Medal of Freedom, the highest civilian honor a president can bestow.

Months after his departure, Webb watched with pride as Neil Armstrong planted the flag on the lunar surface. James Webb today is considered one of the all-time great public managers, and no one is more

THE FIVE ESSENTIAL CHARACTERISTICS OF HIGHLY EFFECTIVE PUBLIC IMPLEMENTERS

Integrity. The biggest barrier to execution is a failure of integrity—it will undermine all efforts to execute anything. Without an honest assessment of the facts, unrealistic expectations will be set—and we have seen how the Overconfidence Trap can doom execution.

Respect. Treat everyone with respect. Failure to respect those we disagree with can lead to Tolstoy syndrome. Those who come from the political universe should respect the knowledge of the bureaucrats ("walruses") on whom they depend, and bureaucrats need to respect political appointees ("those twenty-something smarties") who are, for the moment at least, running the show.

Balance. It takes balance to navigate between the Scylla and Charybdis of the political and bureaucratic worlds. Your ultimate goal is to serve the public, but at the same time you must also serve the political leader voters have placed in charge.

A passion for the mission. A mission-driven organization is the only antidote to cynicism in government. To inspire others, you must aspire to excellence yourself. Good government is a noble pursuit. Effective public leaders leverage mission to inspire employees and recruit people who want to make a difference.

Irrational behavior. The best and brightest can probably make more money on Wall Street or in Silicon Valley. But our nation needs the best to achieve its best—think Richard Riordan, James Webb, or the heroes of September 11. Selfless contribution is an important cultural value rarely celebrated in this era of unbridled public cynicism.

revered at NASA. James Webb embodies the five essential characteristics of successful implementers (see the box). Without question, placing a man on the moon was an enormously challenging technical, bureaucratic, and political achievement. The goal laid down in 1961 by President Kennedy was almost unimaginably audacious. The symbolic impact of this achievement was globally transcendent, altering the way the world viewed America and America viewed herself. Webb had helped put a man on the moon, and in doing so demonstrated that it was possible for democratic government to accomplish great things.

An Ever Steeper Hill: The Pretzel Organization

Webb faced many challenges, but he did enjoy one huge advantage over most public managers. He had the luxury of leading what was in essence a start-up federal agency, absent many of the bureaucratic strictures that tend to multiply over time.

In particular, Webb led the Apollo program at a time when the general bureaucratic and legal environments were far less cumbersome than they are today. While impossible to measure with any precision, virtually everyone agrees that there has been a massive increase in constraints in the public sector in general, including at NASA. One argument says that what Webb accomplished in the 1960s could not be accomplished today, even by an administrator as capable as Webb, because of the proliferation of rules that make leading a public organization harder than ever, particularly one seeking to accomplish something big.

Webb had great appreciation for public management, and after he left NASA, he helped establish the National Academy of Public Administration (NAPA), a nonprofit chartered by Congress. Modeled after the National Academy of Sciences, NAPA was and is dedicated to improving public sector management.[27] In 2007, a NAPA panel reviewed personnel practices at NASA and came to some conclusions that no doubt would have saddened Webb. The NAPA panel found that NASA had become calcified, and needed greater management flexibility to pursue its mission. The greatest challenge was to be found in how NASA managed its most important resource: people. "When agencies have significantly evolving missions . . . the government's rigid, rule-bound civil service system does not facilitate or encourage flexibility in the civil workforce," the report said. "Although the nature of an agency's work requirements changes over time, permanent civil servants with tenure are not forced to adapt."[28]

The NAPA report was also critical of stakeholders—including contractors, universities, and unions—who exert political influence to challenge any change that isn't in their interest:

> *The stakeholders can also impose limitations on the agency by restricting its flexibility in planning and quickly responding to organizational, mission, and programmatic changes . . . [Congress] constrained the agency's options in reshaping and realigning its workforce.*[29]

NASA is not the only public agency laboring under such constraints. The entire federal government, as well as state and local governments, has seen a huge growth in the number of veto players, the number of folks on the bus who have access to a brake. The tangle of rules has led to the need for managers to be master contortionists to get anything accomplished in the pretzel organization of government today.

James Loy, the former deputy at the Department of Homeland Security (DHS), spent more than three decades working for the federal government, including a stint as the commandant for the Coast Guard. He is convinced the constraints of the public operating system have gotten a lot worse since he began his career. "Bureaucratically, we have overwhelmed ourselves," says Loy. "We've reached the point where the bureaucratic trappings have become the albatrosses that we have to bear."[30] Loy points out that over the course of one year, he and then DHS secretary Tom Ridge were asked to testify to Congress 163 times. Considering the immense preparation time that goes into such testimony, he could easily have spent his entire time at DHS responding to Congress instead of protecting our country against threats.

Loy is not alone. In our surveys of federal senior executives and members of the National Academy of Public Administration, both groups cited an increase in administrative and political constraints as *the* top reason for poor program execution in government (see appendixes A, B, and C). One thirty-year veteran of federal service told us: "Every initiative runs up against not only interest groups but also endless hurdles to jump (hearings, studies, court cases). Imagine if it were necessary to build today another Oak Ridge, Tennessee [the secret city built during World War II to refine uranium for the atomic bomb]. It couldn't be done."

The pretzel organization problem doesn't exist only at the federal level. Following the terrorist attacks on the World Trade Center on September 11, 2001, the government made a commitment to erect a monument at the site, a way to show the world that America was bloodied but unbowed. Eight years later, the effort to rebuild at Ground Zero in New York City is mired in a bureaucratic morass, with some nineteen government agencies involved in a process that is way behind schedule and way over budget. The inability to make progress on this task of highly symbolic importance makes government look inept, as *Time* magazine noted in a 2008 article: "It shouldn't escape anyone's attention that in half the time it has taken us to get where we are today at Ground Zero, China has completed construction on the equivalent of a dozen World Trade Center sites in the furiously efficient run-up to the Olympics . . . [W]e shouldn't be happy to be lapped by a command economy."[31] Whereas NASA could put a man on the moon in less than a decade, the tenth anniversary ceremony of the 9/11 attacks is likely to take place at a still unfinished site.

Frustrating? Immensely. Yet we must not forget the flip side of the World Trade Center story. On the day of those scurrilous attacks, some 341 New York firefighters, 2 fire department paramedics, and 60 police officers from the NYPD and Port Authority valiantly gave their lives. These public employees entered the burning towers to rescue others, not because they would get a bonus if they did, but out of a sense of duty. The World Trade Center story illustrates both the frustrating morass of rules as well as the wonderfully irrational commitment of those who gave their lives in public service.

Fixing the pretzel organization without sacrificing public values and accountability is a riddle yet to be fully solved, despite the earnest efforts of the reinventing government movement of the 1990s. Nevertheless, if we want to get better at executing large public initiatives on more than a piecemeal basis, we'll need to find ways to make the hill a little less steep for those who work within government. This means revisiting many of the most challenging and constrictive of the rules and regulations that mushroomed in recent decades, which so often tie the hands of our public servants.

The Double Sisyphus Trap

You know it can't be good if it's called the Double Sisyphus Trap. Well, it isn't.

The point of this chapter so far has been to show the various ways that people respond to the unique forces of the public sector, and how the interplay between government systems and those who work within government has an enormous impact on the success or failure of large undertakings. This is true in all public undertakings. At this point, however, it must be pointed out that while putting a man on the moon was an incredible achievement, it was easier in one sense than many government undertakings for one simple reason: the challenge involved humans on only one side of the equation.

In pushing a rock up a hill or a rocket to the moon, the only thing you are fighting is gravity. But what if your challenge is to try to change people's behaviors? In government drug rehabilitation programs, teen pregnancy prevention programs, or job training programs, the goal is to transform citizens, to change their behavior. Even a less "touchy-feely" program such as the London road pricing scheme was about changing people's driving habits. The challenge Sisyphus faces in these cases is portrayed in figure 5-2.

If the little people in the drawing were getting up the hill on their own, government intervention would be superfluous. In these sorts of undertakings, often the biggest challenge is the ingrained behaviors of the individuals being helped. If no one makes it to the top of the hill, after a while both the helper and those who are being helped become despondent about ever getting to the top. This is the essence of the Double Sisyphus Trap, the variable and sometimes unexpected reactions of the citizens touched by government programs. Rather than promoting racial harmony, busing in Boston schools increased racial hostility and prompted

FIGURE 5-2

The double Sisyphus trap

residents to flee outside the city or to private schools, leading to greater segregation. By some accounts, providing aid for single mothers has encouraged more single motherhood. Moreover, the unintended harm being done over time has an impact on providers as well—the public workers in these programs, like Sisyphus, are working hard but aren't necessarily seeing positive results. These workers can also become dispirited, and lapse into despair.

In the next chapter we'll meet some people trying to turn around the public school system in New Orleans, which has been highly dysfunctional for decades. "The problem we have in New Orleans is that a lot of people for so long have only seen failure that it's hard for them to believe in the possibility of success," says Paul Pastorek, Louisiana's state superintendent of education. When asked if turning around schools in New Orleans is harder than putting a man on the moon, Pastorek doesn't hesitate. "Oh, this is harder than putting a man on the moon, no question," said Pastorek.[32] He should know. Before becoming Louisiana's superintendent of education Pastorek was a senior executive at NASA.

Welfare Reform 1996: Beating the Double Sisyphus Trap

In addition to the interplay between government and those who work within it, there is an interplay between government programs and those who benefit from them. Since their very inception, the great conundrum of federal antipoverty programs has been this: how can we help those in need without establishing a culture of dependency? In his

State of the Union speech of 1935, President Franklin Roosevelt called continued dependence on aid "a narcotic, a subtle destroyer of the human spirit."[33]

By 1970, politicians from both sides of the aisle called for an overhaul of antipoverty programs. Democratic senator George McGovern noted, "Over the past ten years we have sought to end poverty with programs . . . You recognize the programs to which I refer—medical care in public clinics, public assistance, and public housing. All were started by reformers with high hopes. All have turned out badly . . . These programs have efficiently demeaned the poor."[34]

Just weeks after Neil Armstrong planted the American flag on the moon, President Nixon appeared on television and told the nation, "Nowhere has the failure of government been more tragically apparent than in its efforts to help the poor and especially in its system of public welfare."[35]

Fixing welfare proved much harder than putting a man on the moon. During the seventies and eighties, welfare rolls soared. By 1994 about 14 million Americans were receiving Aid to Families with Dependent Children (AFDC) welfare benefits. Nobody was happy about the status quo, but change was hard to come by.

Like the nation as a whole, Wisconsin was struggling to break the seemingly unbreakable cycle of welfare dependency in the early 1990s. State officials introduced reforms that shifted the focus from distributing benefits to moving welfare recipients into jobs. These programs showed great promise.

Taking a cue from the success in Wisconsin, in 1995 the Republican-controlled Congress introduced legislation to transform the existing welfare model from cash handouts to a time-limited, work-based benefit. The bill was met with heavy opposition and vetoed twice by President Bill Clinton. The third time the bill crossed his desk President Clinton signed it, provoking outrage and warnings of catastrophe. Senator Daniel Patrick Moynihan (D-New York), whom we profile in chapter 8, called the proposal "the most brutal act of social policy since Reconstruction."[36] He predicted, "Those involved will take this disgrace to their graves."[37] The widely respected Urban Institute predicted the new law would drive 2.6 million people, including 1.1 million children, into poverty.[38]

Critics and skeptics had plenty of reasons to expect disaster. Other than some small-scale state and local experiments, governments previously had very little success moving people from welfare into jobs. Moreover, the broad congressional goal of moving people from "welfare to work" had to be cascaded all the way down from the federal to the state to the local to the community level. Welfare reform also could easily have gotten caught in the Sisyphus Trap, since the culture at most social service agencies at that time emphasized providing services, not pushing people into jobs. In many cases, the social workers didn't even believe the recipient of the services was capable of working. Given the incongruence with their existing worldview, social services agencies could have rebelled against the new rules, with individuals either subtly sabotaging the effort or gaming the system, as we saw happen with No Child Left Behind.

Welfare reform could have failed in many ways, but it didn't.

Instead of the predicted fiasco, the 1996 welfare reform became one of the biggest public policy success stories of the past few decades. Child poverty and poverty of single mothers declined substantially. Employment among welfare recipients increased significantly, and welfare rolls plummeted by more than 50 percent in the six years after the bill was signed into law.[39] It certainly helped that the economy was strong during these years, but most observers acknowledge the importance of the 1996 reforms.

The question remains: what made welfare reform succeed? Given the complexity of the intergovernmental issues, the culture of the social service world, and the skepticism among many of those charged with implementing the reforms, how did welfare reform escape the Double Sisyphus Trap?

The first thing to understand is that welfare reform didn't succeed equally everywhere. In some states, welfare reform did indeed get tripped up by opposition from social service organizations, the political-bureaucratic differences, and partisan policy disagreements. In New York, for example, policy makers were so divided on the policy issues that decisions about work requirements were left to the counties. In Arizona, the welfare agency was committed to a different approach and resisted what they saw as a political push toward work first.[40]

In a number of states, however, enterprising public officials were able to overcome such obstacles. The best example is Wisconsin, the state widely considered the father of welfare reform, which reduced its welfare rolls by an astounding 82 percent in six years. Wisconsin escaped both the Sisyphus Trap and the Double Sisyphus Trap by changing the incentives (both for recipients and for providers), getting the culture right, and closing the political-bureaucratic divide.

The first reason welfare reform worked in Wisconsin was the bipartisan consensus about the goal. In fact, it was Democrats in the legislature who first proposed abolishing AFDC and replacing it with another model by 1999. The shared commitment to the main goals of welfare reform removed what turned out to be a major stumbling block in other states: achieving goal alignment.

Second, the state built on earlier experiments and successes at the local level in counties like Kenosha. Rather than simply impose an untested top-down solution, policy designers took their cue from implementers; this eliminated much of the friction that typically exists between levels of government. Politicians followed the lead of practitioners in the field, narrowing the political-bureaucratic divide and ensuring a smooth implementation.

Third, Wisconsin got both the incentives and the cultural issues right. It did so by introducing a novel system of competition. It put the administration of the welfare to work programs out for bid in all ninety-two counties, allowing public, private, and nonprofit organizations to bid on running the program. This forced many of the organizations that would be delivering on the reforms—organizations with very different cultures that might previously have operated at cross-purposes—to team up and coordinate their efforts. The state added an important twist by paying only for results; that is, organizations were rewarded for moving welfare recipients into self-sufficiency, as opposed to the old model of paying for effort. This approach led local agencies administering the program to partner with for-profit companies and nonprofit organizations that bought into the new culture of work first. Performance would now be measured in jobs, not counseling sessions. The powerful financial incentives aligned all the players with the primary goal of work and self-sufficiency.

Last, and perhaps most important, the state agency in charge of implementing welfare reform was more than up to the task. Larry Mead, the author of *Government Matters*, an acclaimed book on Wisconsin's welfare reform, argues that "bureaucratic statecraft," the development of a strong, efficient, and engaged administrative structure was—more than anything else—responsible for Wisconsin's success. "The Wisconsin story makes clear how dependent successful social reform is on strong institutions," writes Mead. "The Wisconsin reform is the achievement of legislators and administrators who were unusually able and conscientious by national standards."[41]

Wisconsin's welfare reformers skillfully navigated the interplay of people and systems. By getting the incentives, culture, and politics right, Wisconsin achieved a grand success, proving it is possible for government to beat the Double Sisyphus Trap.

Systems, People, and Results

Large undertakings are hard, whether in the public sector or the private sector. Without a doubt, the constraints of the public sector, with its unique incentives, politics, and culture, can make things especially challenging.

There is no magic formula to ensure success, but it helps to keep in mind that results are a function of both systems and the people who work within them. It's not magic, but those who like formulas can think of it this way: Results = f(Systems + People). In those cases where a government program interacts with the public, results also depend on how those being helped react to that assistance. The human spirit cannot be reduced to mathematical formula, but neglect the human element and an initiative can easily fall victim to the Sisyphus Trap or the Double Sisyphus Trap.

Keeping certain core principles in mind can improve the odds of success. Unquestionably, incentives matter. Second, as both the NASA and Wisconsin stories demonstrate, people can be inspired by a sense of mission, so it is critical to pay careful attention to matters of culture. Finally, as with everything in the public sector, politics play a crucial role. Politics can work with or against the bureaucracy. Sometimes, public leaders will ask imperfect people to achieve near-impossible results with inadequate resources. The best chance for success then lies in getting extraordinary results from the people trying to roll the rock up the hill.

Anybody looking for easy answers or surefire success should set up a lemonade stand, because government isn't a game of perfect. It would be nice, however, if some of the more frustrating constraints of the public sector, the things that make the hill so steep, could be reduced.

In some cases, the best way to achieve results entails rethinking the hill completely, gaining a new perspective on what you are trying to accomplish and how. How to do this is the subject of the next chapter.

FIELD GUIDE: RESULTS PHASE

The problem of getting big things done in government isn't merely a systems problem. It isn't merely a policy problem. It's a human problem as well. It is critical to remember that we are asking real people to do difficult things within a challenging environment. If your effort involves changing people's behaviors, double that. Results are a consequence of the systems of government and the interaction of the people in government with those systems.

Biggest Danger

The Sisyphus Trap. People fall into this trap by failing to comprehend the special challenges of the public sector terrain and how human factors—attitude, effort, desire—can make or break an effort. When a program seeks to change people's behaviors, the Double Sisyphus Trap comes into play.

Guiding Principles

Understand the terrain. The public sector hill is steeper than the private sector hill. To make a difference in government means operating within a sometimes bureaucratic system laden with rules, some of them sensible, many of them not.

Focus on the mission. Having an inspiring mission may be the most important competitive advantage in government. As with the *Apollo* program, mission can inspire people to achieve amazing results. Emphasize the importance of what you are doing. People want to make a difference. *Apollo* engineers worked long hours because they were passionate about the mission. Any undertaking of any significance requires that the organization be aligned to the mission.

Incentives matter. Self-interest is part of human nature. Performance incentives, award ceremonies, recognition—they make a difference. The lack of built-in incentives and feedback, however, makes it harder to get results in government.

Be cognizant of culture. Think twice before asking an organization to work outside its cultural comfort zone. One mismatch, for example, is when social workers are asked to be "enforcers," in essence turning in their clients.

Bridge the political-bureaucratic divide. This requires a leader who can interface between the different worlds—the rare person who can translate the bureaucratic language to politicians and tell the political masters when they are off course. These "bridgers" are critical to execution in government but highly undervalued today.

Tools and Techniques

The key tools for overcoming the Sisyphus Trap involve people and technology—skillfully managing contractors, your own employees, and relationships with legislators and citizens.

Know the people doing the work. Data is important, but getting to know the people in the trenches will foster a different understanding of the challenge ahead. Get out of the office and work the phones, work the line, work something. Attitude is everything.

Invest in your people, develop your people. Government is notorious for underinvesting in the productive capacity of its workers. Training in the tools of process management and change management is a good start. Programs aimed at developing a deep competency can help groom the "bridgers" needed to bridge the political and bureaucratic realms over time. One example: the British Civil Service's Fast Stream program where the best and brightest are exposed to a series of intensive job placements designed to prepare them for senior managerial positions.[42]

Cultural transformation toolkit. Systems you use to manage your workforce have a huge influence on employee attitudes. Civil service systems, union rules, and retirement structures have a huge impact on the public sector workforce and getting big things done. Tools to transform include:

- **Cultural assessment:** This type of survey is distributed widely across an organization to identify the organization's core beliefs and values—both those currently present and those that are desired.

- **Change readiness assessment:** This tool helps quickly assess organizational strengths and challenges to change with respect to leadership, workforce, structure, and process.

- **Flexible retirement approaches:** Greater flexibility in retirement packages allows workers to choose the time when it makes sense for them to stay or move on, and makes it easier to attract young talent.

- **Project-based flexible staffing:** Skills repositories provide information on the skills and capabilities of employees. These can help managers match skills to employees based on their expertise and availability and help to manage project performance.

Network governance. As both the NASA and Wisconsin stories demonstrate, government executives' core responsibilities no longer center on managing people and programs but on organizing resources, often belonging to others, in order to produce public value. Unfortunately, governments regularly underinvest in contract oversight, and contractors continually underestimate the complexity of the government environment, especially the cultural challenges. See *Governing by Network* by Stephen Goldsmith and William D. Eggers for tools and techniques to facilitate networks and complex partnerships.

Resources (Books, Web Sites, and Other Cool Stuff)

For further reading we recommend *Reforms at Risk: What Happens After Major Policy Changes Are Enacted*, by Eric M. Patashnik—a great book that shows how many big reform initiatives are eroded over time during the results phase. To avoid this fate, reformers need to consolidate political support and reconfigure the political dynamic. Two more for your reading list: *The Next Government of the United States*, by Donald Kettl (his chapter equating the skills needed to succeed in government today to those of a rocket scientist is a must-read for managers trying to achieve big things in today's networked government environment), and *The People Factor: Strengthening America by Investing in Public Service*, by Linda J. Bilmes and W. Scott Gould. Other good resources include the National Academy of Public Administration Management Studies Center (www.napawash. org/pc_management_studies/index.html) and Australia and New Zealand School of Government (ANZSOG; http://www.anzsog.edu. au/). A collaborative project of a half dozen universities, this terrific educational institution is dedicated to promoting outstanding public sector leadership and policy.

CHAPTER 6

The Complacency Trap

Changing Times

Idea → Design → Stargate → Implementation → Results
(⟵————————— **Reevaluation** ———————⟶)

CHAPTER GUIDE

- Mickey Landry Returns to New Orleans
- The Complacency Trap
- Sloughing Off Yesterday
- Pruitt-Igoe and Dynamiting Obsolete Structures
- Sunset in the Lone Star State
- Fixing the White House
- Herbert Hoover's Comeback
- Schwarzenegger's Reforms Get Terminated
- NASA's Twin Tragedies
- The Risk of Complacency

You see things; and you say, "Why?" But I dream things that never were; and I say, "Why not?"

—ROBERT F. KENNEDY, PARAPHRASING GEORGE BERNARD SHAW IN *BACK TO METHUSELAH*

"FROM MY PERSONAL EXPERIENCE, I can tell you that the public school system in New Orleans has been troubled for decades," says Mickey Landry. In the 1970s, Landry and his wife both taught in New Orleans, Mickey at Carver High School, his wife at an elementary school. "We used to come home and joke that the best thing that could happen to the Orleans Parish school system would be for someone to blow it up and start all over again."[1]

Landry saw it all. "Despair existed in abundance in New Orleans schools in the 1970s. There were teachers who literally would bring a newspaper to school and read it in class. Whatever happened on the other side of the paper, that really was none of their business," says Landry. There were also some outstanding teachers, Landry recalls, but too many adults had given up on the kids. On one occasion, Landry was making copies at the school's only "thermograph" machine, delaying a school administrator who wanted to head home. "I don't know why you're putting out effort for these kids, Mickey," the administrator said.

Frustrated, Landry left New Orleans, but stayed in education, eventually running a prestigious private school in Colorado. Landry was lured back to post-Katrina New Orleans by the opportunity to run a school without the bureaucratic constraints of the old Orleans Parish school system. When a charter operator stumbled, the board sought out Landry to run Lafayette Academy. "This wasn't just professional for me, it was personal. I was coming home to help my city."

Mickey Landry visited his new school for the first time in July 2007. "When I walked in the front door, I was struck by the stench of human waste," Landry recalls. "The walls were Pepto-Bismol pink and battleship gray. I remember thinking, how could adults let children go to school in a building like this?"

Because Lafayette was a charter school, Landry had a free hand in retooling every aspect of the school. In just three weeks he hired forty-five new staff members, seeking out qualified teachers every place he could, including Craigslist, TeachNOLA (a nonprofit), and Idealist.org. He rewrote the school's charter, fixed the bathrooms, and had the walls repainted. When school started in the fall, he put the focus on teaching kids. The results? According to eleven-year-old Angel Snyder, "Last year, everybody was running through the halls, cursing our teacher," she said. "This year we're just educating."[2]

How did Landry get a chance to wipe the slate clean and start over at Lafayette Academy? First, lawmakers in Baton Rouge changed the state constitution so that individual failing schools could be plucked out of their old district and placed into a state entity known as the Recovery School District. These schools brought with them only the buildings, the students, and their operating money. Teachers, principals, administrators, and all existing contracts were gone. The Recovery School District allowed school leaders to start without inheriting the culture of despair that so often marks failing schools in failing districts.

Then came Hurricane Katrina.

Before Katrina, the Recovery School District had taken over just four schools in New Orleans. After Katrina struck in August 2005, the state legislature swept 107 of the 128 public schools in New Orleans into the Recovery School District. For these 107 schools, all existing school leadership, teachers, contracts, processes, procedures, forms, rules, policies, and the Orleans Parish school board that oversaw them were instantly wiped away. These schools were now a clean slate, a blank canvas, a *tabula rasa*—and a once-in-a-lifetime opportunity not only for local boy Mickey Landry, but for nationally known education transformer Paul Vallas.

Paul Vallas came to New Orleans to run the Recovery School District. In the world of urban education, Vallas is a rock star. He had been a successful superintendent in both Chicago and Philadelphia, with tenures that lasted more than five years in each system. Vallas is capable and ambitious, the sort of public leader who bridges the political and bureaucratic worlds. In fact, Vallas narrowly lost the democratic primary for governor of Illinois in 2002 to a guy named Rod Blagojevich.

In both Chicago and Philadelphia, Vallas had to take over an existing system and try to reform it. In New Orleans, he was able to start virtually from scratch, freed of the "pretzel logic" that dominates so many urban school bureaucracies. "Without question, this is the easier job," says Vallas.[3]

Like Mickey Landry, Paul Vallas gravitated to New Orleans because it offered him freedom. "You can come and, with no restraint on who you hire and no institutional obstacles blocking you, change the whole curriculum, the length of the school day, length of the school year."[4] Vallas did all that and more in his first two years. He had a vision of the Recovery School District as a nonbureaucratic facilitator rather than overseer. As a result, New Orleans today resembles no other urban school system in the country. There are no attendance zones—all schools are schools of choice. There is no teachers' union—Vallas basically sets the salaries. Roughly half the schools, including Lafayette Academy, are run by independent charter operators. National philanthropic organizations, including Teach for America and New Leaders for New Schools, are bringing excited young teachers and ambitious principals like Mickey Landry to the system.

It was a wrenching transition. One elementary school principal, after being displaced by Katrina for six months, came back and had to interview for her old job. "It wasn't fun," she admitted. "But I understand what they're doing."[5] Many educators lost jobs that they would never get back. The New Orleans Parish School Board lost almost all its power. It is hard to imagine a state legislature inflicting such transitional pain in the absence of a crisis such as Katrina, which essentially wiped out the existing system for them.

It is too early to declare the New Orleans reform experiment a success, but without question one can say this: things are different in New Orleans today than when Mickey Landry taught there in the 1970s.[6] Just the fact that Mickey Landry was brought in to run a school after a prior charter operator had failed to live up to expectations shows that the system is to some degree more self-correcting.

The New Orleans experience contrasts sharply with that of most urban districts, where little changes despite continuous reform. Many dysfunctional urban districts hire a new superintendent, hoping that a good leader can make a bad system work. The results generally disappoint. In 1996, retired army general Julius Becton was named superintendent of the Washington, D.C., schools to great fanfare. He was hailed as a tough, no-nonsense leader who would turn around a dreadful district. "Failure is not an option," he declared when he took office.[7] But after sixteen months of waging war against the bureaucracy, General Becton surrendered. His resignation letter explained why: "This debate is no longer about children. It's about power politics . . . I have had it!"[8] A veteran of three wars, Becton said he'd never experienced anything as tough as trying to turn around the district's existing school bureaucracy: "In the Army, I always knew who and where the enemy was. In the school district of Washington, I never did."[9]

The Complacency Trap

Urban education is one example of what we call the Complacency Trap, which occurs whenever the way things are block the path to what might be. The Complacency Trap is caused by a whole host of barriers to change inherent in democratic systems that lock us into "what is" and prevent us from trying "things that could be." The Complacency Trap is the dangerous tack of staying the same when the circumstances of the world around you change.

Some readers may object to the term *complacency* as applied to education, noting that education reform has been a national priority for four decades. But that is precisely the problem. The reform efforts in public education have focused on making the system work, rather than reexamining the system itself. Such systemic reform is painful, but isn't it more painful to watch generation after generation of children robbed of an education? Without Katrina, New Orleans would still be trapped in a never-ending educational death spiral.

We have described the journey to success as running from idea to results. Indeed, results are the end goal when launching a new program. Once the program is in place, however, a continuous reevaluation becomes critical to ensure that the program or agency still makes sense and that complacency doesn't set in.

Management guru Peter Drucker contends that successful business executives periodically reexamine the nature and purpose of everything their corporation does by asking two questions: "If we were not already doing this, would we now go into it?" If the answer is yes, they ask the follow-up question: "If we were to start doing this today, how would we do it?"[10] Drucker's questions get at a simple but profound truth: in some cases *what* is being done no longer makes sense. In other cases, *how* it is being done no longer makes sense. In either case, change is called for, and Drucker referred to this as "sloughing off yesterday" and "purposeful abandonment." Innovation brings change, and while the innovation introduces new and improved ways of creating wealth, it also means that old structures become obsolete. Economists sometimes refer to this as the process of "creative destruction," the removal of what exists to make room for what might be—the organizational equivalent of pruning a bush to make room for new growth. Drucker notes that successful businesses tend to be fanatical at such pruning. This is not because businesspeople are so smart, but because businesses that don't do this don't stay in business.

In 1982, Tom Peters and Robert H. Waterman Jr. published *In Search of Excellence*, which showed how forty-three companies achieved sustained excellence. Unfortunately, within just a few years of the book's publication, several of the companies profiled weren't so excellent anymore. Once successful companies like Data General, Wang Laboratories, and Digital Equipment disappeared. Excellence in the past didn't guarantee excellence for all time. In a competitive market, companies that don't proactively engage in "sloughing off yesterday" become roadkill. Their demise makes room for new ventures. Wang Laboratories is gone, but now we have Google.

Successful companies adapt to changing realities. In the early 1980s IBM was highly successful selling PCs. A near-death experience in the 1990s prompted a massive corporate transformation, and IBM became a consultative technology solutions provider. As a result, the IBM of the

1980s in no way resembles the IBM of today, and neither bears much resemblance to the typewriter manufacturer of the 1940s.

Government, however, generally lacks the painful feedback mechanism of the market that drives this sort of change. While companies evolve or disappear, too often government programs simply endure, operating as they have for decades with only incremental changes. Beating the Complacency Trap means embracing deep, systemic change to both the "what" and "how" of the public sector. The trick is that not all change is good change. Not all innovative approaches work.

Things Seen and Unseen

How does government redesign or altogether eliminate obsolete structures and avoid the Complacency Trap? Well, sometimes the public sector needs to use dynamite. Literally.

In 1955, construction was completed on the Pruitt-Igoe public housing complex in St. Louis. The project was innovative, being one of the nation's first public housing projects, and it was massive. Pruitt-Igoe comprised 33 eleven-story, flat-topped apartment buildings built in a style architects refer to as "high modernism" but which most people refer to as "butt ugly." The complex was built with high hopes, sited to incorporate renowned urban architect Le Corbusier's "three essential joys of urbanism: sun, space, and greenery."[11] That was the plan, anyway.

The reality was different. From the very start, Pruitt-Igoe was blighted by crime, drugs, and vandalism. Less than ten years after completion, the apartment complex was a dangerous, ill-maintained structure decorated primarily by graffiti. The complex included one particularly novel architectural feature: the "skip-stop" elevator system, whereby elevators stopped only on the first, fourth, seventh, and tenth floors. In theory, this was intended to foster community by providing a gathering space in the hallway, 11 feet wide and 85 feet long, on the elevator floors. In practice what it fostered was crime, as the stairways were the preferred hangout of drug-dealing gangs. (Falling into the Double Sisyphus Trap, planners had failed to foresee how residents might behave—or misbehave—in this novel setting.) Cheery metal grilles were added to the windows after three children defenestrated. Common areas were stripped of fixtures and a bleak, almost palpable atmosphere of despair permeated Pruitt-Igoe.[12]

The government's first response was to try to fix what was there.

Millions of dollars later, it was clear the complex was beyond fixing. Demolition was the only answer. Pruitt-Igoe was dynamited into rubble in a spectacular explosion less than twenty years after it was built.

Pruitt-Igoe was razed in part because it was a tangible, visible, and obvious failure. No one could look at the facility and say, "Well, that's not so bad. Maybe if we just plant some shrubs it will be fine." The inescapable reality was that Pruitt-Igoe couldn't be fixed. It had to be torn down. Too often, public failures are every bit as awful but are simply less visible, and rather than removing the offending structures, they enter a state of perma-tweaking, an ongoing earnest hand-wringing exercise that offers shrubs where dynamite is required. The New Orleans school system—like the school systems in Los Angeles, or Washington, D.C., or half a dozen other major cities—haven't worked in decades. Their failure is merely less visible than Pruitt-Igoe's, though no less destructive.

Table 6-1 illustrates just how captive we are to our past. Down the list, each program still reflects the realities of the era in which it was designed rather than the changed reality of our current day. The school calendar we use today is essentially based on the *Farmer's Almanac*, which makes a lot of

TABLE 6-1

Government programs and the context of their creation

Program	Time period initiated
Education delivery	1800s
Unemployment insurance	Great Depression
Social Security	Great Depression
Agricultural subsidies	Great Depression
Employer-provided health insurance	World War II (tax loophole)
HUD	Great Society
Medicare	Great Society
Medicaid	Great Society

sense for a nineteenth-century agrarian society, but not so much for a twenty-first-century information society. Agricultural subsidies of the dust bowl era were designed to assist family farms, and now they subsidize agribusinesses. Our health insurance still reflects the 1940s concept of lifetime employment and provides little portability for frequent job changers. Our Social Security system was created in 1935, when life expectancy was about sixty-two—a far cry from today's seventy-eight. When Medicare was created in 1965, very few people over sixty-five were economically well off, whereas seniors now constitute one of the wealthiest segments of society.

Without a doubt, these institutions could all use a fundamental redesign. Without a doubt, any effort to introduce such a redesign would trigger a political onslaught from those who benefit from the status quo. The structures that exist today create both a political and psychological barrier to what could be.

Not surprisingly, government hasn't done a good job of "sloughing off yesterday." One of the biggest challenges in doing so is that unlike a business, no one "owns" that part of the journey. While the executive branch owns the launch of a program, in many cases no one owns the task of reevaluation.

What if some government agency had, as its sole focus, reevaluating existing programs to see if they still made sense?

Sunset in the Lone Star State

In the mid 1970s, the good government group Common Cause came up with the idea of "sunset laws." Under sunset, the legislature would have to vote to keep an existing program or agency—otherwise, it would disappear.

The idea for sunset laws came from Craig Barnes, an idealistic young lawyer and founder of Common Cause Colorado. Barnes wanted some way to drive change at government regulatory oversight agencies, which he saw as too cozy with the industries they regulated. "I discovered that the state agencies were as much in the pocket of the industries as they were responsive to the public," said Barnes.[13]

Barnes's sunset idea combined two factors. First, under sunset, the legislature has to pass a new law to *save* the entity. In the language of choice architecture, it shifts the default status to "terminate."[14] Second, the review must be done by an independent agency. This makes sunset vastly different from congressional reauthorizations, in which, for example, every five years the farm bill comes up for reauthorization through the Agriculture Committee, whose members are heavily influenced by farm interests. Instead of a chance to pare down the obsolete, the congressional reauthorization process often becomes a chance to add on new goodies—instead of getting rid of obsolete mohair subsidies, the committee creates one for chickpeas. (This actually happened in the 2002 Farm Bill.) In contrast, the concept of sunset is that an independent group takes a peek under the hood.

Sunset held broad appeal. For liberals, it offered the chance to confront agencies that protected big business at the expense of consumers. For conservatives, sunset held the promise of reducing the size of government by eliminating obsolete agencies. In 1976, Colorado became the first state to enact sunset legislation. The idea quickly caught on, and within a decade forty-four states had passed sunset laws.

Sunset came to Texas in 1977, when Austin was a town still largely run by good ol' boys. "Texas was the nation's prime example of an insider governing culture," said Barnes.

In 1977 Common Cause pushed the legislature to create the Texas Sunset Advisory Commission, a twelve-member board consisting of legislators and citizens. A full-time staff of analysts would support the commission in conducting reviews and making recommendations.[15]

Early on, the legislature decided that the sunset commission should dip its toes in the water by examining smaller agencies with funny names like the "Texas Board of Tuberculosis Nurse Examiners." (By the time this agency came up for review in 1981, only four nurses in Texas held this certification—the board's records were stored in a box under the bed of one of the staffers.) The sunset process mercifully ended this obsolete agency. Initially going after smaller, less controversial targets helped drum up positive reviews from the press and from legislators who equipped the commission with the tools it needed to go after bigger targets.[16]

After picking off the low-hanging fruit, in 1983 the sunset commission took aim at some sacred cows of big business.

Regulatory boards reviewed in 1983 included the Texas Railroad Commission, Public Utility Commission, and the boards that oversaw banking and insurance. Driving changes in these areas was seen as a nearly impossible task given the political influence of these heavy hitters. "Industries Facing Sunset Review Step Up Lobbying and Donations," noted a headline in the *Dallas Times-Herald*. One legislator noted: "The utilities want us to leave the PUC [Public Utility Commission] alone, the truckers want us to leave the Railroad Commission alone, the oil companies want us to leave the Railroad Commission alone, the bankers want us to leave the banking board alone."[17]

But the sunset process isn't about leaving things alone.

In 1983, the sunset commission made headlines when it declared that the high-profile Public Utility Commission was too biased in favor of utility companies and recommended that it be abolished. The sunset commission found that regulations weren't protecting consumers; instead, they were protecting established companies against new competitors. Ultimately, the PUC staved off outright elimination, but reformers did manage to push through a complete reworking of the Texas utility regulation process, resulting in significant gains for telephone and electricity ratepayers.[18] Sunset made the impossible possible.

In many cases, the sunset process gave legislators the cover they needed to do the right thing. It served as a way to beat the Complacency Trap.

In Texas, no regulatory agency is more powerful than the Railroad Commission, whose tentacles stretched into oil and gas production, gas utility rates, trucking, railroads, and other fields.[19] Sunset recommended changes that made it easier for newcomers to get permits to enter the oil business and deregulated the hauling of agricultural products.[20] Despite fierce opposition from established industry players, the commission didn't back down from its charge, and many changes that legislators had known were long overdue became law thanks to the sunset process.[21]

The Texas Sunset Advisory Commission had its greatest impact in its first several years. But three decades later, sunset is still a powerful force in Texas, providing a mechanism for the state to rethink how agencies can best fulfill their most important obligations. In 2000, for example, a sunset review demonstrated that one of the state's two job-training programs achieved much better results than the other, which was plagued with financial and operational problems. Sunset recommended the faltering program be shut down. The legislature agreed and eliminated it, saving the state $25 million a year. A few years later, the sunset commission recommended the legislature abolish the Texas Department of Economic Development under the rationale that it was costing the state more money than it was generating.[22] The legislature agreed. All told, fifty-four Texas agencies have been abolished under sunset since its inception.[23]

Moreover, the sunset commission provides an external look at agency operations, opening up new ways of thinking about old problems. When the Texas Department of Criminal Justice came up for review during the 2007 legislative session, eliminating it certainly wasn't an option. With a growing prison population, there was a perceived need to construct more prisons. But the sunset commission recommended reorienting the department's mission from locking up prisoners to reducing recidivism, and called on the agency to allocate more resources on rehabilitation. It was a bold proposal in a state as tough on crime as Texas, but the sunset commission inserted an external, data-driven perspective that prompted change in the prison system.

Replicating Sunset

So, this means that sunset is a triumphant story, the surefire way to beat the Complacency Trap, right? Not quite. Of the forty-four states that passed sunset laws, nineteen have abandoned them entirely. In many states, sunset commissions have themselves become outdated agencies, periodically issuing timid reports that get ignored by the legislature.

Barnes, who has championed the cause since the 1970s, isn't surprised by any of this: "From a government standpoint, sunset represents disorder. This threatens the people in power who want to consolidate power. The forces of stability tend to have the upper hand over reformers."[24]

The most important reason why sunset works in Texas is the state's political culture—the politicians there want sunset to succeed. Sunset has often been the vehicle for getting otherwise politically difficult proposals through the legislature.

At one session during the 1980s, a sunset review of the Texas Air Control Board prompted some amendments that, if passed, would significantly strengthen clean air laws. These amendments were being fiercely opposed by the oil and chemical industries. Time was running out on the

House's session for the year, and the fate of the proposed reforms was still undecided.[25]

About 6 p.m., a young sunset commission staffer named Ken Levine received a call to come over to the office of the Speaker of the House immediately. Levine (now the deputy director of the sunset commission) recalls what happened next:

> *I run over and am ushered directly into the Speaker's office. There sit the Speaker, three House members, and the presidents of the oil and chemical associations. One of the House members immediately asks me to explain what the amendments would do (because, of course, they weren't quite sure themselves). With shaking hands and voice—I was a green, young policy guy—I give an explanation. The Speaker then gets the "cons" from the industry folks. He thinks for a moment or two and turns to the industry folks and tells them, "I'm going to go with my members this time." And with that, there was no more opposition to the bill and Texas clean air laws were considerably strengthened.[26]*

As this story shows, the influence of a sunset commission extends only as far as its political support. It is only to be expected that the presidents of the oil and chemical associations are going to be camped in the Speaker's office—their political influence will always garner them a hearing. Having a sunset commission helped balance the equation, but the reforms became reality because the political leaders took the sunset commission's recommendations seriously.

The legislators who sit on the sunset commission are proud of their independent viewpoint. "We're not constrained by convention," explains Representative Carl Isett, the 2008 chairman of the sunset commission. "We don't come in with any preconceived ideas. We don't care how they've done things in the past. We come in with ideas as reformers."[27]

Sunset in Texas has long had powerful champions across the political spectrum, from Representative Isett, a conservative Republican, to Congressman Lloyd Doggett, a liberal Democrat, who worked tirelessly for the original implementation of sunset. Doggett in fact spent years trying to get sunset legislation passed in the U.S. Congress, but finally gave up after several unsuccessful attempts. The political appetite inside the Beltway simply wasn't there for the sort of reevaluation and self-examination that sunset offers.

Fixing the White House

In his first few years in office, President Harry Truman faced some remarkable international challenges: the start of the Cold War, the rebuilding of Europe, and the occupation of Japan, for example. There were problems at home, too: the national debt was large, labor unrest was crippling major industries, and the Trumans' bathtub was sinking into the floor.

Truman's new home, the White House, was literally falling apart. The floors creaked and swayed. Plaster from the third-floor addition sagged dramatically. A leg of Margaret Truman's piano actually broke through the floor. Truman's new digs "wouldn't pass the safety standards of any city in the country," declared the commissioner of public buildings.[28] Truman called the White House an "old barn" and said it should be turned into a museum.

Not only was the White House in danger of imminent collapse, but more than a century's worth of additions and small-scale renovations from different presidents had rendered it a disjointed collection of rooms. No baths connected to the guest rooms. A main staircase led awkwardly to a hall. Rather than following a coherent plan, the White House was an accidental collection of rooms, some useful, some not. Truman determined that incremental improvements would be inadequate and only cause the house to feel more incoherent. What was required was nothing short of a complete overhaul.

Truman and his family moved across the street to Blair House. Beginning in 1948, the entire interior of the White House was gutted. All that was retained was the outer shell of the house. Inside the shell workers spent four years constructing an entirely new building—a new house within old walls. "The White House we see today is largely Truman's," says Robert Breeden, the former chief executive of the White House Historical Association.[29]

If the White House Truman inherited was outdated, disjointed, and inadequate for the task at hand, so too was the government he inherited. The world was a very different place following World War II, and America's federal cabinet structure and agencies had been built in a different time for different challenges. FDR's New Deal programs and the panoply of wartime activities had essentially been bolted onto a nineteenth-century model of government, much like previous White House additions had been tacked onto a nineteenth-century foundation. So while the White House was undergoing its biggest renovation since it was destroyed in the War of 1812, Truman set about fundamentally overhauling the U.S. government.

Herbert Hoover's Comeback: The Hoover Commission

In 1946, a Republican Congress swept into power after more than a decade of Democratic dominance. The previously obscure Harry Truman was the accidental president, and it was widely assumed that New York governor Thomas Dewey would complete the Republican sweep by winning the presidency in 1948. In anticipation, Congress established a blue-ribbon commission to examine the organization of the U.S. government. In a symbolic move, Congress installed Herbert Hoover, the last Republican president and a vocal critic of the New Deal, as commission chair.

The Hoover Commission was bipartisan, with six Democrats and six Republicans.[30] The inclusion of several Southern Democrats gave the commission a distinctly conservative tilt, however. The Senate Republican Conference characterized the commission as "a major operation on the sprawling, tax-eating patchwork bureaucracy bequeathed to us by the New Deal."[31] Sidney A. Marshall, the executive director of the commission, determined that it would deliver its recommendations "by the end of 1948. Then we would make these the first order of business in the Eighty-first Congress in January 1949"—just in time for President Dewey to enact them.[32]

Despite the *Chicago Tribune*'s insistence to the contrary, Dewey did not defeat Truman. Not only that, but Democrats rebounded to win back significant majorities in both the House and Senate.

Given the shift, many now expected the work of the Hoover Commission to be tossed aside. It wasn't.

Instead, the Hoover Commission ended up being the most successful federal government reorganization initiative of the twentieth century.[33] Hundreds of the proposals from the commission's thirty-four study teams became law. The armed services were merged into the Department of Defense. A cabinet system of government was established. The Post Office and the Departments of Commerce, Interior, Labor, and State were reformed and reorganized. The General Services Commission was created.

Just as today's White House is Truman's, the structure of today's federal government is a product of Truman and the Hoover Commission. The Hoover Commission beat the Complacency Trap, not allowing existing structures to impede needed changes. It took a mishmash of agencies and created the structure of the modern federal bureaucracy. What made it work? For one thing, an unlikely partnership between Hoover and Truman.

Until 1929, the name of Herbert Hoover was synonymous with competence. At the tender age of twenty-five, the Stanford engineering graduate was getting rich rehabilitating mines in Australia.[34] Within a few years, he had revived mines in Australia, China, Russia, and the United States. By the time he was thirty-five he was widely considered the greatest engineer of his generation.[35] When the U.S. government needed someone to lead the drive to organize the famine relief effort at the end of World War I, they sent Hoover. As commerce secretary during the 1920s, he took charge during the Great Flood of 1927, coordinating relief and calming the nerves of the nation. Hoover took a lead role in the planning of one of the most astounding engineering feats of its day: the awe-inspiring Hoover Dam.[36] In 1928, he was elected president in a landslide. Hoover had never known failure.

Then, in his first year in office, came the stock market crash and the start of the Great Depression. From then on, fairly or not, the public perception of Hoover was one of ineptitude and indifference. The tent cities of the homeless were dubbed "Hoovervilles," and he was drubbed by Roosevelt in the 1932 election. For the next twelve years, Hoover was shunned by the Roosevelt administration, which went so far as to change the name of Hoover Dam to Boulder Dam.

Truman's career trajectory was somewhat different. The only twentieth-century president without a college degree, Truman was a failed haberdasher and small-time Missouri politician. He was chosen to run for the Senate by the corrupt Pendergast political machine and was a surprise choice for vice president by the ailing Roosevelt. After serving as vice president for less than three months, Truman assumed the presidency upon Roosevelt's death in April 1945.

Hoover and Truman formed an unlikely friendship. In 1946, Truman sent Hoover to postwar Germany to assist in relief efforts. In 1947, President Truman restored the name of Hoover Dam, the same year that the seventy-two-year-old Hoover assumed leadership of the commission that would bear his name.

Truman's surprising victory in the 1948 election completely changed the dynamic of the Hoover Commission and the more conservative members realized that to accomplish anything they would have to temper their recommendations.[37] In a way, Truman's election helped the Hoover Commission avoid the Tolstoy syndrome, because they were now forced to take into account the views of their political opponents. Rather than focusing on undoing the New Deal, the Hoover Commission now focused on how to improve the structure of government to enhance its effectiveness. Most of the commission's reports were hailed as balanced and of high quality by both sides of the aisle.

The Hoover Commission benefited from the sincere friendship between Hoover and Truman. Despite their differences, the mutual respect they shared eclipsed partisan concerns. Years later, Truman wrote Hoover that their friendship "reached deeper into my life than you know."[38] In an effort to prove his competence, both to his new friend Truman and to the country, Hoover worked hard to make the Hoover Commission successful, working tirelessly on its recommendations.

Subsequent presidents have tried to reorganize the federal bureaucracy to modernize or eliminate obsolete programs. But neither Ronald Reagan's Grace Commission nor Bill Clinton's National Performance Review had the lasting impact of the Hoover Commission, which altered the basic organizational structure of the federal government. If Hoover were alive today, however, he would be dismayed to learn that the federal government hasn't undergone a comparable reexamination since the commission bearing his name. The engineer in him surely would argue that modern technologies and business practices have rendered obsolete many of the organizational structures established after World War II. Programs, structures, and regulations designed twenty, forty, or sixty years ago—even highly successful ones—need periodic and thorough reevaluation.

Schwarzenegger's Reforms Get Terminated

One politician who pushed for the reexamination of government is California governor Arnold Schwarzenegger. In true action-hero fashion, Schwarzenegger muscled his way into the California governor's mansion in 2003 promising to rescue the state from fiscal disaster in the wake of a $34.6 billion budget deficit. "For people to win, politics as usual must lose," he told constituents in his victory speech.[39]

For several months after his inauguration in November, the new governor rode a wave of popularity. He had a job approval rating above 70 percent, "Governator" T-shirts were selling like hotcakes, and he even had his own bobble-head doll. But "politics as usual" was still holding sway in Sacramento. One Saturday in July 2004, just eight months into office, Schwarzenegger lashed into the recalcitrant lawmakers. "I call them girlie men!" he famously declared to a crowd at a California shopping mall. Schwarzenegger went on to decry a political culture that was "out of shape, that is out of date, that is out of touch, and that is definitely out of control in Sacramento."[40]

In his first state of the state speech, Schwarzenegger called the state government "a mastodon frozen in time and about as responsive" with "multiple departments with overlapping responsibilities." He pledged to "blow up the boxes" of state government.[41] Soon after the speech, the new governor launched a major reform initiative, the California Performance Review, whose goal would be a "total review of government—its performance, its practices, its cost." The final report proposed some of the most sweeping and radical reorganization changes ever proposed in the state, including eliminating more than a hundred boards and commissions, realigning many existing agencies and departments, and completely restructuring the state's prison system.

Not content to stop there, the governor followed up these proposals by sponsoring four major ballot initiatives. These would limit state expenditures in line with revenues, change the state pension plan for new hires, introduce merit pay for teachers, and alter how the state drew up its election districts.[42] The initiatives, if passed by voters, would have significantly altered the political equation in Sacramento.

Arnold was essentially staking his governorship on breaking the Complacency Trap. He recruited a performance review guru from Texas to help run his reevaluation program. He barnstormed up and down the state to get his proposals on the ballot. He helped raise tens of millions of dollars to fund the signature drives and a media blitz. And he never stopped warning Californians of the consequences of sticking with the status quo: ever larger budget deficits and a state government that was becoming virtually ungovernable.

A year later, after all the dust had settled, only a handful of the hundreds of reform recommendations from his 2,500-page performance review had been enacted by the legislature. The promised grand reorganization never occurred. The California Performance Review was never even submitted to the legislature after Democratic leaders had proclaimed it "dead on arrival." As for the ballot initiatives, the November 2005 special election was decisive. Final score: interest groups opposing initiatives 4; governator 0.

Schwarzenegger's failure to convince both the legislature and California voters of the need for a fundamental rethinking of the way the state does business demonstrates how difficult it is to succeed during the reexamination phase of the journey. At the height of his popularity, Schwarzenegger had been campaigning against the status quo. Once he tried to alter the status quo in specific, concrete ways he faced a buzz saw of opposition that he couldn't overcome. Like Prime Minister Koizumi in Japan, he took his case to the people. Unlike Koizumi, Schwarzenegger lost.

The sad truth is that Schwarzenegger was correct. His prophecy of doom if the state didn't change its ways came to pass in 2009, when the state found itself looking at a $21 billion budget gap. The Complacency Trap fooled people into believing that the day of reckoning could be put off forever. It can't. Sometimes, we all have to learn the hard way. Sometimes you see clearly only through tears.

NASA: Two Tragedies, One Underlying Cause

"By the second day of the investigation, I said to myself, 'I've seen this movie before,'" says Sally Ride, referring to the 2003 *Columbia* space shuttle accident. Seventeen years after the 1986 *Challenger* disaster, Ride said, "history had repeated itself."[43]

Sally Ride, a physics professor at the University of California, San Diego, is best known as America's first female astronaut. In both 1983 and 1984, she spent days circling the earth aboard the *Challenger*. Ride has another important distinction: she is the only person to have served on the commissions investigating both the *Challenger* and the *Columbia* accidents, and the tragedy of these two avoidable disasters haunts her still. When the *Challenger* accident occurred, Sally Ride was in training for her third *Challenger* mission, scheduled for just a few months out. Four of those killed were in her NASA astronaut training class. They were her colleagues, her friends.

Most frustrating were the parallels between the two accidents. "It is clear NASA didn't learn from its mistakes," says Ride. "Yes, the agency changed for a couple of years after the *Challenger* accident, but then the culture bounced back." The story of the two shuttle accidents is the story of how bureaucracy deals with risk. Risk is invisible, but as the shuttle experience proves, it can be deadly. The story illustrates a facet of the Complacency Trap we haven't yet explored: the propensity to develop a false sense of security. Humans in general and government agencies in particular tend to get comfortable over time—to get complacent—with high-risk environments.

What makes the shuttle disasters particularly frustrating to Ride is that for NASA, managing risk is not just a side job, something to be shunted off to the actuaries and auditors. Managing risk is a core competency. "At NASA even the smallest problem can kill you," notes Ride. "If failures like this can happen in NASA given its reputation for risk management, they can happen anywhere."

Challenger: *1986*

The *Challenger* was scheduled for launch on the morning of January 28, 1986. This was one of the most anticipated NASA launches in years, since the crew would include Christa McAuliffe, a thirty-seven-year old mother of two, a civilian who was to be the first school teacher in space. President Ronald Reagan would be giving his State of the Union address later that evening, and he planned to highlight McAuliffe and the *Challenger*.

It was unseasonably cold in Florida, however, with temperatures well below freezing. The day before the launch, engineers at Morton Thiokol, a NASA contractor, learned of the weather forecasts and told NASA they were concerned that the frigid temperatures at Cape Canaveral would cause the shuttle's rocket booster "O-rings" to fail—which would mean catastrophe for the shuttle. Just hours before liftoff, Thiokol engineers were recommending that the launch be delayed.

This was not a message that NASA officials wanted to hear.

Concerns regarding the O-rings were nothing new. In eight previous shuttle flights, NASA had found evidence that the O-rings had allowed hot exhaust to burn through the primary seal. Since 1982, the O-rings had been designated a "Criticality 1" issue. The January shuttle flight in cold weather just a year earlier had shown significant burnthrough. Paradoxically, the repeated incidence of burnthrough had desensitized officials to the seriousness of the problem. "The first time they saw it, they thought, 'Oh, my gosh, we dodged the bullet here. We need to do something about this,'" explains Ride. But each time NASA saw evidence of leakage around the O-ring seal, the risk *seemed* less serious. "Finding a solution became less urgent each time, and the problem started to become a normal occurrence," says Ride. "Singed O-rings in the booster seal became acceptable, when in reality they should have triggered the grounding of the space shuttle fleet. Instead, NASA said, 'Oh, we saw a little bit of singe. We've seen that before.'"

Just as engineers on the Big Dig tunnel saw repeated evidence of slipping bolts, NASA and Thiokol were aware of repeated evidence of O-ring failures. This "normalization of deviance" led to a sense of complacency. Replace the slipping bolts, replace the singed O-rings—and move on.

On the eve of the *Challenger* launch, at 8:45 p.m. eastern time, a conference call was convened with thirty-four participants, sixteen from NASA and eighteen from Morton Thiokol. During this nearly three-hour call, the engineers from Morton Thiokol argued forcefully for delaying the launch because of the cold weather and its possible impact on the O-rings. The risk was too great, said the engineers, who recommended that the O-ring temperature should be at least 53 degrees Fahrenheit. NASA pushed back hard, with one senior NASA official asking, "My God, Thiokol, when do you want me to launch, next April?"[44] As one engineer later testified, "We were being put in a position to prove we should not launch."[45]

It was nearly midnight when Thiokol officials finally gave in. Thiokol managers—excluding the engineers—decided to approve the launch. Certain inconvenient voices would be ignored. "It appeared that NASA managers would have stayed on the teleconference as long as they needed to in order to get the answer they wanted," says Ride. "The management process wasn't receptive to engineering input." At the request of NASA, at 11:45 p.m., Thiokol faxed NASA a signed statement approving the launch. The presidential commission later concluded that Thiokol's management reversed its position and recommended the launch "at the urging of [NASA] and contrary to the views of its engineers, in order to accommodate a major customer."[46]

The next morning, millions of Americans watched in horror as the *Challenger* exploded seventy-three seconds after launch. Many of these viewers were school children, as the presence of teacher Christa McAuliffe on board had been of great interest to the education community. Other interested viewers included the thirty-four individuals who had participated in the long, contentious conference call the night before. Unlike the rest of the nation, they knew instantly what had gone wrong.

Columbia: *2003*

The *Challenger* and *Columbia* disasters were different in particulars but eerily similar in how the organization mismanaged risk. "Most troubling for me in comparing the *Columbia* and *Challenger* accidents is that NASA as an organization did not learn from its previous mistakes," Ride says.

As with *Challenger*, the *Columbia* experienced problems moments after takeoff. About eighty-one seconds into flight, a briefcase-size piece of foam from the shuttle's external fuel tank broke off and hit *Columbia's* left wing.

Once again, the foam problem had occurred on numerous previous flights, and on some flights hundreds of small pieces of foam had fallen off. Once again, a group of engineers had tried in vain to get NASA management to take action. Explains Ride:

Foam had been falling off the tank since the very first shuttle flight, and NASA had long been trying to fix it. One shuttle was hit by a piece of foam on the underbelly during launch. The foam knocked off a thermal tile, and the exposed aluminum had begun to melt on reentry because of the damage to the thermal protection system. But in each case, NASA decided it was okay to keep flying. Over time, this led to a significant understating or a collective ignoring of an actual risk.

The foam strike didn't cause any immediate problems and *Columbia* entered orbit. In fact, engineers at NASA only became aware of the foam impact the day after launch while reviewing high-resolution film of the launch. Once discovered, the Debris Assessment Team became concerned because this was the largest foam incident yet. A 1.7-pound piece of foam about the size of a briefcase had hit the shuttle's wing traveling at roughly five hundred miles an hour, and no one knew for sure what sort of damage the wing might have sustained. If there was a hole in the wing, that would cause a disaster upon reentry. Engineers at NASA wanted management to ask the Department of Defense (DOD) to use some of its ground-based telescopes or imaging satellites to take a picture to assess the damage.

This was not a difficult decision. There was no undue pressure to launch, no State of the Union address to worry about. The *Columbia* was already in orbit. Asking DOD to take a picture of the wing wasn't a big deal. Previous foam incidents, however, had "trained" NASA leadership not to worry, and they declined to make the request to the DOD. Although the low-level engineers on the Debris Assessment Team grew frantic, that sense of urgency was lost as information traveled up the hierarchy. As it happened, one unofficial request from NASA actually did reach the DOD—and this was seen as a breach of protocol. "The Department of Defense was processing the request to examine the shuttle when the request was cancelled by NASA," says Ride. "The Department of Defense might have been able to spot the hole in *Columbia*'s wing, and there were actions that NASA could have taken to rescue the astronauts on board."

Without the DOD images, both Mission Control and the *Columbia* crew were unaware that they were orbiting in space with a hole in the shuttle's wing. For two weeks, the crew performed its mission. A video of the crew members preparing for reentry shows them joking around, eager to get home, and blissfully unaware of their peril.

RIDE'S RULES FOR MANAGING RISK

Six rules for risk management emerged from our interviews with Sally Ride:

1. **Ask "what if?"** If things are going well, there is a tendency to assume that they will continue to go well. We become desensitized to deviations from the norm. To counter this human tendency, organizations need a process that actively creates what-if scenarios—tiger teams whose job it is to come up with a range of possible disaster scenarios.

2. **Avoid smugness about your successes.** Past successes can be a step toward future failures.

3. **Learn from your mistakes.** Before the *Columbia* accident, NASA had never used the *Challenger* accident as a case study in risk management. They never internalized it. To paraphrase Yogi Berra: If you don't learn from your mistakes, you will face déjà vu all over again.

4. **Develop effective feedback loops.** Organizations need both a process that allows them to identify problems—risks—and a feedback loop to actually address them.

5. **Leadership should value—even demand—minority opinions.** NASA didn't and paid a very big price for it. Web 2.0 technologies, says Ride, can make an enormous difference. "Leaders can use these technologies to bypass the hierarchy and quickly get down to the midlevels of the organization and frontline employees who see the problems first," says Ride.

6. **Welcome the negative.** A big problem in many organizations, says Ride, is the difficulty of communicating bad news. Managers don't want to hear bad news and staffers don't want to give it to them. But without hearing bad news, leaders can't fix the problems until it is too late. Creating a culture that encourages everyone in the organization to speak up about problems can counter this tendency.

Once the shuttle reentered earth's atmosphere, however, plasma air superheated to more than 2,000 degrees Fahrenheit entered the breach in the wing and began melting the aircraft. The shuttle became aeronautically unstable while traveling about 12,000 miles an hour and disintegrated thirty-eight miles above Texas. All aboard perished.

In both cases, NASA had seen evidence of the technical problem but engaged in an "insidious and unconscious waiving of the standards over time," says Ride. As disaster failed to materialize, the O-ring and foam problems went from being important signals to not even being recognized as close calls. In both cases, it was organizational failure to handle risk appropriately that transformed a technical problem into a fatal disaster. "Ultimately it's not enough to spot risks; it's how you address them that counts," says Ride.[47]

In forty-plus years of space travel, NASA has had an exemplary safety record. But possibly because of its stellar record, the agency was lulled into the Complacency Trap and experienced two tragedies that were both preventable.

The Risk of Complacency

The Complacency Trap occurs when the way things are blocks our vision of what could be. In many cases, this means that risk will go unappreciated until after a disaster has occurred.

The attack on the World Trade Center in 1993 was evidence of risk, the risk of a much more deadly attack to come. But as with the singed O-rings, the message was missed. After all, America hadn't experienced a serious foreign attack since Pearl Harbor, and we had grown complacent. The nature of the external risk had changed since 1941, of course. It would no longer require a fleet of planes to inflict massive damage; now it could be done with a suitcase filled with anthrax, or hijackers armed with box-cutters taking over a commercial aircraft. We had sophisticated defenses to protect against the threat of Soviet bombers, while at the same time letting supertankers chug into busy urban seaports with no idea what was in their cargo holds.

Financial risk is even more insidious. Following the Great Depression, the government instituted the Federal Deposit Insurance Corporation to guard against the risk of bank failure. In the 1980s Congress changed the rules around banking and at the same time raised the level of insurance from $40,000 to $100,000 per account. The risk that people might lose their life savings was gone, but the new risk was that banks would make bad bets and leave taxpayers to bail them out. That is precisely what occurred in the savings and loan crisis, and the mismanagement of risk cost taxpayers $124 billion.[48] That was considered a lot of money until the financial meltdown of 2008.

Before 2008, no one on Main Street worried about the credit rating of mortgage-backed securities. Very few people worried about collateralized debt obligations and asset-backed securities. It seemed a little odd, perhaps, that banks and mortgage companies were advertising "liar loans" that required no money down and no income verification. At the time, people on Main Street were blissfully unaware that they were implicitly underwriting the risk of the great lending orgy that was taking place. Some experts like economist Robert Schiller were warning anybody who would listen of the huge risks. Like the Thiokol engineers, these inconvenient voices were ignored. No crisis, no reform.

The 2008 collapse of many private financial institutions is the equivalent of the Truman piano leg going through the White House floor. As we write this chapter, it is likely that financial regulation will undergo a fundamental overhaul, similar to the "down to the studs" rehab the White House underwent sixty years ago. The problem is the overhaul will come after the damage has been done. What governments need but so sorely lack is a mechanism to force changes before the crisis takes place.

Of all the traps, the Complacency Trap is perhaps the most challenging to alter given the political reality of democracy. The recovery of the New Orleans schools and the demolition of the Pruitt-Igoe housing project represent one possible model: the clean slate approach. Though the most radical of the approaches, it has the advantage of clearing away the psychological barriers to change. It's easier to imagine "what could be" once you remove "what's already there."

In theory, the sunset approach offers a great mechanism to ensure a regular reevaluation. Changing the default from "keep it" to "eliminate it" gives reformers more of an even playing field against defenders of the status quo. Sunset also has the advantage of unearthing problems before they fester, but to work the sunset approach needs the buy-in of legislators.

The Hoover Commission model, due to its breadth and scope, must be used far more sparingly than the other approaches. As Governor Schwarzenegger's experience shows, it inevitably generates strong opposition. However, by looking at government as a whole—at the entire enterprise—instead of agency by agency it can help reformers to envision a different and better structure than currently exists.

Today, we need all of these approaches and more. Most of all, we need a sense of urgency throughout our democracy, for our current course is unsustainable. We have evidence in many forms that we are facing a significant danger. The challenges we face are big, but they are not insurmountable. The bigger risk is that our political institutions won't change until it's too late.

FIELD GUIDE: REEVALUATION PHASE

Sometimes, the way things are stand in the way of how they might be. The challenge here is for government to continually evaluate *what* it does and *how* it does it. Right now, nobody owns that job. The result is a government that often tries to do too much, while at the same time fails to respond to the changed reality of its external environment, particularly with respect to risk.

Biggest Danger

The Complacency Trap. Needed change doesn't happen. Don't let the way things are become a barrier to what could be.

Guiding Principles

Don't let "what is" prevent you from trying "things that never were." What exists today can be both a political and a psychological barrier to what could be. It took Katrina to bring real change to the schools in New Orleans.

Improve your focus—do less, better. Constantly reevaluating *what* government does and pruning nonessential activities is essential to improving *how* government operates.

Change the default status. By changing the default from *keep* to *eliminate*, the sunset process provides an ongoing mechanism for government to rethink how agencies can best fulfill their obligations.

Ask "what if?" When things are going well, the tendency is to assume that they will continue to go well. To counter this tendency, you need a process that actively creates "what-if" scenarios—tiger teams whose job it is to come up with a range of possible disaster scenarios. Don't wait for a tragedy to address risk.

Tools and Techniques

Idealized design. Try to imagine the ideal way to accomplish your policy goals, irrespective of how you do things today. Then look backward from where you want to be to where you are today and identify the obstacles to getting to your ideal state. (For more info, see *Idealized Design*, by Russell Ackoff, Jason Magidson, and Herbert Addison.)

Sunset review. This action-forcing mechanism encourages elimination, reform, and merger. (For more info, see www.sunset.state.tx.us.)

BRAC model. A variant of the sunset review, the Base Realignment and Closure model used an independent commission to recommend military base closures. Congress had to vote up or down on a package of proposals within forty-five days. This process helped to overcome parochial political interests in Congress. Similar thinking could be applied to other areas of government. (For more info, see www.brac.gov.)

Look out for the black swans. Periodic risk analyses can help guard against complacency by identifying big-consequence, hard-to-predict, and rare events. Monitoring metrics for unexplained changes can help to uncover such "black swans" and other hidden risks. (Read *The Black Swan*, by Nassim Nicholas Taleb.)

Strategic options analysis. This tool identifies various strategies across a range of potential futures for the organization. (Read *Strategy Paradox*, by Michael Raynor.)

Resources (Books, Web Sites, and Other Cool Stuff)

Recommended further reading: *The Reinventor's Fieldbook*, by David Osborne and Peter Plastrik, and "Executing Government Transformation: Case Studies of Implementation Challenges," by the Lyndon Baines Johnson School of Government. The latter is the output of a year-long research project we engaged in with Professor Kevin Bacon and his class, which resulted in a first-rate report analyzing a handful of government redesign cases (http://www.utexas.edu/lbj/pubs/isbn/089940-777-7/). Two great Web sites for information on this subject are the National Governors Association Best Practices Center (www.nga.org/center) and Kennedy School Innovations in American Government Program (www.ashinstitute.harvard.edu).

CHAPTER **7**

The Silo Trap

The Walls Between Us

Idea → Design → Stargate → Implementation → Results
(←——————— Reevaluation ———————→)

CHAPTER GUIDE

- Energy Bill Celebrations
- Four Decades of Groundhog Day
- The Silo Trap
- 9/11 and Silos of Excellence
- Katrina and the Weakest Link
- Chickens in Manhattan
- Lessons from Reengineering
- Setting Goals, Measuring Progress
- The Common Link Between Bad Movies and Bad Policy

Our society has reached a point where its progress and even its survival depend on our ability to organize the complex and to do the unusual.

—JAMES WEBB, FORMER NASA ADMINISTRATOR

PRESIDENT GEORGE W. BUSH'S energy secretary was very excited. Speaking in San Francisco, Samuel W. Bodman was telling his audience about the recently passed Energy Policy Act of 2005.

"The bill Congress passed," Bodman said, "is a landmark achievement. It will truly help bring about the energy and economic security that the American people deserve." Bodman oozed superlatives for the bill, which had passed in the Senate with bipartisan support and was on its way to the president's desk:

> *The step Congress took last week to pass comprehensive energy legislation represents a momentous decision for our future. Passage of such a vitally important bill represents a fateful decision to break away from the policies of the past toward a future marked by safety, security and prosperity. And just as important, it means taking critical steps to safeguard the environment for future generations to enjoy.*[1]

Freedom from world energy markets, safety, security, prosperity—and a clean environment for generations to come—these claims sounded almost too good to be true. Bodman was realistic, of course, admitting that passage of the law "won't change things overnight. Gasoline prices won't sink as an immediate result of the passage of an energy bill." Nonetheless, Bodman had high hopes, because the Energy Policy Act of 2005 had, at long last, settled once and for all the question of America's energy future:

What is important is that with passage of comprehensive energy legislation last week, we are finally headed in the right direction. After years of indecision, partisan squabbling and disjointed policies, we are committed finally to making the changes necessary to secure our energy future.[2]

The reaction? Few people took Bodman's remarks seriously. It's not clear that anyone was intended to. Unlike normal human speech, in which people use words to communicate ideas, Bodman's speech was a form of political Kabuki, the public-policy equivalent of a late-night infomercial, designed to reach only the most credulous. You don't need to listen to an infomercial—you recognize the script instantly. The man in the Hawaiian shirt has developed a method to make millions in real estate, and he wants to share it with *you*. Why, just a few years ago, he was struggling to make ends meet, but then he figured out this amazing real estate system. Today, he's living large, hanging out on that big boat with his bikini-clad friends. His program could help you make $100,000, maybe more, in the first six months—and your cost is just three easy payments of $49.95.

You don't believe the man in the Hawaiian shirt. Your wisdom and experience tell you that get-rich-quick schemes don't work. What you expect from an infomercial are grandiose claims for a product that delivers disappointing results. Most of you don't believe Energy Secretary Sam Bodman, either, for much the same reason.

Here's a sampling of what editorial boards around the country had to say about the 551-page Energy Policy Act that Mr. Bodman was so enthused about:

New Jersey Star Ledger: "[An] inadequate energy bill."

Orlando Sentinel: "Unworthy of becoming a law."

Cleveland Plain Dealer: "A smorgasbord of tax breaks."

Baltimore Sun: "No redeeming value."

Columbus Dispatch: "Yet again, Congress has failed . . ."

Washington Post: "Don't believe the spin."

Los Angeles Times: "Laden with pork."

Oregonian: "Congress stages a depressing retreat."

Detroit Free Press: "Bears little resemblance to the kind of foresighted planning America needs."

Philadelphia Inquirer: "This bill is a lobbyist's dream and a citizen's nightmare . . . "

The tendency to see the enactment of legislation as an end unto itself, to claim credit for a great achievement upon the creation of a new law, is one of the most destructive tendencies in democratic governance. When a major reform is passed, no one really knows whether it will achieve its intended results or not. Shouldn't we hold off on the celebration until some results have started rolling in?[3]

Four Decades of Groundhog Day

We don't mean to pick on Mr. Bodman. After all, this isn't the first time our nation has celebrated the passage of an energy bill, only to be disappointed by the results. When it comes to energy policy, America is like Bill Murray in the movie *Groundhog Day*, waking up again and again to the dawn of a bright new morning that, on closer examination, looks a lot like the day before.

It began with Richard Nixon. In response to the OPEC oil embargo, his administration announced the launch of Project Independence, which promised to free us from world oil markets.[4] "Let this be our national goal: At the end of this decade, in the year 1980, the United States will not be dependent on any other country for the energy we need to provide our jobs, to heat our homes, and to keep our transportation moving," Nixon urged.[5] In addition to being an ill-advised and unattainable goal—the United States gets a lot of energy from Canada, for instance, and that doesn't seem to be a problem—Project Independence never produced any legislation. It didn't produce any results, either.

The following year, President Gerald Ford signed the Energy Policy and Conservation Act.[6] In signing the law, Ford declared America "on the road toward energy independence." Result? By 1980, net imports of oil to the United States were four hundred thousand barrels per day *higher* than they were in 1973.[7]

This was just a warm-up for the Carter administration. That's when the country got really serious about energy independence—or at least really serious about passing legislation promising energy independence. Carter signed both the National Energy Act in 1978 and the Energy Security Act in 1980.[8] "The keystone of a national energy policy is finally being put into place," Carter declared, just twenty-five years before Bodman would make almost the identical claim. "Passage of the Energy Security Act is the highlight of our efforts to develop and implement a comprehensive national energy policy—a policy that meets our energy problems, a policy that sets out a program for Americans to follow in the future, a policy that gives us weapons to wage and to win the energy war."[9] While promoting a host of alternative energies, the sun was to be Carter's secret weapon in the battle for energy independence. Carter claimed the new law would help the country "to reach our goal of deriving 20 percent of all the energy we use by the end of this century directly from the sun." Result? By the turn of the century the sun was providing about seven one-hundredths of one percent of all the energy used in the United States.[10]

Next up was the Energy Policy Act in 1992 signed by the first President Bush.[11] Surely this bill would set our nation on the right path. "That means there will be less reliance on foreign oil, foreign energy. And it will promote conservation and efficiency. And it will create American jobs," claimed Bush the Elder.[12] Result? In 1992, we imported 44 percent of our petroleum. By 2007, that figure had reached 58 percent.[13]

The second President Bush ushered the country into yet another era of energy independence when he signed the Energy Policy Act of 2005, the one Bodman described as a landmark.[14] George W. Bush wasn't content to rest on his laurels, however, and followed the 2005 law with another, the Energy Independence and Security Act of 2007.

That won't be the end of it, either. The 2008 presidential election had both major party contenders, Senators Barack Obama and John McCain, offering competing versions of the solution to our latest energy crisis, which saw prices spike to $4 per gallon of gas. One observer offered a compromise policy:

> *Barack wants to focus on new technologies to cut foreign-oil dependency, and McCain wants offshore drilling. Well, why don't we do a hybrid of both*

candidates' ideas? We can do limited offshore drilling with strict environ-
mental oversight, while creating tax incentives to get Detroit making hybrid
and electric cars. That way, the offshore drilling carries us until the new tech-
nologies kick in, which will then create new jobs and energy independence.
Energy crisis solved.

That proposal belonged to Ms. Paris Hilton, delivered to the nation wearing a leopard-print bikini and high heels. This certainly beats the heck out of the guy in the Hawaiian shirt, and in terms of content it sounds a lot like what's gone on for the past thirty-five years.

The grim history of federal energy legislation highlights a peculiarity of the political world, in which our political system places a huge premium on passing a law in order to be seen as "doing something." The self-congratulatory celebrations at energy-bill signing ceremonies are akin to stopping a football game after the calling of a play to celebrate. You don't declare victory after sending in a play. You wait to see if the play actually works. In the case of energy policy, the promised touchdowns of energy independence have failed to materialize. After nearly four decades of fabulous legislative "accomplishment," America faces an energy challenge every bit as daunting today as it was in the 1970s.

Why so many celebrations for such dismal results? Think of the journey to success as a relay race in which various runners carry the baton for a portion of the trip. Too often in government, these individual runners don't see themselves as part of a relay team—they experience only their segment of the race. When their job is finished, they celebrate. This incomplete view of the process can lead to dropped batons or other bad exchanges.

A successful relay team sees itself as a team, practices as a team, and wins as a team. An enormous amount of time is spent perfecting exchanges, ensuring smooth transitions between runners. Government doesn't do enough of that.

The Silo Trap

Unlike something as simple as a relay race, which involves only a series of straightforward linear handoffs, a complex public undertaking has numerous systemic interdependencies. How these interdependencies are handled often makes the difference between success or failure. The Silo Trap is the failure to put all the pieces together. Democratic government creates many walls of separation. As a consequence, those who work in government are often stuck in silos, disconnected from others involved in what should be an integrated process.

Democracy establishes distinct roles for the legislative and executive branches of government. Once lawmakers toss an energy bill through the Stargate, their work is largely done (save for oversight), and they immediately move on to the next piece of legislation on the docket. Since those who craft an energy bill will rarely play a part in implementation, they are often oblivious to the fact that they are part of a larger process. Their "goal" was to pass an energy bill, and they did that—so why not celebrate? Sociologists refer to the phenomenon by which a lesser goal substitutes for the ultimate objective as "goal displacement." We call it the Silo Trap.

The Silo Trap is the failure to put all the parts of the journey to success together. It's not simply the boundaries between the policy designers and the policy implementers that cause problems. The fragmentation of authority in government prompts individuals to lose sight of the larger goal, focusing instead only on their part of the journey. Countless public undertakings underperform because of the failure of participants to see the end-to-end process of reaching a result as a set of related, interdependent steps, and to behave accordingly. The Silo Trap is a serious problem, and one not easily fixed. Creating alignment that crosses boundaries is not easy, particularly in the public sector.

The Failed Silos of Excellence

The heinous attacks of September 11, 2001, shocked America. But they shouldn't have come as any great surprise. As the 9/11 Commission report makes clear, during the summer of 2001, the nation's intelligence warning systems were blinking red—but those warnings were missed. Examining the evidence after the fact, the commission found that various intelligence agencies had uncovered pieces of evidence that, taken together, might have enabled officials to thwart the attacks. But, as the report notes, "the U.S. government did not find a way of pooling intelligence . . ."[15]

The 9/11 Commission report cites numerous instances in which information was trapped within silos. Some of the examples are painful to read. In the summer of 2001, certain FBI intelligence officers learned that an Islamist extremist named Khalid al-Mihdhar, who had been linked to the bombing of the USS *Cole* in Yemen, had entered the United States, flying into New York's JFK airport on July 4, 2001. A search for Mihdhar commenced. One FBI officer reached out to an FBI agent identified as "Jane" in the New York office, who had access to files containing information on Mihdhar and his possible whereabouts. Within the FBI, however, there are strict rules that create a "wall" designed to keep certain intelligence information from being shared with criminal agents, and the requesting agent was designated a "criminal agent." The Mihdhar case had been designated as a criminal matter, but the information about Mihdar was in "intelligence" files, and "Jane," according to the commission report, "appeared to have misunderstood the complex rules" regarding information sharing. "Jane" refused to allow the intelligence officer access to the files. As the commission report noted, this meant that operatives familiar with Al Qaeda and experienced in tracking down terrorists were excluded from the search for Mihdhar. After his request for access to the files was denied, the frustrated officer lashed out on August 29, 2001, in a searing email sent to "Jane":

> *Whatever has happened to this [request]—someday someone will die— and wall or not—the public will not understand why we were not more effective . . . especially since the biggest threat to us now, UBL [Usama bin Laden], is getting the most "protection."*[16]

Two weeks later, on the morning of September 11, Kalid al-Mihdhar boarded American Airlines Flight 77, which he helped to hijack and then crash into the Pentagon, killing 125 people. The commission, noting that Mihdhar had been using his real name during the weeks before the attack, concluded that if the investigation had been handled differently, Mihdhar might have been apprehended. The commission felt that his detention might have thwarted the entire operation.

You may be feeling as angry at "Jane" as her colleague was. When hearing of this failure to share vital information, it's easy to assume it stemmed from a turf battle or some other bureaucratic pettiness. But "Jane" wasn't engaged in some foolish power-play squabble. She was simply trying to do her job in an environment steeped in complex rules. How complex? The commission noted: "Everyone involved was confused about the rules governing sharing of information gathered in intelligence channels."

Think about that: *Everyone was confused about the rules.* The rules that limit information sharing and create a "wall" within the FBI exist because if a criminal investigator gains illegal access to information, a prosecutor's case might get thrown out of court and the bad guys might walk. "Jane," in fact, had sought the advice of the agency's lawyers in helping her determine whether she was permitted to give the officer the information he had requested.[17]

Few people understand the challenges of sensitive information sharing within government better than Michael Wertheimer. Wertheimer, whom we met briefly in chapter 1, is the assistant deputy director of national intelligence. Since 2005, he has been charged with transforming how the intelligence community gathers, shares, and analyzes information, trying to break down the silos and enable appropriate, effective information sharing. His career in intelligence began in 1982, when he put his PhD in mathematics to use breaking codes for the National Security Agency (NSA).

Wertheimer recalls that arriving for work on his first day was like entering a new universe. The moment he set foot within the NSA facility, his actions became governed by an entirely new set of rules. "On the other side of the threshold, as a United States citizen, you may do absolutely anything you choose to do which is not prohibited by law. Period," says Wertheimer. But once across the threshold, "You may not do anything whatsoever which you are not specifically authorized to do. Those are the rules." In some ways, these rules make eminent sense—you can't have a cowboy culture where agents feel free to share the sort of highly sensitive personal information such agencies possess. Wertheimer notes that tight constraints are in many ways appropriate "and serve as one of the mainstays of my enthusiasm for working in government." The challenge is that sometimes information should be shared, and these rigid rules within an agency can foster an attitude of complete distrust of anyone else in the government or the intelligence community. "It has created that culture that we know as silos of excellence, each agency a self-contained unit," says Wertheimer.[18]

The silo approach, as 9/11 so painfully demonstrated, isn't terribly effective in an era of global terror threats. (One CIA agent who focused on Southeast Asia discovered that Mihdhar had a U.S. visa—but didn't mention that to his FBI counterpart. As the 9/11 report notes: "He was worrying solely about Southeast Asia, not the United States.")[19] Our ability to collect data has outstripped our capacity to place that data into meaningful context, to transform the disparate scraps of information into actionable intelligence. "The last frontier that we have yet to really take on is, 'How do we get analysts and human brains linked up through social networks to give us a competitive edge that we never had before?' We have not done that," says Wertheimer. Decades of institutional policies tightly controlling information handling have created a work environment where employees live in fear of doing the wrong thing. Something as simple as synching the address books in your Blackberry and laptop can be a career-limiting violation. "Everyone is told, 'Take a risk, take a risk,'" says Wertheimer. But, he adds, they also get a conflicting message: *"Just do not get it wrong!"*

To figure out better ways to foster collaboration, Wertheimer looked outside of government and became a corporate tourist, visiting such cutting-edge firms as Google, Industrial Light & Magic, and Pixar. Instead of hanging out with a bunch of spies, Wertheimer figured he might learn something from people who make cartoons. He did. He found that at Pixar headquarters, Steve Jobs had put all the restrooms in the center of the building, often at some distance from work areas. "People hated it," said Wertheimer. "If you have to go use the restroom, you have to get out of your office, walk all the way down to where the cafeteria in the central area is. [Steve Jobs] was trying to get people to bump into each other to have collaboration." It opened Wertheimer's eyes to just how differently government operated. "We are the reverse on almost everything. Our security policies are designed against collaboration," says Wertheimer.

Inroads are being made. In 2006, Wertheimer helped introduce Intellipedia, a secure, Internet-based collaboration tool that enables sixteen intelligence agencies to share information. In 2008, Wertheimer was instrumental in the launch of A-space, a social networking site for intelligence analysts modeled after MySpace and Facebook. The paradox is that these tools, by allowing for the independent, decentralized distribution of intelligence, actually enhance the effective centralization of intelligence. Rather than rigid hierarchical "channels" of permitted information flow, these are free-wheeling "spaces" in which unplanned and uncontrolled exchanges are encouraged. Says Wertheimer, "It is about doing things that you never thought you could do before. It is making connections. It is mashing up . . ." In effect, Wertheimer is using cyberspace to foster virtual collaboration in the same way Jobs used physical space. Just how effective this all is remains an open question. The horrible truth about 9/11—that our nation's intelligence agencies had all the pieces of the puzzle but failed to put them together—has demonstrated how dangerous the Silo Trap can be. Armed with that awareness, Wertheimer and the intelligence community are taking steps to counteract the natural tendency toward organizational isolation.

The Silo Trap isn't limited to intelligence efforts. Imagine the increased effectiveness of law enforcement efforts if information flowed freely between the Coast Guard, the U.S. Border Patrol, the Drug Enforcement Agency, and local police departments. It won't be easy, however, to break through the walls that keep the left hand of government from knowing what the right hand is doing. Some of these walls are built into the design of democracy. There are technical challenges, but those are ultimately surmountable. By far the bigger challenge is changing the organizational barriers and cultural attitudes that permeate the public sector.

Katrina and the Weakest Link in the Chain

Earlier, we likened the journey to success to a relay race. To be successful, each member of a relay team must be successful individually, and their actions must also be coordinated with those of the other team members. In many complex public undertakings, officials rightly break down a job into component parts. As the saying goes, "The only way to eat an elephant is one bite at a time." But in breaking a big job into component parts, someone better be making sure the parts work together. It is easy to lose sight of the linkages, and as we all know, a chain is only as strong as its weakest link.

In 1965, Hurricane Betsy raced across the Gulf of Mexico and slammed into New Orleans. When levees failed, water from Lake Pontchartrain put much of New Orleans under water, especially the Lower Ninth Ward. The massive devastation caused by Betsy prompted Congress to give the U.S. Army Corps of Engineers the task of constructing a hurricane protection system. The system was specifically intended to protect New Orleans from a similar hurricane in the future.

Forty years later, Katrina hit.

Katrina was a powerful storm, but one for which the corps was supposed to have protections in place. Nine months after Katrina, an official postmortem, the 6,615-page Interagency Performance Evaluation Task Force (IPET) report, put the blame for submerging New Orleans not on Katrina, but on the Army Corps of Engineers. "The Corps has had to stand up and say we've had a catastrophic failure at one of our projects," acknowledged corps commander Carl Strock.[20]

The IPET report explained the reason behind the failure of the hurricane protection system, concluding: "The system did not perform as a system." According to the report, the corps had treated its various levees, pumps, and canals as independent components rather than the interconnected, interdependent system that it was. For example, pump stations were not designed to operate during a hurricane or handle overflow in the case of a levee breach. This made them virtually useless during Katrina. Moreover, flood walls along the 17th Street and London Avenue canals were designed with a smaller safety factor than other nearby levees— meaning these structures would (and did) behave like the weakest link in a chain:

> *At no time has the entire New Orleans and Vicinity area had a reasonably uniform level of protection around its perimeter. At no time has any individual parish or basin had the full authorized protection planned for in 1965.*[21]

The corps had fallen victim to the Silo Trap. Instead of looking at the whole, it had broken the job into its component parts. As the American Society of Civil Engineers bluntly put it: "The hurricane and flood protection system was a system in name only."[22]

This is not an isolated example. The process by which we conduct large public undertakings tends to be treated not as a coherent system, but rather as a set of steps with little appreciation for the interdependencies between them.

Chickens in Manhattan: Fostering Alignment

Who is in charge of getting the right number of chickens to Manhattan every day? After all, few chickens live there, but a lot of chickens get eaten there. The typical Manhattanite downs about sixty pounds of chicken a year, in every imaginable form, from chicken chow mein to chicken nuggets, from organic chicken to those little cubes that float in your can of chicken soup. Untold thousands of people participate in providing for Manhattan's ever-changing chicken needs, from truck drivers to restaurant owners, from grocery store managers to Arkansas chicken farmers. Who is in charge? Who makes sure that New York winds up with the right amount of the right kind of chicken?

The answer, of course, is no one. The chaos of the uncontrolled buying and selling of the market produces an orderly pattern of exchanges that coordinates the activities of independent yet interdependent participants. The result, without any central planning, is an adaptable and ever-changing arrangement that generally meets the needs of Manhattan's chicken eaters. The government provides certain oversight—the U.S. Department of Agriculture watches over chicken farms and the city's Board of Health licenses and inspects restaurants—but it is the invisible workings of supply and demand that align the productive activities of a loose network of thousands of people (and companies) in making sure New Yorkers get their chicken potpie, chicken vindaloo, and extra-spicy buffalo chicken wings.

Author Francis Fukuyama believes we are just beginning to understand the paradox of how chaos can create order:

> *The study of how order arises, not as the result of top-down mandate by hierarchical authority, whether political or religious, but as the result of self-organization on the part of decentralized individuals, is one of the most important intellectual developments of our time . . . In an information*

*society, neither governments nor corporations will rely exclusively on formal,
bureaucratic rules to organize the people over whom they have authority.*[23]

In our chicken example, information that shapes behaviors travels
through the market through prices. The mind-boggling complexity boils
down to a set of choices. How much chicken should I order this week for
my restaurant? Should I hire another chicken plucker? How much should
we charge for the chicken schwarma? Should I get the chicken marsala for
$14.95 or the veal marsala for $17.95? Prices and profits give signals to
both producers and consumers.

There are two areas in which large numbers of people are occupied in
productive activities in which they are not exposed to price feedback: large
corporations and government. For example, a twenty-person legal department at a corporation generally does not charge an hourly fee to its "internal clients." In contrast, a twenty-person law firm not only charges its
clients, it also keeps a close eye on the difference between resources consumed (costs) and value created (revenue), since the difference between the
two will be the firm's profit or loss. It is relatively easy to assess how the law
firm is doing and much harder to assess how the legal department is doing.

For both large corporations and government, the problem of alignment—
of coordinating the productive activities of individuals—is made more
difficult by the absence of monetary measures on outputs. Large corporations enjoy a significant advantage over government because they at least
get profit feedback in aggregate. You may not know how profitable the
legal department is, but at least you know how profitable the company
is overall. In government, the lack of a single measure of organizational
performance—profit—makes it more challenging for managers to coordinate the activities of those who work within it.

Government does not, cannot, and should not measure itself strictly in
terms of dollars and cents. In the for-profit sector both inputs and outputs
can be measured in dollars, while in government, inputs are measured in
dollars but outputs have to be measured using—and here it gets tricky—
something else.[24]

What does all this have to do with beating the Silo Trap?

A great deal, actually. An enduring challenge of the public sector is
how to foster alignment, or "goal congruence," among those who work

within it. As the problems the public sector deals with get more complex, these challenges will only get bigger. Taking a cue from the corporate world, which struggles with a similar challenge, can provide some valuable lessons here.

One of the best-selling business books of all time was *Reengineering the Corporation*, by Michael Hammer and James Champy, published in 1993. Their critical insight was that large corporations tended to organize around function, and this undermined the organization's ability to efficiently produce value. Corporations had devolved into a set of "stovepipes" or "organizational silos." Over time, activities within those silos had become insulated, divorced from the reality of producing value for the customer. Reengineering set out to fix that. Reengineering was defined by Hammer as the "radical redesign of business processes for dramatic improvement . . . The key word in the definition of reengineering is 'process'; a complete end-to-end set of activities that together create value for the customer."[25] This meant taking a process-based view of the organization, and reducing handoffs, ensuring smooth transitions between departments, and breaking down the silos between functional parts of the organization.

Reengineering meant thinking about every activity by every employee and seeing it as part of an end-to-end process, and asking about every activity along the way, "How does this produce value for our customer?" When companies began thinking seriously in this way, they saw that they had to radically alter existing practices to improve their processes. Aligning the activities of all parts of the organization meant that it wasn't good enough for manufacturing to blame the design group for designing a flawed product. Design and manufacturing had to act in tandem to design a buildable product. As production processes grew in complexity, including relationships that crossed organizational boundaries, it became increasingly important to coordinate the productive efforts of employees. During the 1990s, it became the responsibility of top management to create alignment, to break down interdepartmental rivalries, and to ensure that every part of the organization was in alignment, focused 100 percent on efficiently delivering a great end result.

Reengineering as a movement has had its share of both successes and failures. The important thing here is not the specifics of particular restructurings, but a mindset that looks at productive activity within the context of a larger process. What is the ultimate goal? How do the activities of each player contribute to the larger goal? Does the value created exceed the resources consumed? The corporate world struggles with the Silo Trap, and the challenge is even greater in the public sector.

What is the best way to beat the Silo Trap? First off, take to heart the lessons and the main messages from this book. The journey to success is a single process with a single result. It involves a series of phases, often performed by different people, but it is a single process. Initiatives in the public sector are particularly vulnerable to being undermined by a failure to see the whole process. Great results can be delivered only if the pieces work together: designers and implementers, politicians and bureaucrats, government agencies and private contractors.

Once aware of the Silo Trap, there are strategies that can help align all the pieces. These strategies generally center around three things: a clear goal; systems to measure performance; and goal congruence, particularly integration of the designers and implementers of policy.

Setting Goals, Measuring Progress

One reason organizations fall prey to the Silo Trap is a lack of clarity about the end goal. To counteract this tendency, in the words of author Stephen Covey, you must "begin with the end in mind."[26]

A well-articulated goal paints a clear image of what success would look like. In May 1961, President Kennedy told Congress: "This nation should commit itself to achieving the goal, before the decade is out, of landing a man on the moon and returning him safely to the Earth."[27] Specific, time-based, and unambiguous, President Kennedy's challenge is often cited as a textbook example of how to articulate a goal. The goal helped guide choices at NASA—the agency's full effort was devoted to the moon mission.

In the same way, President George H. W. Bush's objective in the Gulf War was made crystal clear in a nationally televised speech on January 16, 1991, at the commencement of hostilities: "Our goal is not the conquest of Iraq. It is the liberation of Kuwait." Once that goal was accomplished, he stopped the advance of the army rather than continuing to Baghdad, despite strong pressure from some to topple Saddam's regime. Years later, Bush would talk about how his stated goal guided that decision: "We had an objective. We had formed a coalition based on, not on killing Saddam, not on conquering or capturing Baghdad, but ending the war, ending the aggression. We did what we said we were going to do."[28]

In contrast, President George W. Bush's speech to the nation at the beginning of the Iraq War in 2003 contained multiple articulations of purpose that made it hard to answer the key questions: What are we trying to accomplish? How will we know when we are finished? The following statements from the president's address to the nation on March 19, 2003, reveal ambiguity with respect to the goal in Iraq:

- "We have no ambition in Iraq, except to remove a threat and restore control of that country to its own people."

- "You can know that our forces will be coming home as soon as their work is done."

- "Helping Iraqis achieve a united, stable, and free country will require our sustained commitment."

- "We will defend our freedom."

- "We will bring freedom to others."[29]

Establishing a stable Iraq is a very different goal from removing an outlaw regime. Defending our freedom is a very different goal from bringing freedom to others. Depending on the goal, you'll either be able to bring the troops home soon, or you'll have to prepare for a sustained commitment. The ambiguity in the goal translated into ambiguity in execution, and the prolonged struggle to secure the peace in Iraq had its roots in the unclear expectations at the start.

Setting a clear goal and then holding everyone involved accountable is an evolving art in the public sector. "The whole performance accountability movement has been critical. No question, from my point of view, great strides have been made in setting performance expectations and commensurate accountability, and I think that's a good thing," says Jenna Dorn, president of the National Academy of Public Administration. "Having clear benchmarking and performance expectations can make a positive difference."[30] Despite the progress, much work in this area remains. As the No Child Left Behind debates have shown, there are often fundamental disagreements about what results are being sought, in this case what children are actually learning. In other areas, identifying quantifiable outputs can be a daunting challenge.

The Common Link Between Bad Movies and Bad Policy

Art begins as an idea in the mind of an artist. The idea is worked, explored, and developed, perhaps into a sketch. Through an act of creation, the idea takes form in some medium—clay or watercolor or bronze. It is unveiled, displayed for viewing, and judged not once but many times, by many people. Sometimes, the artwork takes on a life of its own, eliciting reactions unimagined by the artist.

As we've shown, public policy also begins as an idea. This idea is then worked through a political process, a Ouija board involving lobbyists, legislators, think tanks, and the media. The result is not a finished work, but a blueprint in the form of a new law, an executive order, or other directive. This policy "sketch" (design) is then executed, brought into reality by a public bureaucracy (or by a private contractor or some network of providers). Once unveiled, the public policy is judged by many people at different times, creating an overall impression in the public consciousness. And like a piece of art, it may have unintended consequences, prompting unforeseen reactions and behaviors. Like art, the initial reception of a program may be very different from how it is judged after the passage of time.

The analogy is imperfect. In most cases, a single artist conceives, designs, and creates a finished product—a sculpture, a novel, or a painting, for instance. The final result reflects the consistent, coherent vision of the artist. If one person comes up with an idea, another creates the blueprint, and yet another person creates a final product based on that blueprint, the result can be a disaster unless there is some consistent vision of the end goal.

This is a familiar occurrence in Hollywood. A brilliant author writes a story of depression. A team of scriptwriters turns it into a screenplay, but lightens it up with some humor and a little romance. The director adds in some steamy bedroom scenes, maybe a car chase. This is how truly awful movies are created. This is how truly awful public policy is created, too. And as we've shown throughout this book, this unfortunately is too often the way large public undertakings are designed and implemented today. It is a challenge for various participants at each phase of a large public undertaking to see their role as part of a larger process. Each participant in the process tends to see *his* end product as *the* end product.

Visualizing the journey to success as a continuous process helps highlight the fact that everyone should be pointed toward the ultimate result. It also shows one of the biggest "walls" along the way: the Stargate, which creates a gap between policy designers and policy implementers. This gap can be disastrous, as we saw in Boston's school busing fiasco and California's electricity deregulation. The question is how to fix it. We've offered several suggestions previously, including an "implementability review" that would allow bill drafters to more regularly gain the perspective of implementers in determining what makes a well-written bill. As Tim Wiest, a colleague at Deloitte Consulting, who has spent a career helping government agencies execute big initiatives, puts it: "If you show me a draft bill, my brain immediately starts thinking about all the potential downstream issues it will cause. That's just how my brain works. I'm an operations guy. I'm looking for all the things in there that are going to cause a lot of grief down the road."[31] We need more people like Wiest who are trained in implementation poring over the policy designs of major initiatives before they come out of Stargate.

Another option is to actually place some of the designers on the implementation team and vice versa, where feasible. Doing this helped make the rollout of London's congestion pricing initiative so successful. "We couldn't afford the luxury of having the implementers revisit the design," said Derek Turner, who led the implementation team.[32] "We had to have seamless integration—from design to implementation to operation. The typical handoffs between design and implementation cause all sorts of problems, from the hiatus period in which the implementers try to understand the design to the attitude of 'We could have done the design better,' which causes incongruence."

In effect, those who had designed the plan would be put in charge of implementing it. "I was looking for people who had a commitment to the idea [of road pricing] and were hell bent on delivery," said Turner.

Seeing the journey to success as a continuous process geared toward producing an end result can help avoid the Silo Trap. To be successful, everyone must understand what the ultimate goal is, and what their role is in achieving it. To be successful, the system must behave as a system.

FIELD GUIDE: OVERCOMING THE SILO TRAP

The challenge is to see the journey as an integrated whole and to create alignment, a shared sense of purpose among the various participants through the various stages of an undertaking.

Biggest Danger

The Silo Trap. Those who fall into this trap mistake part of the journey for the whole by failing to see the journey to success as an integrated process.

Guiding Principles

Articulate your goal. What is the problem you are trying to solve? How will you know when you're finished? Achieve agreement on a desired future state and a shared commitment to create the future. A clear goal to put a man on the moon helped everyone at NASA to focus their efforts to that end. Unclear goals in postwar Iraq led to role confusion and premature celebration.

Define roles. Know your role. Once people are clear on the goal, the players need to understand how their individual contributions will lead to that goal.

Foster alignment. Promote coordinated effort between participants in different parts of the public sector. Unlike a business initiative, in government there is often no overarching "owner" who oversees the entire journey to success. Different parts of the process report to different political authorities: Congress doesn't report to the president; mayors don't report to governors.

Plan for the entire journey. Cover every step of the journey to success. One bad idea, a single design flaw, an implementation error—any weak link in the chain can doom an initiative, just as a few weak levees doomed New Orleans.

Practice your handoffs. The blame game is lots of fun, but the real cause of failure often lurks in hidden, systemic causes—the invisible gaps between the people. When things go wrong, recognize that the *process* and its many handoffs can generate problems as easily as the *people* doing the work. Toyota says it gets great results from average people by having better processes than its competitors.

Tools and Techniques

SMART goals. A smart leader articulates a SMART goal (specific, measurable, attainable, results-oriented, and time-based), as President Kennedy did when he urged "achieving the goal, before this decade is out, of landing a man on the moon and returning him safely to the earth." Anybody unclear on that?

Visual reminders. These can help link activities to the end goal and bring purpose to employees' work. Remember the Rosie the Riveter posters during World War II showing a strong female factory worker flexing her muscles? It helped people to visualize every day how women were helping America and its allies to win World War II.

Process mapping. Map the journey early on, with a big box at the end showing the goal—the hoped-for result. Tools like Gantt charts and Microsoft Project can help. Seeing the journey as a single endeavor can encourage the integration of the political and the bureaucratic, of the designers and the implementers.

Systems thinking. Systems thinking helps in understanding how the structure of complex systems influences the behavior of various participants in a process who are exposed to different information. This book applies a systems-thinking mindset to policy initiatives.

Resources (Books, Web Sites, and Other Cool Stuff)

For further reading, we recommend *The Fifth Discipline*, by Peter Senge (a classic on systems thinking); *Business Dynamics*, by John Sterman (a good book on how to apply system dynamics modeling to the analysis of policy and strategy, with a special focus on business and public policy applications); *Execution Premium*, by Robert S. Kaplan and David P. Norton (presents a six-stage management framework to link strategy and operations; the focus of the book is the private sector but public organizations can also benefit from many of the ideas and tools); and *The Four Pillars of High Performance*, by Paul Light. Another great resource is the Lean Enterprise Institute (www.lean.org/). Lean thinking is all about looking at the whole process from beginning to end. The Lean Institute has great materials on process mapping, defining value, and seeing the whole from the parts. Read their book: *Lean Enterprise Value: Insights from MIT's Lean Aerospace Initiative*.

CHAPTER **8**

Creating a Better Future

The Execution Mindset

CHAPTER GUIDE

- Mr. Moynihan Goes to Washington
- LBJ Declares War—Twice
- Moynihan's Obsession
- The Remarkable Dwight Ink
- The Alaska Earthquake of 1964
- "Mr. Implementation" in the White House
- Closing an Agency for Ronald Reagan
- Taking Government Work Seriously
- The Courage to Make Yourself Heard
- Your Turn

The reasonable man adapts himself to the world. The unreasonable man persists in trying to adapt the world to himself. Therefore, all progress depends on the unreasonable man.

—GEORGE BERNARD SHAW

T HE FUTURE HEALTH OF DEMOCRACY depends on government's ability to successfully execute on wisely selected undertakings. Given the challenges we face, if we consistently choose the wrong course of action or regularly fail to accomplish what we set out to do, our troubles will only worsen.

In a democracy, each of us contributes to creating our future. The media's focus on those at the top of the power pyramid often makes it seem as though leadership is the province of the chosen few. No doubt those in positions of power can make a big impact. But so can you. This chapter tells the stories of two individuals—one from the political world, one from the bureaucratic—who made a difference without always wielding a great deal of formal authority. What set these two apart was their execution mindset.

Mr. Moynihan Goes to Washington

In 1961, thirty-three-year-old Daniel Patrick Moynihan came to Washington with President John F. Kennedy, armed with a PhD in sociology and a belief in the ability of government to improve the human condition. Like many of his New Frontier colleagues, Moynihan had served in the military during and immediately after World War II. After the war, he attended graduate school in London on that much-beloved federal program, the GI Bill. His first stint at public service was with New York governor Averell Harriman. When Moynihan came to Washington, he was part of a cadre of "junior officers," including Lieutenant John F. Kennedy, who were now taking leadership from their former commanders, symbolized by General Dwight D. Eisenhower. As with so many of Moynihan's generation, WWII had merged personal experience with national experience. Those now in positions of leadership had seen firsthand America's ability to achieve great things. They had lived through the Manhattan Project, D-Day, the Marshall Plan, the occupation of Japan, and the Berlin Airlift. They knew what a democratic government could do when called upon.

The experiences of this generation fueled optimism. One imagines Moynihan listening to Kennedy's 1961 inaugural address and soaking in the bold vision of the "New Frontier," ready to do battle against "the common enemies of man: tyranny, poverty, disease, and war itself."

It was an exciting challenge and a noble one, worthy of the exertions of those who might be called the best and the brightest—before that term was doomed to irony. Moynihan joined an administration that attracted luminaries such as Arthur Schlesinger Jr., Chester Bowles, John Kenneth Galbraith, Sargent Shriver, and Bill Moyers. It was a time when high achievers felt called to public service. It was also a time of passionate commitment. In 1963, a twenty-nine-year-old lawyer named Ralph Nader hitchhiked to Washington, where he was promptly hired by Pat Moynihan at the Department of Labor to work on the issue of automobile safety.

Moynihan was not initially charged with solving America's big problems. In fact, one of his first assignments should have been a real snoozer, a time-wasting exercise of the first order. But in part because of Moynihan's optimistic outlook, this dead-end project ended up leaving an enduring mark on the landscape of Washington—literally.

From Shabby to Chic

During his inaugural parade, heading down Pennsylvania Avenue on January 20, 1961, President Kennedy noticed that the nation's capital city was more shabby than chic. That afternoon, he mentioned the seedy condition of Pennsylvania Avenue to his secretary of labor, Arthur J. Goldberg, wondering if there wasn't something that could be done about it. Goldberg handed over this thankless project to his young aide Pat Moynihan.

The effort was inauspiciously titled the "Ad Hoc Committee on Federal Office Space." One participant described it as "mainly bitching about parking in federal buildings."[1]

Pat Moynihan decided to make the most of this limited opportunity. In the spring of 1962, the committee issued its report. Far more than just a routine analysis of office space and parking shortages, the report also included a Moynihan-penned document entitled "Guiding Principles for Federal Architecture." Moynihan's guidelines offer a glimpse into his thoughts about government. A federal office building, wrote Moynihan, "must provide visual testimony to the dignity, enterprise, vigor and stability of the American Government."[2] The report also recommended that the president launch an effort to revitalize Pennsylvania Avenue. On June 1, 1962, the President's Council on Pennsylvania Avenue was formed, with noted architect Nathanial Owings as chairman. The council members included Daniel Patrick Moynihan.[3]

Moynihan, a junior official in the Department of Labor, had taken a trivial review of office buildings and elevated it into one of the most high-profile redevelopment projects in the country. On November 21, 1963, President Kennedy requested a meeting with Moynihan and others, after his return from Dallas, to discuss their plans.[4]

Moynihan's high hopes for Pennsylvania Avenue did not perish with the president. When President Lyndon Johnson inquired whether there was anything he could do for her, Jacqueline Kennedy responded by mentioning the Pennsylvania Avenue restoration.[5] It took years, but Moynihan's initial effort became the Pennsylvania Avenue Development Corporation, which built many of the parks, monuments, and plazas along that thoroughfare. In a poetic twist, in 1990 Moynihan, then a senator, took up residence with his wife in an apartment on Pennsylvania Avenue, surrounded by the grandeur he had envisioned nearly three decades earlier.

LBJ Declares War—Twice

We have in 1964 a unique opportunity and obligation—to prove the success of our system; to disprove those cynics and critics at home and abroad who question our purpose and our competence.

—PRESIDENT LYNDON JOHNSON, 1964 STATE OF THE UNION ADDRESS

After his death, many of President Kennedy's New Frontier initiatives were continued—strengthened even—by President Johnson and his Great Society. In January 1964, less than two months after Kennedy's assassination, President Johnson used his first State of the Union address to declare war. "This administration today, here and now, declares unconditional war on poverty in America," the new president told Congress. In Johnson's own words, this was to be an "all-out war on human poverty and unemployment in these United States."[6] Kennedy no longer walked among us, but his spirit endured. So did his advisers, most of whom stayed on with Johnson.

As part of Kennedy's New Frontier, and subsequently with President Johnson's Great Society, Moynihan and his colleagues found themselves in positions of authority with vast financial resources at their disposal. The economy was strong, and unprecedented federal dollars flowed into ambitious new initiatives.

Under Johnson, Moynihan was placed on an antipoverty task force. He knew his subject. The son of an absent, alcoholic father and a mother on public assistance, young Pat Moynihan hustled newspapers on the streets of New York to make ends meet. His PhD from Tufts and Fulbright studies at the London School of Economics gave him impeccable academic credentials, while his hardscrabble upbringing gave him "street cred." At six feet five inches, Moynihan possessed both physical and intellectual stature. In 1964, he helped Johnson win passage of the Economic Opportunity Act, which created the Office of Economic Opportunity, VISTA (Volunteers in Service to America), the Job Corps, the Neighborhood Youth Corps, and the Community Action Program. This was a hint of what was to come.

The Democratic landslide of November 1964 may have been the high-water mark for the Democratic Party in the twentieth century. In one of the most lopsided results in history, Lyndon Johnson trounced Barry Goldwater, winning more than 60 percent of the popular vote. Democrats also significantly increased their numbers in both the House and the Senate, gaining a veto-proof two-thirds majority in both chambers. The vote was seen as a clear mandate for a more expanded federal role in domestic policy.

After the 1964 election, Johnson's domestic programs multiplied as he fought the war on poverty on multiple fronts. The federal government launched ambitious programs in education and health care.[7] But the main theater of the war on poverty would be the hard-core urban poor.

In 1965, as Johnson's assistant secretary of labor, Moynihan wrote a report entitled, "The Negro Family: The Case for National Action." In it, Moynihan pointed out that the rate of babies born to single mothers among African Americans was around 24 percent, more than six times the rate for whites and 40 percent higher than it had been in 1940. Moynihan argued that the crisis of the African American family was bad and growing worse—and he offered a solution.

> *Measures that have worked in the past, or would work for most groups in the present, will not work here. A national effort is required that will give a unity of purpose to the many activities of the Federal government in this area, directed to a new kind of national goal: the establishment of a stable Negro family structure. This would be a new departure for Federal policy.*[8]

Eradicating poverty, ending unemployment, and fixing the family— these unprecedented federal objectives were far more ambitious than Roosevelt's New Deal. These efforts involved changing people's personal and economic behaviors, the hardest rock to roll up the public policy hill and one prone to the Double Sisyphus Trap.

Moynihan wouldn't be around to see the results, at least not from within the Johnson administration. The increasingly bitter relationship between President Johnson and Robert Kennedy diminished Moynihan's standing with the president; he was seen as a "Kennedy man." In 1965, Moynihan left the administration to run for the City Council of New York. He lost and retreated to academia—for the time being, anyway.

Moynihan's Obsession: Results

It was a good time to get out of Washington because the unsatisfying results of the War on Poverty were starting to roll in. In his 1967 State of the Union address, President Johnson delivered a caustic one-liner: "Three years ago we set out to create these new instruments of social progress. This required trial and error—and it has produced both."[9]

Meanwhile, the departed Moynihan was pointing out the dismal results from his ivory tower. In 1967, as director of the MIT-Harvard Joint Center for Urban Studies, he mused: "All the things we've tried to help the cities with aren't working out very well, are they?"[10]

In 1968, Moynihan wrote *Maximum Feasible Misunderstanding*, an inside look at just one part of the War on Poverty, the Community Action Program (CAP). Moynihan described the program as "a debacle," characterized by "soaring rhetoric" and "minimum performance."[11] The idea behind CAP was to provide federal dollars to local community groups in depressed neighborhoods, and to enable "maximum feasible participation" of local residents in these local antipoverty efforts. Moynihan remained supportive of the Community Action Program's goals, but he was highly critical of the execution. It was hard not to be. Some of the local CAPs saw their role as shadow city governments, others as centers of social criticism. Conflicts between the federally supported CAPs and the local city hall were common. Many well-intentioned programs bogged down in red tape. Attracting a mishmash of ideological extremists, these community-centered programs were plagued by mismanagement and infighting and generated precious little community benefit. The federally funded mimeograph machines were often put to use inflaming local residents with radical pamphlets, which hardly endeared CAP to the existing power structure and contributed to the program's rapid loss of political support. As Moynihan put it in *Maximum Feasible Misunderstanding*: "To see an effort begun with such great hopes remorselessly dismantled is to know a disappointment not easily got over."[12]

Moynihan offered a scathing critique of the failed execution within the Great Society programs:

The first judgment, then, must be that during these years in Washington, a good many men in the anti-poverty program, in and about the Executive Office of the President, and in the Congress, men of whom the nation had a right to expect better, did inexcusably sloppy work. If administrators and politicians are going to play God with other people's lives (and still other persons' money), they ought to at least get clear what the divine intention is to be . . . The poorest performance was that of the high-level staff aides, some nominally political, some nominally in the career service, but far more like one another than otherwise, who busied themselves with the details of community action but never took time to inform themselves, much less their superiors, that the government did not know what it was doing.

This is the essential fact: The government did not know what it was doing. It had a theory. Or rather, a set of theories. Nothing more. The

U.S. government was no more in possession of confident knowledge as to how to prevent delinquency, cure anomie, or overcome that midmorning sense of powerlessness, than it was the possessor of a dependable formula for motivating Vietnam villagers to fight Communism . . .

A big bet was being made. No responsible person had any business acting as if it were a sure thing.[13]

This is certainly not the first we have heard of disappointing leadership, unclear goals, and overconfidence. Such pitfalls, as we've seen earlier, have bedeviled many efforts to transform big ideas into big results.

Moynihan's prophetic insights won him the reward traditionally reserved for prophets: he was stoned by his own people. Like a war critic in any era, he was pilloried as a defeatist, excoriated as a traitor, and castigated for undermining the war effort. A 1991 article summed it up in the title: "Slumlord; Pat Moynihan Has Done Some Great Things—But Betraying the Poverty Warriors Isn't One of Them." That article contained a revealing line, referring to Moynihan's 1965 report on the Negro Family: "Today, the Moynihan Report stands as probably the most refuted document in American history (though its dire predictions about the poor black family all came true)."[14] The report was refuted by everyone but borne out by the results.

To Moynihan, however, the results were what really mattered. Noble intentions without sound execution, he pointed out, were of no value to those you were trying to help. This was not a message some people wanted to hear. In 1970, Moynihan himself identified the most egregious of his perceived sins: "Few assertions in *Maximum Feasible Misunderstanding* evoked more widespread disagreement than the statement that '*The role of social science lies not in the formulation of social policy, but in the measurement of its results.*' "[15]

It seems like common sense that real-world results should be the ultimate test for any theory, but as we saw in our examination of the Tolstoy syndrome in chapter 1, humans are loath to abandon a dearly held belief, and most will cling tenaciously to a theory despite an accumulation of contrary evidence. This was true of both the War on Poverty and the war in Vietnam. President Johnson and his military advisers believed that America's military might would overwhelm the North Vietnamese.

When troops and bombs didn't work, they sent more troops and dropped more bombs. To try something different would be to admit error. Humans, it turns out, aren't terribly rational. Even if we are deeply conflicted prior to making a tough decision, we find it really hard once that decision is made to alter course—even when new evidence tells us we should. Psychologists refer to this as "escalation of commitment" or "commitment bias," the tendency to increase our attachment to an earlier poor decision. Poker players refer to it as "throwing good money after bad." Whatever you choose to call it, it happens a lot, and it isn't terribly effective as an approach to public policy.

Facts are stubborn things, however, and eventually disappointing results at home and abroad spelled doom for President Johnson. In early 1968, the war in Vietnam was going as badly as the War on Poverty. After a poor showing in the New Hampshire primary, Johnson decided against seeking reelection. He had become a casualty of two wars of his own making.

As for Moynihan, he went back to the White House as Nixon's urban policy advisor and then served President Ford as ambassador to India and the United Nations. In 1977, he became a U.S. senator from New York, where the lifelong Democrat earned a reputation for intellectual independence. Journalists always had a hard time pinning him down ideologically— labeling him everything from a neoconservative to a New Deal liberal. Moynihan himself never flinched from the label "liberal," but as a social scientist, he was far less concerned with ideology than with empirical results. His data-driven analysis led to his concerns about urban poverty, and his data-driven analysis then prompted his disappointment in federal efforts to fix it. Facts mattered to Moynihan. The story is told of Moynihan engaging in a heated political disagreement, when his opponent finally said, "Well, you may disagree with me, Pat, but I'm entitled to my own opinion." To which Moynihan hotly replied, "You're entitled to your own opinion. You're not entitled to your own facts."[16]

Troubled by what he termed "the leakage of reality from American life," Moynihan was often the skunk at the party during his four terms in the Senate, continually insisting on real-world results when his colleagues wanted to focus on policy and ideology, or congratulate themselves for their good intentions.[17] In 1994, the Senate debated a major education bill. The legislation had two key goals: a high school graduation rate of at least 90 percent by 2000 and American students "first in the world in mathematics and science." Moynihan inconveniently compared the two goals to Soviet grain production quotas, those empty declarations of a rosy future that never seemed to materialize.[18]

Around the same time, as chairman of the Senate Finance Committee, Moynihan opposed the Clinton health care plan on the simple grounds that it wouldn't work. "Anyone who thinks [the Clinton health care plan] can work in the real world as presently written isn't living in it."[19] He instead brokered a bipartisan bill that would have cut the number of uninsured Americans in half—an approach rejected by the White House. When Hillary Clinton later was running for Moynihan's seat in 2000 after he decided to retire from Congress, she wrote him a long letter expressing regret that she didn't follow his advice on health care reform. "If I had listened to you about health care in 1994, I would be far better off today—but more importantly—so would the nation's health care system," wrote Clinton.[20]

Pat Moynihan had many admirable traits, not the least of which was that he always kept an open mind when it came to public policy, refusing to succumb to confirmation bias. Perhaps more than any other legislator in modern times, he also cared passionately about execution—about what came after the bill was passed. He continually forced his fellow senators to care about—or at least to consider—whether a given policy would actually work in the real world. As a social scientist, he looked for data, and he accepted that data even when it told those in power a message they didn't want to hear. When Moynihan died in 2003, he was heralded across the political spectrum. But it was columnist George Will who penned perhaps the most poignant description of the senator from New York: "The Senate's Sisyphus, Moynihan was forever pushing uphill a boulder of inconvenient truth."[21]

The Remarkable Dwight Ink

On October 27, 1964, the strongest earthquake ever documented on this continent—a 9.2 on the Richter scale—ravaged the main population center of Alaska. The state's populace was very much at risk. About one-third of its citizens faced the prospect of having to abandon the state. It was among the worst natural disasters in America's history, though few people today have ever heard of it.

Thankfully, Alaska managed to survive. In fact, the rebuilding of the state is a textbook example of post-disaster recovery. One year after the quake, the *Anchorage Daily News* wrote that the comeback from disaster had been so remarkable that "the recovery period was almost as dramatic and breathtaking as the earthquake."[22] Alaska was not saved by a charismatic governor or a four-star general, or by the Federal Emergency Management Agency, which did not yet exist. Instead, President Johnson tapped an unassuming career bureaucrat with thick, metal-rimmed glasses and a receding hairline to lead the recovery operations.[23] It was not the first or the last time an American president would call on this lifelong public servant to do the impossible. If Daniel Patrick Moynihan represents the model for a politician with an execution mindset, Dwight Ink embodies the model bureaucrat.

Dwight Ink served in senior executive positions for seven consecutive presidents of the United States. His rise to some of the highest echelons of government didn't result from family connections or an Ivy League pedigree. Born during the Great Depression, Ink, like Moynihan, came from humble origins. He was raised on a family farm in rural Iowa, and he walked several miles a day—often barefoot—to a one-room schoolhouse. "We were dirt poor," recalls Ink. "Twice I had to drop out of school for a time when cold weather arrived before my father could buy me shoes."[24]

After serving a four-year stint in the U.S. Army Air Corps and then obtaining undergraduate and graduate degrees from Iowa State University and the University of Minnesota, he landed a job working for Leroy Harlow, a reform-minded city manager in Fargo, North Dakota. He helped Harlow root out the endemic corruption that had characterized Fargo's city hall. "The harsh lessons of Fargo made an indelible impression on me about personal courage in the public service," Ink recalls. "And they taught me that serious problems call for bold, innovative management strategies that often have few, if any, precedents."

His first job with the federal government began in the early 1950s when he went to work for the Federal Bureau of Reclamation building small dams in the Missouri River basin, but he soon moved on to the

Atomic Energy Commission. At age thirty-two, he became control officer, charged with expediting the largest and most urgent construction project in the free world: the huge "H-bomb" plants in Savannah River, South Carolina, critical facilities in America's race with the Soviet Union to develop an arsenal of hydrogen bombs.

After being transferred to Washington headquarters, he helped develop the concept for a limited nuclear test ban agreement with the Soviet Union. The idea was to ban atmospheric nuclear tests that poisoned the atmosphere, but to allow underground tests to continue, in part because violations of this sort were nearly impossible to detect. This idea was controversial, but after vigorous internal debate, the limited test ban proposal became a key element of President Eisenhower's foreign policy.

Ink had high regard for Ike's management skills. "He was more effective than people realize," says Ink. "He came across as imprecise in press conferences. Nice, and likeable, but indecisive. He was the opposite in private—brisk, with a temper on occasions."[25]

By the time President Kennedy took office, Ink was the assistant general manager of the Atomic Energy Commission. In that role, he served in a small ad hoc group of key national security officials who gave advice to President Kennedy early in his administration. The White House member of the group was the historian Arthur Schlesinger, a close advisor to the president. In the first two meetings of the group, Ink and Schlesinger locked horns over the limited nuclear test ban proposal. The historian, along with many in the Department of State, thought Kennedy should oppose it.[26] In general, a bureaucrat treads lightly with political appointees, particularly famous ones close to the president. Nonetheless, Ink passionately made the case for the limited ban, refusing to back down. During one of their heated debates Ink found himself in over his head.

> *I was aghast to suddenly realize that sitting in a chair along the wall behind Arthur was Bobby Kennedy. Apparently, Arthur had reported my unseemly behavior and Bobby had come to see for himself. I concluded instantly that my days in the government were definitely over and could not wait for the session to end so I could exit from this hole I had dug.*

Ink went back to the commission and tendered his resignation, believing the White House would want him, a carryover from the Eisenhower administration, removed from the government. That didn't happen. Bobby Kennedy evidently appreciated Ink's candor. "To my complete surprise, [they] kept me in that role, and at the next meeting Schlesinger was absent and never attended another one," says Ink. "Apparently Bobby realized that while Schlesinger was a brilliant historian, and valued by the president in many ways, test ban treaties were not his strength."

Ink didn't have much in the way of formal authority, but his data-driven arguments had influence. President Kennedy in fact came to support the notion of a limited test ban, and successfully negotiated such a treaty with the Soviet Union in 1963. It was not the last time a president would take the advice of this career civil servant over one of his political appointees.

It was also during the Kennedy administration that Ink first got to know James Webb of NASA. The two of them oversaw the Nuclear Joint Space Program together, with Ink leading the nuclear side and Webb the space side. "Webb had a lot of good, plain sound judgment," says Ink. "He was one of the best there ever was in dealing with both Congress and the career service."

By the time Lyndon Johnson became president, Ink was garnering a reputation for being an effective implementer. As president, Johnson tapped into Ink's ability time and time again. His assignments included revamping the Office of Education ("Everyone else would have been under the control of the National Education Association," Johnson told Ink) and helping to start up the new Department of Housing and Urban Development. Each of these assignments would be a career highlight for most public servants, but were cakewalks compared to the other big job Johnson gave him: Alaska reconstruction.

Dwight Ink Rescues Alaska

Even as he watched televised pictures of the devastation caused by the Alaska earthquake, Ink was already thinking about the recovery effort. "I remember on a Good Friday, watching television footage of the earthquake," recalls Ink. "It looked like utter chaos. I remember feeling sorry for whoever was going to have to put things back together. It looked like an almost impossible task." Several days later, Ink got the news that Johnson wanted him to be the executive director of the rebuilding effort.

Ink didn't know how to react. He had never been to Alaska, never dealt with earthquakes, and had no experience in disaster recovery. But it wasn't an assignment he could turn down. "I recognized from the beginning that it was going to be an unusual kind of assignment, but I didn't have any opportunity to think about whether I wanted to do it or not," he recalls. "I wasn't given the option to say no to the president."

Why did Johnson choose Ink for this critical assignment? There was his reputation for getting things done. But there was also something else. "He knew I had worked for Eisenhower and in those days, Republicans were regarded as highly fiscally responsible—not any more of course. He told me he thought it would be good to have someone there who wouldn't run away with the Treasury on this job," recalls Ink, laughing at the memory.

To expedite interagency coordination, Johnson departed from the customary approach in disaster recoveries by appointing most of his cabinet members to a temporary reconstruction commission for Alaska and took the unprecedented step of appointing a powerful senator, Clinton Anderson, Democrat from New Mexico, as chair. With Ink serving as executive director of the commission and reporting to the president, everyone knew he was in charge of recovery operations.

Ink's initial assessment was not auspicious. Every engineer he met when he arrived in Alaska agreed that the rebuilding of critical utilities could not be completed during Alaska's short construction season. (There are four seasons in Alaska: almost winter, winter, still winter, and construction season.) Without a water and sewer system, Anchorage and other harbor communities couldn't function. Without functioning harbors, there would be no fishing, and without fishing, the economy would collapse. Alaskans would abandon the state if Ink couldn't get key infrastructure working before a deep freeze halted progress. "It was a very, very dismal first night," he recalls, "I got no sleep at all."

During that sleepless night, however, he had an epiphany. He had to think in reverse of the typical approach to managing construction projects, beginning with the results needed to enable families to stay in Alaska:

> We had to figure out, no matter how impossible it might seem, what had to be done by the time the construction season ended, then work backwards with milestones that we would have to meet, no matter how seemingly

impossible. Then, [we'd have to] figure out new management and engineer-
ing approaches that would enable us to do what had never been done before
in peacetime.

Simply putting forth unrealistic schedules that could not be met in the
vain hope that conventional management could be expedited—a more
typical approach—would be the worst sort of disaster. By thinking in reverse, however, Ink concluded that the only way to finish the job in time
was to suspend those administrative processes that would jeopardize meeting the impossible milestones. So that's what he did. With the acquiescence of congressional leaders, whenever necessary he either streamlined
or suspended government procurement timetables and public hearings
that typically make government move so slowly. This enabled him to dramatically collapse the planning phase of the rebuilding.

He took other steps to speed the recovery. All major construction contracts were made incentive based: large financial bonuses were awarded to
contractors for getting the job done early, and financial penalties were imposed for missed deadlines and cost overruns. To stave off time-consuming
congressional hearings and inquiries from key members of Congress, he
recruited several highly qualified congressional staffers to be part of his
management team, ensuring that Congress was fully informed of both
progress and setbacks. This openness reinforced congressional willingness
to permit innovative management approaches.

Without an existing bureaucracy to assist him, Ink established a small
but powerful temporary entity that could plan and implement recovery
efforts without bureaucracy. This encouraged innovation, creativity, and
rapid action. The engineering experts who had offered their dismal estimates weren't wrong—they were merely constrained in their thinking.
They fell victim to the Complacency Trap; their thinking regarding how
long it would take to rebuild was anchored in the existing procurement
systems. Because of what was in place, they couldn't imagine what Ink
and his colleagues would create, namely, a rescue operation unencum-
bered by red tape. Ink, as director of the commission who reported to the
president, had near unlimited ability to act, so there were no jurisdictional
battles, no power struggles, no elaborate reviews. Yet, as a publicity-shy
bureaucrat with a short-term appointment, Ink represented a turf threat
to no one. The result of this innovative approach: peacetime records in

rebuilding harbors, highways, and water and sewer systems. And Alaskans did not have to abandon their state.

Mr. Implementation

The LBJ years were some of Ink's most fulfilling in public service. According to Ink, Johnson didn't know a lot about management, but he trusted those who did. "Johnson had a high regard for the civil service," says Ink, "He felt that they were better qualified to operate the government than political appointees. He made a distinction between the political leadership being accountable for policy and the career leadership being accountable for implementing policy through professional operations."

The Nixon presidency meant new opportunities and new challenges for Dwight Ink. This president was unusually focused on implementation, but Nixon didn't trust the bureaucracy. He decided he needed a management expert in the White House who could help him get his policy initiatives through the federal labyrinth. He naturally turned to Ink, by now considered Mr. Implementation. Ink became the first career executive to participate in the daily 7:30 a.m. senior White House staff meetings. "They gave me a voice in developing legislation and other initiatives," explains Ink. "I would advise them if the legislation made the implementation too complex or imposed an unnecessary burden on state and local governments, and help them with the workability of it." Imagine that, an implementation expert weighing in on policy design.

In essence, Ink was working to help the administration avoid the Design-Free Design Trap. In this role, Ink worked closely with Pat Moynihan, then Nixon's urban policy advisor. During this time, a young White House Fellow, Major Colin Powell, was also assigned to Ink's tutelage.

Nixon also charged Ink with leading the New Federalism initiative to return decision making to states and cities. In this role, Ink applied more generally many of the ideas he had pioneered with the Alaska recovery. He led an interagency initiative that slashed processing time for state and local grant approvals and cut red tape. There was a common thread to the reforms: simplification. "They were born out of a growing recognition of Moynihan's earlier criticisms about implementation of Great Society programs as well as analyses showing the programs to be too centralized and complex," explains Ink.

"The Nixon I saw was very different from the Nixon you read about in the tapes," says Ink. "He was very interested in good government and for several years stood up to special interests in this area better than other presidents. His first term was the best of what I'd been involved in from a management perspective." Nixon's second term? "Terrible. The whole White House atmosphere changed overnight with the 1972 election. He let secrecy and politics pervade."

After a short stint as acting administrator of the General Services Administration for President Ford, where he led the president's initiative to cut the federal government's energy use by one-third in ninety days during the Arab oil embargo, Ink faced his next big challenge when Jimmy Carter became president. Carter asked Ink to design the reform of the civil service system. Working with the White House, the head of the Civil Service Commission, and a task force of career employees, Ink designed the most comprehensive overhaul of civil service since it had been established nearly a century earlier. One provision Ink was especially proud of was the creation of the Senior Executive Service, an elite corps of senior civil servants. Ink hoped the SES, as it is known, would allow more of his colleagues a chance to serve at the highest levels of the federal government, as he had. "I want to thank you for leading and accomplishing the most fundamental and comprehensive review of Federal personnel management ever undertaken," President Carter later wrote Ink.[27]

Reforming civil service would have been a nice crowning achievement for this outstanding civil servant, but Ink wasn't quite done. In fact, it was under President Ronald Reagan that Dwight Ink would encounter the ultimate test.

Closing an Agency for Ronald Reagan

Soon after taking office, President Reagan nominated Ink to lead the Community Services Administration (CSA), an agency that ran a variety of leftover Great Society antipoverty programs assisting local community action groups that worked with and represented the poor. This time, there was a catch: Reagan wanted the agency eliminated. Ink's job? Close it down.

For a career public servant, almost any assignment would be preferable. "I really didn't want it, but my wife said 'Dwight, you should take the job. You've always said that given the right leadership, career people would respond, even if it went against their interests.' "

There was another motivator for Ink. He agreed with Reagan that the agency should be shuttered. The agency had been established in the Kennedy administration as a temporary agency—Daniel Patrick Moynihan had been involved in its genesis. Its charge had been to experiment with innovative antipoverty approaches, and those that worked were supposed to be woven into existing departments, after which the CSA would be terminated.[28] It hadn't worked out that way, and CSA came to house a hodge-podge of orphaned programs. Nixon attempted to eliminate the agency, but the highly contentious effort had failed miserably. The conventional wisdom inside the Beltway was that this "temporary" agency had become a permanent fixture, largely ineffective but politically untouchable.

Ink accepted the job. He soon learned there weren't many precedents for what he was asked to do. Other than wartime agencies, the only example Ink could find of an independent federal agency being closed was the New Deal's National Recovery Administration, whose work had been found unconstitutional by the Supreme Court. Once again Ink would have to craft his own approach.

Many conservative Republicans were uneasy that Reagan had appointed a career employee to lead the closure. These hard-liners pressured Ink to distance himself as much as possible from the career leadership at the agency, who they were convinced would sabotage the effort. Ink ignored their advice. He believed his success depended on gaining the trust of the CSA's career employees. "I gambled that most of them would be willing to respond to the presidential decision to close the agency in a responsible manner, provided it was done in a professional way that showed respect for people even if they disagreed strongly with the policy."

Ink went to great pains to garner and retain that trust. One day he found out that political "advisers" had been sent by his deputy, a political appointee, to watch over each of the agency's regional directors to make sure they kept in line. "Within an hour, I immediately removed every one of the watchers," says Ink. Ink established a closure steering committee and included the president of the local public employee union, further annoying some of Reagan's people. Reagan had no doubt been guilty during the presidential campaign of scoring political points by blaming bureaucrats for the failures of the bureaucracy, but in choosing Ink he was ensuring a more measured approach, one more respectful of those who worked within government. Ink's deft touch and impeccable integrity was just what was needed for this assignment. He worked hard to find jobs for those being displaced. His unassuming presence didn't hurt either. One Reagan appointee told the *Wall Street Journal* at the time that the Ink appointment "was brilliant. He looks like the ultimate bureaucrat."[29]

Where Nixon had failed, Reagan succeeded. The Community Services Administration was killed off and it stayed dead. The shutting down of the antipoverty agency, the first elimination of a federal agency in fifty years, was carried out not by a right-wing ideologue, but by a pragmatic bureaucrat who grew up in poverty. The irony was not lost on Ink. "It was a traumatic experience for the people there and a draining one for me," recalls Ink. "I had to prove that career people are capable of doing whatever the president asks them to do, as long as it's legal."[30] Ink had only praise for the career employees who helped him shut the doors of their place of employment. "They were a hardworking group. There was hardly a person in the agency who agreed with closing it down, and yet we had an excellent relationship." Also deserving praise, says Ink, was Reagan himself, who resisted the urgings of his more strident political advisers by selecting a career bureaucrat to carry out the task. In doing so, Reagan signaled that he wanted the closure handled in a professional, not a political, fashion.

Ink served Reagan in several other important roles. As an assistant administrator of the Agency for International Development, he helped Latin American and Caribbean countries develop democratic institutions. By the time he finished that work, every significant country in the region except Cuba and Haiti had largely democratic government. In this role, Ink played a significant part in the forefront of the War on Drugs. At one point, this career bureaucrat must have felt like Indiana Jones when, working to curtail drug production in South America, he was kidnapped by drug lords while inspecting coca plots in the upper reaches of the Bolivian Amazon. Whoever said working as a bureaucrat is boring?

When Reagan completed his second term, Ink chose to retire from federal service.

Taking Government Work Seriously

Dwight Ink is retired now. His eyesight is failing him and his walk is slower, but his mind is still sharp. The study of his Virginia home is filled with autographed photographs straight from the pages of history—Ike, JFK, LBJ, Nixon, Ford, Carter, and Reagan. These pictures show the leading men of our modern history, and behind them, in the background, stands a bespectacled bureaucrat, the nondescript fellow who actually got so many of the important jobs done. Ink's career embodied all the characteristics of successful public servants—respect, integrity, balance, passion, and an "irrational" dedication to public service.

Dwight Ink doesn't at all fit the image of Indiana Jones, the swashbuckling hero. He doesn't fit our mental model of a leader, as did so many of the confident, powerful politicians he served. The West Wing of the White House has always had more than its share of office politics, but Ink was able to cut through it all and, despite little formal authority and a humble persona, to achieve some rather heroic results.

The political class respected the skills that Dwight Ink brought to the table. Too often today, political appointees bring their politics into operational roles. As the number of political appointees continues to increase, the senior civil servants don't get the opportunities that Ink did. "I was given the opportunity to work at the highest levels for president after president," notes Ink. "Think what that did for me in terms of accumulating valuable experience and gaining credibility with Congress." In recent years, probably only a handful of career officials have gotten into the Oval Office to see more than one president, never mind leading critical presidential initiatives for seven consecutive ones.

The careers of both Dwight Ink and Pat Moynihan show that you don't need to be president to be a leader. Not surprisingly, both men had a few key traits in common. Both brought an execution mindset to their tasks. They both had open minds that generally allowed them to follow the evidence rather than cling to preconceived beliefs. They took the responsibility of making government work seriously. They were students of process, of data, of the mechanics of governing, because they understood that making government work is a serious endeavor that deserves serious attention.

The media has helped turned government into a celebrity gossip game, a horse race, a reality television show packed with strong-willed and dysfunctional characters. The squabbles inside the Beltway today call to mind a school we visited where a group of students had left a mess at their table following lunch. Their teacher brought them back and scolded them all, telling them to clean it up. Instantly, the children began bickering about who among them had made the mess. Finally, one of them cried, "Who cares who made the mess? Let's just clean it up."

Cleaning up our public sector challenges won't be easy.

If our government is to reclaim a reputation for competency, we will need more Dwight Inks and Pat Moynihans. We will need a political culture that values and honors the capable management of public undertakings; a political culture that values the public servants who tell the unpleasant truths to their political masters. We don't have enough of either today.

The Courage to Make Yourself Heard

It can be hard to use your voice in government. When you are sitting in a meeting holding an unpopular opinion, the temptation will be to remain silent. At that moment, keep in mind the Morton Thiokol engineers who argued to ground the *Challenger* because of the risk the O-rings would fail at low temperatures. Although their arguments didn't carry the day, to their enduring credit they forcefully expressed their views despite enormous political pressure.

Speaking up requires courage. After Dwight Ink argued with Arthur Schlesinger in front of Bobby Kennedy, he thought his career was over. Instead, his arguments eventually helped convince President Kennedy to sign the Limited Test Ban Treaty—an important milestone in reducing nuclear tensions during the Cold War. Using your voice can be a challenge even for those in more elevated positions of power. Arthur Schlesinger was firmly opposed to the Bay of Pigs invasion, but even as a senior advisor to President Kennedy, he was reluctant to voice his concerns before the disastrous invasion. "In the months after the Bay of Pigs, I bitterly reproached myself for having kept so silent during those crucial discussions in the Cabinet Room," Schlesinger later wrote. The historian Schlesinger, surrounded at the table by cabinet secretaries and generals, later noted that others at the meeting "could strike virile poses and talk of tangible things—fire power, air strikes, landing craft and so on." It takes a lot of courage to voice namby-pamby concerns while surrounded by others who are confidently urging bold action. Schlesinger attributed his reticence in those critical days to "the circumstances of the discussion."[31]

One silver lining of the Bay of Pigs fiasco was that it changed the way the Kennedy White House conducted deliberations. During the Cuban missile crisis, not only were outside experts brought in to share their views, but at key times senior officials, particularly President Kennedy, would absent themselves so as to encourage vigorous debate. It shows that government can learn from its past, that we can avoid repeating dangerous mistakes.

Like the slipping bolts on the Big Dig, democracy is showing ominous signs of slipping in terms of its ability to accomplish what it sets out to do. To acknowledge the mounting evidence of a growing execution problem isn't a sign of weakness, nor does it diminish the achievements for which our nation may be justifiably proud. Acknowledging our shortcomings is a necessary step toward making things better. Ignoring signs of incipient failure can lead to disaster, as the *Challenger* and *Columbia* tragedies sadly proved.

Your Turn

Democracy is not a spectator sport. All of the participants in democratic government—elected leaders, those who work in the public sector, and citizens—play a role in creating the future. The goal of this book is to advance the art and practice of public sector management, particularly on large undertakings. Our hope is that no matter who you are, there will be something of benefit to you as together we engage in the democratic process.

For those who work in the public sector, we hope the book illuminates the systemic challenges of government and serves as a useful guide as you navigate the treacherous terrain on the journey to success.

For political leaders, both elected and appointed, we hope the book provides insights that will help you achieve results on the issues about which you care passionately. A clearer understanding of the perils of implementation may even lead some of you to a greater appreciation for the bureaucrats on the other side of Stargate.

For citizens, we hope this book is a reminder that it is voters who ultimately shape the future most of all. Our political leaders take their cue from their electorate. We hope this book opens the eyes of more citizens as to how their government actually works. Better informed citizens can be more discerning voters, more attuned to the challenges of political execution. After all, as Moynihan and Ink have taught us, it is not good intentions but the results that matter.

We hope the many successes profiled in the book can inspire everyone in the process to strive to make government better. At the same time, everyone who reads this book should heed the cautionary tales of the smart, capable people who have learned the hard way that failure is, indeed, an option. Whenever someone is pushing for a particular program or proposal, they should be expected to answer the question, "How exactly is this going to work in the real world?" After all, a policy will be implemented by flawed people working in a difficult environment. Recognizing that high hopes alone don't guarantee results would be a big step in the right direction.

Democracy has a proud history, and despite its flaws, it is the greatest system of government yet devised by men and women. The six American flags that stand on the moon are reminders of what we can achieve, but these flags, like our past glories, are fading with the passage of time. While it is true that our nation has faced great challenges before and prevailed, that is no guarantee that it will always do so. Neither our greatest triumphs nor our most humbling defeats determine what will come next. Our future depends not upon our past but on our present, on what we do both as individuals and as participants in the grand enterprise of democracy. The only way we will make a better future is by making wise choices about what government does and then executing those undertakings effectively. We hope this book contributes to that effort, but ultimately the future depends on you.

Appendix A

Case Studies Analyzed

Policy Initiatives

G.I. Bill (1944)

War on Poverty (1964–1968)

Negative income tax (NIT) (1969–1971)

Energy independence initiatives (1970–2005)

Nixon wage-price controls (1970s)

ICRA Immigration Reform Law (1986)

Clinton national health care reform plan
(1993–1994)

North American Free Trade Agreement
(NAFTA) (1994)

No Child Left Behind Act (NCLB) (2002)

London congestion pricing (2003)

Medicare Part D Prescription Drug Plan (2005)

McCain-Kennedy Immigration Bill (2006)

Reform

Hoover Commission (1947–1949)

Texas Sunset Advisory Commission (1977–present)

Grace Commission (1982–1984)

Texas Performance Review (1991–present)

School voucher programs

Missouri Commission on Management & Productivity (1992)

UK railway privatization (1993)

National Performance Review (1993–1998)

Welfare reform (1990s)

EMPOWER Kentucky (1996)

State of Florida charter school initiative (1996–present)

Washington, D.C., charter school initiative (1996–present)

Defense transformation (2001–2007)

U.S. Department of Interior cooperative conservation initiative (2001–2008)

New York City School Reform (2002–present)

Public Private Partnerships for Infrastructure in Texas (2003)

California Performance Review (2004)

Massachusetts health care reform (2006)

New Orleans Recovery School District (2004)

Japanese postal privatization (2007)

Regulatory

Airline deregulation (1978)

Trucking deregulation (1980)

Acid rain cap and trade program (1990)

California electricity deregulation (1998–2001)

European Union emissions trading scheme (2005)

Creating New Institutions

Marshall Plan (1947–1951)

Defense Advanced Research Projects Agency (DARPA) (1958)

Department of Homeland Security (2002)

Process and IT Initiatives Improvement

IRS modernization (1980s–present)

Government consumer service revolution (1990s)

California State Automated Child Welfare Information System (1994–1997)

Standard Terminal Automation Replacement System (STARS) (1996)

NSA Trailblazer (1999)

Federal Aviation Authority Wide Area Augmentation System (WAAS)

U.S. Census Bureau handheld computers

Colorado State Titling and Registration System (CSTARs) (2001–2007)

FBI Virtual Case File (VCF) (2001)

Navy Marine Corps Intranet (NMCI) (2000)

Human resources outsourcing in Florida (2002)

Human resources outsourcing at the Texas Health and Human Services Commission (2004)

Department of Homeland Security eMerge2 (Electronically Managing Enterprise Resources for Government Effectiveness and Efficiency) (2003–2005)

New York City 311 (2003)

Capital Projects

Manhattan Project (1941–1946)

Interstate highway system (1956–1992)

Project Apollo (1961–1975)

V-22 Osprey (1981)

NASA *Challenger* accident (1986)

Superconducting super collider (1987–1993)

Denver International Airport (1989)

Boston's "Big Dig" (1991–2007)

Crusader Artillery System (1994)

Future imagery architecture (1999)

Mars Climate Orbiter (1998)

World Trade Center rebuilding (2002–present)

NASA *Columbia* accident (2003)

Disaster/Crisis response

Alaska earthquake recovery (1964)

Louisiana hurricane protection system (1960s–present)

Peacekeeping/Defense

World War II

Berlin Airlift (1948–1949)

Bay of Pigs invasion (1961)

Korean War (1950–1953)

Vietnam War (1963–1973)

Iran Hostage Crisis/failed rescue (1979–1981)

Gulf War (1990–1991)

Iraq War (2003–present)

Iraq reconstruction (2003–present)

Appendix B

National Academy of Public Administration Survey Results

The National Academy of Public Administration (NAPA), a nonprofit established in 1967, is a coalition of distinguished leaders and public management experts providing independent and qualified advice and solutions to government on current and future challenges. Its 550 fellows, who are outstanding public servants or scholars, lead the academy's research and other activities. About one-third of the fellows, or 165, responded to our survey between November 2007 and March 2008 on the government's ability to execute.

Nearly 93 percent of the respondents have more than two decades of experience. They have worked in diverse sectors: from social service and health care to defense and the environment. It is their combined knowledge gained over the years serving at different levels of government (federal, state, municipal, university, and others) that is reflected in the survey results.

At the time of the survey, approximately 68 percent perceived the government less likely to successfully execute projects today than at any time in the past. Reasons why government is less capable today according to the respondents include a rise in administrative and political constraints, lack of political leadership, an increase in complexity, and more partisanship (figure B-1).

FIGURE B-1

Perceived reasons for why government is less capable today by years of experience

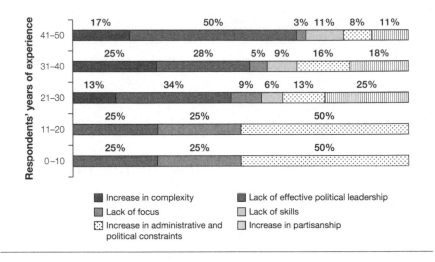

There was a fairly high degree of consensus that failures in public policy are a result of poor policy design, with proficiency of design declining as we move from local to federal government (figure B-2). Nearly 85 percent of respondents say that policy makers "rarely" or only "sometimes" provide clear guidance to those who implement policy. The most important aspect of policy design is considered to be provision of "sufficient resources," followed by "realistic goals."

Local governments are also considered much more proficient than state or federal governments in implementation; around 70 percent rate local government as "good" or "excellent." Lack of stakeholder management and operational deficiencies are considered important barriers to successful implementation, but political factors are considered the biggest barriers. Partisan politics, legislative politics, and leadership shortcomings are "always" or "often" the cause of implementation failure.

In line with the above findings, the top three leadership traits relevant to public policy implementation are consensus building, good communication, and experience. Nearly 70 percent of respondents say that if a popular public figure were to champion the policy, this would increase its chances of success.

Proficiency of policy design by level of government

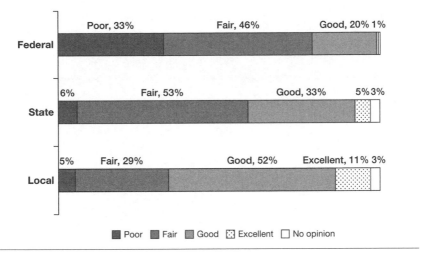

Appendix C

Senior Executive Service Survey Results

The Senior Executive Service (SES) is composed of a dedicated corps of executives selected for their exceptional leadership abilities to transform the federal government and make it more citizen focused and result oriented. They act as the link between the top presidential appointees and the rest of the federal workforce. Partnering with *Government Executive* magazine, we reached out to the membership of the SES between March and April of 2008 to get their input on what government can do to improve its execution ability.

Most of the 217 respondents have more than thirty years of experience at the federal level. Ninety-eight percent are between forty and eighty years of age; 97 percent have worked more than ten years in various government sectors.

Fully 76 percent say the federal government's image has deteriorated in the past three decades. Around half the respondents deem government to be less capable today than ten years ago, while only 1 percent think government is much more capable today. Similar to the NAPA survey, the primary reasons identified for this decline in execution ability are an increase in administrative and political constraints and lack of effective political leadership.

Perceptions regarding proficiency of policy design across levels of government are similar to those in the NAPA survey: proficiency declines with the level of government. Forty-five percent think it is rare that policy

FIGURE C-1

Reasons behind poor policy design

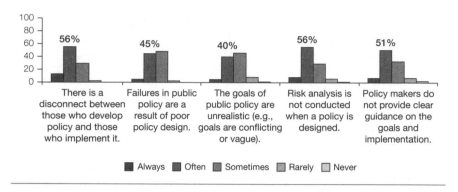

is designed by those with relevant experience. The reasons behind poor policy design? Policy designers fail to connect with those who implement policy, do not provide clear guidance on goals and implementation, and fail to conduct risk analysis (figure C-1).

Unrealistic costs and time lines are the biggest culprits leading to the failure of policy initiatives. Not surprising, then, that sufficient resources

FIGURE C-2

To what extent is Congress exercising its oversight duties responsibly?

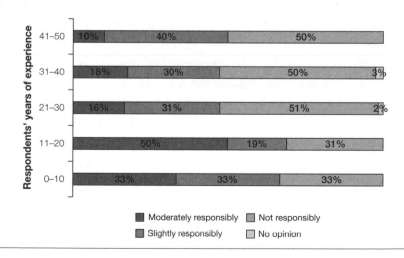

and realistic goals are believed to be the most important prerequisites of successful policy design.

Nearly half the respondents think implementation of large initiatives today is only slightly successful, while another 14 percent believe government is not successful at all. Lack of consensus among political parties is the biggest barrier to successful implementation. More experienced SES members have a less positive opinion of Congressional oversight today (see figure C-2). Good communication and consensus building, therefore, are believed to be the most important leadership traits. Only 3 percent are highly confident that a new generation capable of successfully executing large projects is in place.

Appendix D

Policy Execution Survey Results, Canada

In partnership with *Canadian Government Executive* magazine, a survey of 124 senior Canadian public sector leaders at the federal and provincial levels was conducted in Canada between July and August of 2008 to gauge their assessment of government's ability to execute on big initiatives.

The survey respondents were younger relative to the respondents from the United States: only 63 percent were over forty compared to 98 percent of U.S. respondents. Drawn from fourteen government sectors, all had at least ten years of experience in the public sector. The Canadian responses turned out to be somewhat more optimistic than those from the United States, though the broad trends remain the same.

Sixty-five percent think that government's image has deteriorated over the last thirty years; 41 percent feel that government is less capable of successfully executing large projects compared to ten years ago. The reasons for this are somewhat different than in the United States: increase in complexity and lack of focus are considered more important reasons than an increase in administrative complexity (figure D-1). However, there is consistency in thinking that local government is more successful at policy execution than provincial or federal government.

Governments are perceived as moderately or slightly successful in designing effective public policy. A failure to connect with those who implement policy and an inability to provide clear guidance on the goals and

FIGURE D-1

Reasons why government is perceived to be less capable today

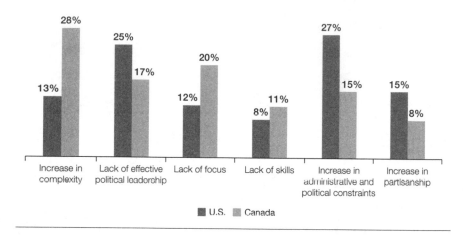

Increase in complexity — 13% / 28%
Lack of effective political leadership — 25% / 17%
Lack of focus — 12% / 20%
Lack of skills — 8% / 11%
Increase in administrative and political constraints — 27% / 15%
Increase in partisanship — 15% / 8%

■ U.S.   ▨ Canada

implementation are considered the biggest barriers to success. Risk analysis is often not conducted during the policy design stage—only around a quarter of the respondents believe that it is conducted when policy is designed. Characteristics of successful policy design closely mirror those in the United States: sufficient resources and clear, realistic goals.

Most respondents (57 percent) view policy implementation as being moderately successful, a relatively more positive view than in the United States. When governments fail at implementation, it is primarily due to poor timing of the launch, partisan politics, and unrealistic costs. Coordination failures and lack of leadership are other major shortcomings.

Good communication and consensus building rank among the top three leadership traits for success, as in the United States. The additional trait is "visionary" leadership (figure D-2). Sixty-five percent believe that a popular public figure improves the chances of success "always" or "often." Though a majority of respondents believe that elected representatives are exercising their oversight duties responsibly, only 4 percent are highly confident of the next generation's ability to address future challenges.

Soft skills far outweigh hard skills as important leadership traits

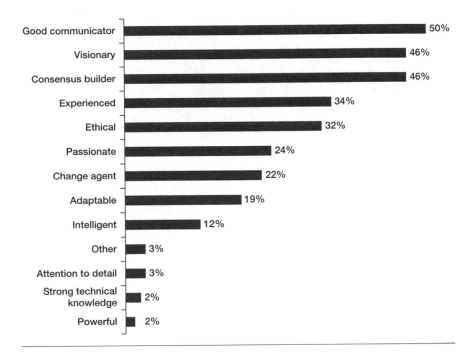

Notes

The opinions expressed in this book are solely those of the authors and not of Deloitte. This book contains general information only, and no person or entity is, by means of this book, rendering accounting, business, financial, investment, legal, tax, or other professional advice or services. This book is not a substitute for such professional advice or services, nor should it be used as a basis for any decision or action that may affect your business. Before making any decision or taking any action that may affect your business, you should consult a qualified professional advisor. Neither the authors nor Deloitte shall be responsible for any loss sustained by any person who relies on this book.

Preface, pages vii–xii

1. W. Henry Lambright, *Powering Apollo: James E. Webb of NASA* (Baltimore: The Johns Hopkins University Press, 1995), 10.

2. President Richard Nixon speech on domestic issues, August 8, 1969, from John T. Woolley and Gerhard Peters, *The American Presidency Project* [online]. Santa Barbara, CA: University of California (hosted), Gerhard Peters (database) at http://www.presidency.ucsb.edu/ws/?pid=2191.

3. President Jimmy Carter speech to the nation, July 15, 1979, from "The American Experience," www.pbs.org.

4. *Charlie Rose* show, May 2, 2008.

5. "Forty years of astronauts, moon craft in the Presidential Inaugural Parade," collect SPACE.com, January 19, 2009. Inaugural parade participants included space veterans from the crew of the shuttle *Endeavour*. The 12-wheeled moon buggy featured in the parade is a prototype of the vehicle NASA is planning to use on its next moon mission, scheduled for the year 2020. President Carter's 1977 inaugural parade featured a NASA public relations employee portraying an astronaut, but no real astronauts.

6. Barack Obama, "Faith in One Another as Americans," *Parade*, July 6, 2008.

Introduction, pages 1–18

1. Most of the technical details regarding the Big Dig ceiling failure were taken from a report of the National Traffic Safety Board, *Ceiling Collapse in the Interstate 90 Connector Tunnel, Boston Massachusetts, July 10, 2006*, Highway Accident Report NTSB/HAR–07/02, July 10, 2007. On October 7, 1999, Modern Continental, the company installing the ceiling, informed Bechtel/Parsons Brinckerhoff (B/PB), the private consortium overseeing the Big Dig, about the bolt slippage problem.

2. Ibid., 47.

3. Ibid., 96–97.

4. Ibid., 46. Tested on November 10, 1999, this bolt (which we have nicknamed the red herring bolt) failed a load test and pulled entirely out of the ceiling. The NTSB cited this finding from a B/PB field report: "Upon examining the pulled-out bolt, it appeared to lack sufficient epoxy to fully fill the drilled hole. Also, there was a significant amount of concrete dust adhered to the epoxy surrounding the bolt, usually an indication that the drilled hole was not completely cleaned out prior to installation. The epoxy nearest to the embedded tip of the bolt was brittle and easily crumbled, usually an indication of improper mixing of resin and hardener. The epoxy near the exposed end of the bolt (but still in the embedded portion) appeared to be fully and properly cured. This would indicate the mixture of resin and hardener was not uniform during the injection of epoxy into the drilled hole. In spite of this combination of installation deficiencies, it appears the bolt was able to develop just enough strength to pass the pull-out [proof load] test. However, after several weeks of constant loading by the ceiling module, the bond was broken, and the bolt began to slip out." The NTSB report does not speculate as to how the discovery of this bolt's multiple flaws influenced the thinking of engineers, but it is reasonable to suppose that the existence of this bolt would support a theory that the installation technique was causing the slippage problem.

5. Ibid., 76: "The accident investigation found no evidence that any inspections had been performed to determine the physical and functional condition of the ceiling system in the D Street portal between the time the tunnel was opened to traffic on January 18, 2003, and the day of the collapse. Nor did records indicate that periodic inspections were performed on any of the ceiling systems in the I-90 connector tunnel." Photographs in the report show bolts visibly slipping out of the roof of the tunnel.

6. The lack of inspections reflects poorly not only on the private contractors, but also on the public oversight provided by the Massachusetts Turnpike Authority; the NTSB report was critical of the performance of a number of project participants.

7. Andrea Estes, "3 Senators Want Big Dig Manager Barred," *Boston Globe*, July 12, 2007.

8. There are ongoing lawsuits attempting to sort out precisely what happened. In December of 2007, Powers Fasteners, the manufacturer of both the Standard Set and Fast Set epoxies, reached a settlement with the Del Valle family for a reported $6 million. As of that time, the Massachusetts attorney general still had an outstanding criminal complaint against the firm. See Megan Woolhouse, "Big Dig Firm, Family Reach $6 Million Accord," *Boston Globe*, December 25, 2007. Certain packaging and branding confusion may have contributed to the misapprehension regarding which epoxy was being used. See NTSB report, *Ceiling Collapse*, 23 and 31–33. Nonetheless, this mystery shouldn't have taken a "Columbo" to solve it, and it shouldn't have taken a fatality for officials to uncover the root cause of the failure.

9. Jonathan Saltzman, "U.S. Attorney's Faulted on Big Dig," *Boston Globe*, December 21, 2007.

10. Michael Levenson and Sean P. Murphy, "Let's Not Allow Another Life to Be Taken; Family, Officials Mourn Victim of Tunnel Accident," *Boston Globe*, July 16, 2006; and Ken McGuire, "Pastor at Victim's Funeral: Fix Big Dig," *Washington Post*, July 15, 2006.

11. NTSB, *Ceiling Collapse*, 14–15: "The suspended ceiling structure in the D Street portal was removed. During subsequent tunnel evaluations, it was determined that, because of the short length of this tunnel section and its proximity to a tunnel opening, the suspended ceiling was not necessary for adequate tunnel ventilation. The ceiling structure was not replaced."

12. In 2006, the law regarding command of the National Guard was changed. At the time of Hurricane Katrina, the governor had full authority of the National Guard during state deployment; the president assumed authority only if the unit was called into federal service. Following the 2007 Defense Authorization Bill, the president can now command National Guard troops during an emergency response. See Kavan Peterson, "Governors Lose in Power Struggle over National Guard," January 12, 2007, http://www.stateline.org/live/details/story?contentId=170453.

13. See Donald F. Kettl, *The Next Government of the United States* (New York: W.W. Norton, 2009), for an excellent treatment of this issue.

14. Ibid., 40.

15. See, for example, U.S. Government Accountability Office, "Medicare: Covert Testing Exposes Weakness in the Durable Medical Equipment Supplier Screening Process," GAO-08-955, July 2008.

16. The initial public reaction to General Marshall's idea was mixed, but over time it came to be viewed favorably.

17. See Stephen Johnson, *The Ghost Map* (New York: Riverhead Books, 2007), for an excellent account of the cholera epidemic.

Chapter 1, pages 19–49

1. You could also believe in the idea's intent, implementability, and instrumentality, but argue that unintended consequences still make it inadvisable ("people will make themselves homeless in order to collect the $500 with no way to discern the true homeless from the scammers").

2. This list includes powers granted not only under the ESA of 1970, but also in subsequent amendments to that act passed in 1971.

3. Robert Higgs, "Nixon's New Economic Plan," *The Freeman*, January 2009.

4. Daniel Yergin and Joseph Stanislaw, "Nixon, Price Controls, and the Gold Standard Excerpt," in *The Commanding Heights: The Battle for the World Economy* (New York: Free Press, 1997), 60–64.

5. Richard Nixon, interview by Frank Gannon, transcript, 1983, University of Georgia media archives, http://www.libs.uga.edu/media/collections/nixon/index.html.

6. Donald Rumsfeld, May 9, 2002, remarks at White House tribute to Milton Friedman, http://www.freetochoosemedia.org/freetochoose/tribute_dhr.php.

7. Statement of Richard Nixon, December 22, 1971, from John T. Woolley and Gerhard Peters, *The American Presidency Project* [online], Santa Barbara, CA: University of California (hosted), Gerhard Peters (database), http://www.presidency.ucsb.edu/ws/?pid=3273.

8. Ibid.

9. Lanny Ebenstein, *Milton Friedman* (New York: Palgrave MacMillan, 2007), 149, 171. Inflation here refers to general inflation, a general rise in prices throughout the economy, as opposed to the rise in the price of one resource based on a change in supply or demand. For example, the price of orange juice may skyrocket due to a freeze in Florida, but that is not general inflation. The phrase attributed to Friedman comes from his *Newsweek* column as cited by Ebenstein.

10. The anti-inflation programs of the 1970s failed because public officials didn't appreciate the power of incentives in driving human behavior. The antipoverty programs of the 1960s failed because public officials in the 1960s didn't appreciate the power of incentives in driving human behavior. There is a pattern. These major, transformational policies attempted to alter human behavior with an imperfect understanding of human beings and an imperfect understanding of the impact of new incentives, and hence resulted in a host of unintended consequences.

11. In 1963, Friedman and colleague Anna Schwartz had published the 800-plus page scholarly work, *A Monetary History of the United States, 1867–1960* (Princeton, NJ: Princeton University Press), which demonstrated through exhaustive analysis the relationship between the money supply and general price inflation.

12. President Gerald Ford, Address to a Joint Session of Congress on the Economy, October 8, 1974, from Gerald R. Ford Presidential Library and Museum, http://www.ford.utexas.edu/LIBRARY/speeches/listkey.htm.

13. U.S. Government Accountability Office, Report to Congressional Committees, *Troubled Asset Relief Program: Status of Efforts to Address Transparency and Accountability Issues*, January 2009, GAO 09-296, 7.

14. Robert J. Samuelson, "Lessons from the Great Inflation," *Reason*, January 2009, 51, 55, http://reason.com/news/show/130352.html.

15. Leo Tolstoy, "The Kingdom of God Is Within You," Chapter III, taken from Wikipedia article on confirmation bias, http://en.wikipedia.org/wiki/Confirmation_bias.

16. Leo Tolstoy, "What Is Art?" taken from Wikipedia article on confirmation bias, http://en.wikipedia.org/wiki/Confirmation_bias.

17. Emory University Health Sciences Center, "Emory Study Lights Up the Political Brain," *Science Daily*, January 31, 2006, http://www.sciencedaily.com/releases/2006/01/060131092225.htm.

18. This treatment of the genesis of our current health care system is incomplete. In addition to wage and price controls, employer guilds and companies aggregated the risk pool by grouping employees, and sometimes used member dues to provide medical care for members.

19. Tim Murphy, interview with the authors, May 19, 2008. All subsequent quotes from Murphy are from the same interview.

20. James Surowiecki's *The Wisdom of Crowds* (New York: Anchor Books, 2005) is an excellent introduction to the phenomenon of collective wisdom.

21. Scott McCartney, "Getting in Line: Fliers Self-Sort at Security," *Wall Street Journal*, May 13, 2008, D1.

22. Ibid.

23. "Inconsistencies, Part 1," Evolution of Security Blog, www.tsa.gov/blog/2008_01_01_archive.html.

24. Stephen Goldsmith, interview with the authors, June 2008.

25. Cited in Jenna Dorn, "Web 2.0: Rebooting the Public Square," *Federal Computer Week*, November 30, 2007, http://fcw.com/Articles/2007/11/30/Web-20-Rebooting-the-public-square.aspx.

26. See http://www.xprize.org.

27. Those forgotten guys were Clarence Chamberlin and Charles Levine, and Charles Levine was actually the world's first trans-Atlantic airplane passenger. For an amusing description, see Herb Geduld, "Charlie Levine and His Flying Machine," *Jewish World Review*, June 29, 1998, http://www.jewishworldreview.com/0698/geduld1.html.

28. Congressional Budget Office, "Federal Support for Research and Development," June 2007, viii.

29. Statement by Vivek Kundra in 2009 online Urban Policy Advisory Group conference, February 23, 2009, attended by authors.

30. Jonah Lehrer, *How We Decide* (New York: Houghton Mifflin Harcourt, 2009), 208–210.

31. Philip Tetlock, *Expert Political Judgment* (Princeton, NJ: Princeton University Press, 2006), 23.

32. Mike Wertheimer, speech at the Deloitte Public Leadership Institute and National Academy of Public Administration conference on Web 2.0, Washington, DC, June 5, 2008.

33. http://www.copenhagenconsensus.com/.

34. Bjørn Lomborg, "How to Think About the World's Problems," *Wall Street Journal*, May 22, 2008, A15.

35. Gary W. Yohe, Richard S. J. Tol, Richard G. Richels, and Geoffrey Blanford, "Global Warming," Copenhagen Consensus Challenge Paper, Copenhagen Consensus Center, April 3, 2008, http://www.copenhagenconsensus.com/Default.aspx?ID=1148.

36. Ronald Bailey, "The Rational Environmentalist," *Reason*, October 2008, 49–50, http://www.reason.com/news/show/128896.html.

37. Deloitte Consulting LLP is a subsidiary of Deloitte LLP. Please see www.deloitte.com/us/about for a detailed description of the legal structure of Deloitte LLP and its subsidiaries.

Chapter 2, pages 51–77

1. Quotes come from a variety of sources, including John Yang, "Elderly Confused by Medicare Prescription Plan," ABC News, November 13, 2005, http://abcnews.go.com/WNT/Health/story?id=1306814; Robert Pear, "Confusion Is Rife About Drug Plan as Sign-Up Nears," *New York Times*, November 13, 2005, http://www.nytimes.com/2005/11/13/national/13drug.html?pagewanted=1&ei=5088&en=11b7be609408995c&ex=1289538000&adxnnl=1&partner=rssnyt&emc=rss&adxnnlx=1184357003-yaRCmpgw8cvbTgp3JqIN9w; Joe Fahy, "Confusion, Frustration Abound as Drug Program Gets Under Way," *Pittsburgh Post-Gazette*, November 6, 2005, http://www.post-gazette.com/pg/05310/600360.stm; and anonymous Medicare benefits counselor, "Special Report on Medicare Part D," March 2006, The Senior Citizens League, http://www.tscl.org/NewContent/102600.asp.

2. For some of the problems that beset the launch, see Julie Rovner, "Problems Plague Rollout of New Medicare Drug Plan," *Morning Edition*, National Public Radio, January 11, 2006, http://www.npr.org/templates/story/story.php?storyId=5148817; and Robert Pear, "Rolls Growing for Drug Plan as Problems Continue," *New York Times*, January 18, 2006, http://www.nytimes.com/2006/01/18/national/18medicare.html?ex=1295240400&en=8fdebaf052b5c3c8&ei=5088&partner=rssnyt&emc=rss. The Harrington quotes are from interviews with the authors.

3. Christian Berthelsen, "Genesis of State's Energy Fiasco: String of Bad Decisions on Deregulation Could End Up Costing Consumers $40 Billion," *San Francisco Chronicle*, December 31, 2000, http://www.sfgate.com/cgi-bin/article.cgi?file=/chronicle/archive/2000/12/31/MN167927.DTL. This includes the $23 billion already paid by customers when rates were frozen at artificially high levels, the $7.5 billion in bonds financing consumers' own rate reduction, and the share of the $11 billion in debt that state utility regulators decided customers should pay.

4. See Jerry Taylor and Peter Van Doren, "California's Electricity Crisis: What's Going on, Who's to Blame, and What to Do," Cato Institute Policy Analysis 406, July 3, 2001; and James Walsh, *The $10 Billion Jolt: California's Energy Crisis: Cowardice, Greed, Stupidity and the Death of Deregulation* (Los Angeles:

Silver Lake Publishing, 2002), 32. Also, W. Pinkston, "Rival States Pitch Power to Woo California Firms," *Wall Street Journal*, January 26, 2001, A4, cited in remarks by Daniel William Fessler at the Fourteenth Annual Utility M&A Symposium, New York City, January 29, 2001.

    5. Walsh, *The $10 Billion Jolt*, 37.

    6. Congressional Budget Office, "Causes and Lessons of the California Electricity Crisis," September 2001, http://www.cbo.gov/ftpdoc.cfm?index=3062&type=0.

    7. Technically, there was no legal cap on competitive electricity prices in the retail market; there was only a cap on the prices the regulated electric utilities could charge for their "provider of last resort" (POLR) services" to retail. The outcome was effectively a cap. Once market prices went above the POLR cap no one would buy from the "marketers," and markets collapsed. The rules were established with the expectation that, since the utilities would need to provide only a small amount of retail electricity to a few "holdout" customers on POLR, the utilities would not need to buy much power. Thus they would not "need" long-term contracts, and they were required to buy on the daily market for their anticipated "limited" needs. These provisions worked for the year in which wholesale prices were below that estimated in the utilities POLR costs because the combination of competitive wholesale electricity prices plus transmission and distribution delivery charges were below POLR. When the wholesale market shot up, everyone with sense switched off POLR and went to the lower POLR prices, which were frozen. As the utilities had no generation, they bought on the rising wholesale market to meet their POLR obligations (now near 100% of the market) and sold at the low POLR prices. Did we mention this could get complicated? Thanks to Branko Terzic for providing this explanation to the authors—any errors remain the authors.

    8. Rachel Gordon and Marianne Costantinou, "Breeze Eases Killer Heat," *San Francisco Examiner*, June 15, 2000, http://www.sfgate.com/cgi-bin/article.cgi?f=/e/a/2000/06/15/NEWS6539.dtl&hw=rolling+blackout&sn=005&sc=866.

    9. Henry Norr, "Searing Heat Tests PG&E Limits," *San Francisco Chronicle*, June 15, 2000, http://www.sfgate.com/cgi-bin/article.cgi?f=/c/a/2000/06/15/MN23394.DTL&hw=rolling+blackout&sn=006&sc=838.

    10. Sarah, age 17, "Losing Power in California," posted on NewsHour Extra, a *NewsHour with Jim Lehrer* Special for Students, January 24, 2001, http://www.pbs.org/newshour/extra/speakout/mystory/power.html.

    11. Janet Kornblum and Jonathan Weisman, "Few Prepared for Outages in Calif.," *USAToday.com*, January 18, 2001, http://www.usatoday.com/news/2001-01-17-blackouts.htm.

    12. The wholesale market in California at this time was fully regulated by the FERC, which could have stepped in at any time to establish caps and floors, and close down the market.

    13. Chi-Keung Woo, "What Went Wrong in California's Electricity Market?" published on GenEnergy Web site, February 5, 2001, www.genenergy.com.

    14. Interview with David Freeman from *Enron: The Smartest Guys in the Room*, Magnolia Pictures, 2005.

    15. Mark Martin, "'Smoking Gun' Enron Memos," *San Francisco Chronicle*, May 7, 2002, A1.

    16. Tapes from *Enron: The Smartest Guys in the Room*.

    17. Interview with Charles Wickham from *Enron: The Smartest Guys in the Room*.

    18. Branko Terzic, interview with the authors, September 2007.

    19. Tamar Lewin, "I.R.S. Sees Evidence of Wide Tax Cheating on Child Care," *New York Times*, January 6, 1991.

    20. Berthelsen, "Genesis of State's Energy Fiasco."

    21. As James Walsh points out, the main problem with the California plan was that the deregulation was incomplete: "The market wasn't totally free. State-regulated utilities were ordered to sell their plants and forbidden to enter into long-term contracts that could hedge against sudden price fluctuations. These same utilities had price caps on what they could charge customers, so that they couldn't pass the higher fuel costs on to customers" (*The $10 Billion Jolt*, 35).

    22. John Simerman, "Wilson Says Idea Was Right; California Power 'Deregulation,'" *Contra Costa Times*, April 15, 2001, http://www.freerepublic.com/forum/a3ad9afe16367.htm.

    23. Severin Borenstein, interview with the authors, July 2007.

    24. Simerman, "Wilson Says Idea Was Right."

    25. Walsh, *The $10 Billion Jolt*, 33.

    26. The first two steps are all about really understanding the market, the problem, and customers through in-depth user observation. This means going beyond surveys and time-worn focus groups and

getting out there and interacting with customers and partners in real-life situations. The third step, envision, means visualizing a better future by encouraging wild ideas and making lots of rough prototypes.

27. Peter Coughlin, interview with the authors, March 31, 2008.

28. Tim Brown, "Strategy by Design," *Fast Company*, June 2005, 54.

29. "Introduction to Shell Global Scenarios to 2025," http://www.shell.com/home/content/aboutshell-en/our_strategy/shell_global_scenarios/ceo_introduction/scenarios_2025_introduction_ceo_3010 2006.html.

30. PBS *Frontline*, "Blackout," transcript from interview with Loretta Lynch, April 1, 2001, http://www.pbs.org/wgbh/pages/frontline/shows/blackout/interviews/lynch.html.

31. Ron Haskins, interview with the authors, March 5, 2009.

32. Ms. Spelling appeared on *NewsHour with Jim Lehrer*, August 14, 2007. Her full quote is: "Are some kids being left behind? You bet. Are some people gaming the system, and we ought to be watchful about that and . . . and hawkish about it? You bet. And that's . . . you know, we do our very best to do that." Illinois test data taken from the John Merrow Report on that same show.

33. "Black America: Nearer to Overcoming," *The Economist*, May 8, 2008, http://www.economist.com/world/unitedstates/displaystory.cfm?story_id=11326407.

Chapter 3, pages 79–105

1. J. Anthony Lukas, *Common Ground: A Turbulent Decade in the Lives of Three American Families* (New York: Vintage, 1986), 239–241.

2. Ibid., 239.

3. Ibid., 240. As Lukas put it: "By stressing his ignorance of the details, Garrity seemed to be saying, 'If, as some predict, this plan causes violence in the fall, don't blame me.'" Garrity did give the Boston School Committee an opportunity to propose an alternative remedy during the summer, but this offer—to a committee steadfast in its opposition to forced busing—was declined and, given the time line, the offer was more symbolic than anything since it had little realistic chance of being accepted. Judge Garrity had the authority to delay implementation until September 1975, but chose instead to take the "best plan available"—indeed, the only plan available.

4. Ibid., 606.

5. Mathew Richer, "Boston's Busing Massacre," *Policy Review*, November/December 1998.

6. Ibid.

7. John W. Kingdon, *Agendas, Alternatives, and Public Policies* (Boston: Little Brown, 1984).

8. Rick Hampson, Dennis Cauchon, and Paul Overberg, "Officials See New Urgency to Improve USA's Bridges," *USA Today*, August 2, 2007, updated August 6, 2007, http://www.usatoday.com/news/nation/2007-08-02-bridge-cover_N.htm.

9. National Commission on Excellence in Education, "A Nation at Risk: The Imperative for Educational Reform," April 1983, http://www.ed.gov/pubs/NatAtRisk/index.html.

10. U.S. Environmental Protection Agency, "Acid Rain," http://www.epa.gov/acidrain/index.html.

11. Kathy McCauley, Bruce Barron, and Morton Coleman, "Crossing the Aisle to Cleaner Air: How the Bipartisan 'Project 88' Transformed Environmental Policy," University of Pittsburgh Institute of Politics, 2008, 7–8.

12. Ibid., 7.

13. Ibid., 27.

14. Ibid.

15. Senator Tim Wirth, interview with the authors, March 2009.

16. McCauley, Barron, Coleman, "Crossing the Aisle to Cleaner Air," 11.

17. Ibid.

18. Robert Stavins, interview with the authors, March 2009.

19. U.S. Environmental Protection Agency, "EPA Clean Air Markets: About the Acid Rain Program," http://www.epa.gov/airmarkt/progsregs/arp/basic.html.

20. D. Ellerman, P. L. Joskow, R. Schmalensee, et al., *Markets for Clean Air: The U.S. Acid Rain Program* (Cambridge, MA: Cambridge University Press, 2000), 1. The program's establishing rule was promulgated in 1995; it consisted of two phases. Phase I, spanning 1995 to 1999, capped emissions on power plants generating more than 100 megawatts; Phase II, starting in 2000 and continuing indefinitely, caps emissions on power plants generating at least 25 megawatts of power.

21. McCauley, Barron, Coleman, "Crossing the Aisle to Cleaner Air," 9.

22. Ibid., 16–17.

23. Senator Tim Wirth, interview with the authors, March 2009.

24. McCauley, Barron, Coleman, "Crossing the Aisle to Cleaner Air," 29.

25. Ibid.

26. Ellerman, Joskow, Schmalensee, *Markets for Clean Air*.

27. Juan Pablo Montero, "Voluntary Compliance with Market-Based Environmental Policy: Evidence from the U.S. Acid Rain Program," *Journal of Political Economy* 107, no. 9, 1999.

28. McCauley, Barron, Coleman, "Crossing the Aisle to Cleaner Air," 33.

29. Lauraine G. Chestnut and David M. Mills, "A Fresh Look at the Benefits and Costs of the U.S. Acid Rain Program," *Journal of Environmental Management* 77, no. 3, May 2005. Also see McCauley, Barron, Coleman, "Crossing the Aisle to Cleaner Air," 34.

30. Isao Iijima, "Secret Memoirs from the Koizumi Cabinet," *Nikkei Shimbun*, December 8, 2006.

31. "Prime Minister Koizumi's Political Drama Drew Cheers, Boos," *Knight Ridder Tribune Business News*, September 18, 2006, 1.

32. The idea of postal privatization was not unique to Japan. It had been implemented successfully and unsuccessfully in other countries such as Germany and New Zealand. In Germany, the privatized postal service, Deutsche Post, successfully extended its business internationally and multilaterally. Conversely, New Zealand's attempt at privatization led to harsh criticism of the savings department for degradation in its customer service and returned to being a state-owned organization.

33. His zeal for economic reform in fact was a big reason why he was elected prime minister. After a decade of stagnant economic growth in the country, the Japanese public finally seemed ready for strong medicine, and Koizumi was just the man to administer it.

34. Amelia Porges and Joy M. Leong, "The Privatization of Japan Post," special section on Japan's economy, *The Economist*, September 27, 2007.

35. Ibid.

36. The "postal tribe" (*yusei zoku*) is the group of politicians within the LDP that controlled the policies and budget related to postal and postal banking services.

37. He did this by establishing the Council on Economic and Fiscal Policy (CEFP), a derivative under the Cabinet office established in January 2001 as a part of the central government reform started by Prime Minister Hashimoto. The gambit eventually paid off when on September 10, 2004, the Cabinet adopted the CEFP's basic policy proposal of splitting and privatizing the state-run Japan Post into four units, effective in 2007; see http://www.keizai-shimon.go.jp/english/about/index.html#deliberation.

38. *International Herald Tribune*, September 28, 2004.

39. *The Asahi Shimbun*, Tokyo, Japan, September 29, 2004, http://www.asahi.com/english/.

40. The prime minister's official Web site, January 2005, http://www.kantei.go.jp/jp/koizumispeech/2005/01/21sisei.html.

41. "Koizumi Dismissals Stir Up Kasumigaseki," *Japan Times*, June 3, 2005, http://search.japantimes.co.jp/cgi-bin/nn20050603b1.html.

42. This right is authorized by Article 68 of the Constitution. The prime minister shall appoint the ministers of state. However, a majority of their number must be chosen from among the members of the Diet. The prime minister may remove the ministers of state as he chooses.

43. Iijima, "Secret Memoirs from the Koizumi Cabinet."

44. "The Lower House," July 2005, http://www.shugiin.go.jp/index.nsf/html/index_honkai.htm.

45. *Nikkei*, August 6, 2005.

46. The Upper House, August 2005, http://www.sangiin.go.jp/japanese/frameset/fset_b04_01.htm.

47. *Nikkei*, August 15, 2005.

48. Prime Minister Koizumi, press conference, August 5, 2005.

49. Jim Frederick, "Koizumi's War," *Time Asia*, September 5, 2005, http://www.time.com/time/asia/2005/koizumi/story2.html.

50. "Wrapup," *Japundit*, September 13, 2005, www.japundit.com/archives/2005/09/13/1180/.

51. Ministry of Internal Affairs and Communications, September 2005, http://www.soumu.go.jp/senkyo/senkyo_s/data/shugiin44/index.html.

52. The Lower House, October 2005, http://www.shugiin.go.jp/index.nsf/html/index_honkai.htm.

53. The Upper House, October 2005, http://www.sangiin.go.jp/japanese/frameset/fset_b04_01.htm.

54. Anthony Failoa, "Japan Approves Postal Privatization," *Washington Post*, October 15, 2005, A10.

55. Congressman Davis is now a colleague of Mr. Eggers in his position as a director at Deloitte Consulting. Unless otherwise noted, all quotes are from conversations with the authors February–April 2009.

56. Peter Baker, "Tom Davis Gives Up," *New York Times Magazine*, October 5, 2008, http://www.nytimes.com/2008/10/05/magazine/05Davis-t.html?fta=y.

57. Ibid.

58. See "Action in Tonkin Gulf," *Time*, August 14, 1964, which cites the Pentagon statements quoted.

59. See Marc Selverstone and David Coleman, "Gulf of Tonkin, 1964: Perspectives from the Lyndon Johnson and National Military Command Center Tapes," Miller Center for Public Affairs, University of Virginia, Tape WH 6409.03, citation #4632, http://tapes.millercenter.virginia.edu/exhibit/gulf-tonkin-1964-perspectives-lyndon-johnson-and-national-military-command-center-tapes.

60. See the declassified article by Robert J. Hanyok, "Skunks, Bogies, Silent Hounds and Flying Fish," declassified by the National Security Agency November 3, 2005, http://www.nsa.gov/public_info/_files/gulf_of_tonkin/articles/rel1_skunks_bogies.pdf. The article dissects in detail how errors in analyzing intercepted signal data contributed to a false official description of events. Interestingly, the article cites as the root cause of these errors the Tolstoy syndrome (though it doesn't use that term), describing how NSA officials selected evidence that supported the attack theory and discarded disconfirming evidence. The article's author notes: "The NSA personnel in the crisis center who reported the second Gulf of Tonkin incident believed that it had occurred. The problem for them was the SIGINT evidence. The evidence that supported the contention that an attack had occurred was scarce and nowhere as strong as would have been wanted. The overwhelming body of reports, if used, would have told the story that no attack had happened. So a conscious effort ensued to demonstrate that the attack occurred."

61. David E. Sanger, "New Tapes Indicate Johnson Doubted Attack in Tonkin Gulf," *New York Times*, November 6, 2001.

62. *Congressional Record*, 88th Congress 2nd session, August 6–7, 1964, 18132-33, 18406-7, 18458-59, and 18470-71.

63. Hanyok, "Skunks, Bogies, Silent Hounds and Flying Fish."

64. Barry Machado, *In Search of a Usable Past: The Marshall Plan and Postwar Reconstruction Today* (Washington, DC: George C. Marshall Foundation, 2007), ch. 3.

Chapter 4, pages 107–134

1. Ken Livingstone, interview with the authors, December 12, 2007. Except where noted otherwise, all subsequent quotes from Livingstone are from the same interview.

2. "Randy Pausch Last Lecture: Achieving Your Childhood Dreams," http://www.youtube.com/watch?v=ji5_MqicxSo.

3. The article by Garrett Hardin, "The Tragedy of the Commons," *Science*, December 13, 1968, was an important exploration of the concept and helped popularize the term.

4. For more than you probably want to know about the rules for grazing cows in 17th century England, see Susan Jane Buck Cox, "No Tragedy on the Commons," *Environmental Ethics* 7, Spring 1985.

5. William Vickrey, "Pricing in Urban and Suburban Transport," *American Economic Review* 53, no. 2 (1963): 452–465.

6. In 1975, Singapore began charging for the right to enter a 2.3-square-mile zone covering the city's busiest central area during morning peak hours. The system used a paper decal displayed on the windshield that drivers could buy for about $1 a day (in 1975 dollars). Observers at twenty-two roads leading into the central area enforced the scheme by noting the plate numbers of violators. The Singapore program is still in existence and now employs electronic tolling instead of paper decals.

7. Martina Smit, "Congestion Charges Explained," BBC News, February 26, 2002, http://news.bbc.co.uk/1/hi/uk/1841869.stm.

8. Anonymous member of ROCOL group, interview with the authors, December 13, 2007.

9. Livingstone had been a stalwart of the Labour Party, but when the party selected someone else to be its candidate for mayor in 2000, he decided to run as an independent and was promptly kicked out of the Labour Party. As a man without a party, Livingstone was politically isolated and considered a long shot to win.

10. According to Transport for London, 43 percent of Londoners opposed congestion charging and 38 percent supported it. The rest were neutral.

11. Derek Turner, interview with the authors, December 2007. Unless noted otherwise, all subsequent quotes from Derek Turner are from the same interview.

12. One of the book's authors, William D. Eggers, is a director at Deloitte LLP in the United States, but was not involved in the London congestion pricing project.

13. Simon Burton, interview with the authors, December 6, 2007. All subsequent quotes from Simon Burton are from the same interview.

14. In fact, London First played a lead role in pulling together the ROCOL report.

15. Harry Mills, *Artful Persuasion* (New York: AMACOM, 2000), 22.

16. Installing the infrastructure required coordinating myriad work streams: when the camera installers showed up, the utilities had to make sure that they had power and the local authorities had provided the right permits. Enforcement systems also had to be developed. TfL had to be able to issue penalty charge notices, hear appeals, consider representations, take offenders to court to enforce against nonpayers, and tow away repeat evaders' vehicles. A call center and other customer services had to be set up to answer motorist queries and take payments by telephone, text messages, and the Web or through retail outlets such as shops and gas stations. Road works had to be carried out so they would not disrupt London traffic but also would be completed with enough time to allow for testing.

17. Linda Swinburne, interview with the authors, December 2007. All subsequent quotes from Linda Swinburne are from this interview.

18. Deloitte refers to a member firm of Deloitte Touche Tohmatsu, a Swiss Verein, and its network of member firms, each of which is a legally separate and independent entity. Please see www.deloitte.com/about for a detailed description of the legal structure of Deloitte Touche Tohmatsu and its member firms.

19. Brian Green, interview with the authors, December 2007.

20. Elaine Galloway, "Congestion Chaos Exposed," *Evening Standard*, February 12, 2003.

21. Ivor Gaber, "The Great Traffic Light Conspiracy," *New Statesman*, May 17, 2004.

22. Luke Blair, interview with the authors, March 7, 2008.

23. This fortunately did not happen. It turns out the combination of the doomsday warnings from the press and Mayor Ken Livingstone's admonition to drivers to stay away from central London if possible on day one had so spooked motorists that the first week of the scheme saw an artificially low number of motorists.

24. Interview with former TfL manager.

25. "Ken Leads the Charge," *The Economist*, February 20, 2003.

26. The reductions in traffic congestion were larger—over 20 percent—in the earlier years of the charge. These gains were eroded by a series of policy decisions, such as adding bike lanes, that removed capacity from the London road network.

27. Jonathan Leape, "The London Congestion Charge," *Journal of Economic Perspectives* 20, no. 4 (Fall 2006): 165.

28. Transport for London, September 2008.

29. This includes the increased revenues from the 2007 Western Extension of the charge.

30. Mark Pothier, "A Beautiful Place to Die," *Boston Globe*, August 17, 2008.

31. Thomas Ricks, *Fiasco: The American Military Misadventure in Iraq* (New York: Penguin Press, 2006), 97–98.

32. The material on the National Defense University meeting and the removal of Warrick and O'Sullivan is from Ricks, *Fiasco*, 100–104, as well as the transcript of the interview with Thomas Ricks, PBS *Frontline* Web site, June 28, 2006, www.pbs.org/wgbh/pages/frontline/yeariniraq/interviews/ricks.html.

33. PBS *Frontline* Web site, transcript of interview with Thomas Ricks. An in-depth look into the details of post-war Iraq can be found in Ricks, *Fiasco*.

34. PBS *Frontline* Web site, transcript of interview with James Dobbins, June 27, 2006, www.pbs.org/wgbh/pages/frontline/yeariniraq/interviews/dobbins.html.

35. http://en.wikipedia.org/wiki/National_Museum_of_Iraq.

36. Roger Cohen, "The Ghost in the Baghdad Museum, *New York Times*, April 2, 2006.

37. *Charlie Rose* Show, May 2, 2008.

38. Ricks, *Fiasco*, 179.

Chapter 5, pages 135–166

1. Charles Taylor Kerchner, "Politics May Still Save the LA Schools," *Education Next* 7, no. 3 (Summer 2007).

2. Howard Blume, "The Best School Board Money Can Buy," *Los Angeles Times*, April 15, 1999.

3. Rick Young, "The Outcome of the Rampart Scandal Investigations," PBS *Frontline*, "LAPD Blues."

4. LAPD official Web site, crime statistics summary.

5. Michael Keeley, interview with the authors, quoted from a previous book by the authors, *Revolution at the Roots* (New York: Free Press, 1995), 150.

6. Howard Blume, "Dorsey High Rejects Aid from Riordan Group," *Los Angeles Times*, October 15, 2008.

7. Terry Moe, "Put to the Test," *Stanford Magazine*, July/August 2006.

8. One of the best books to explore the role of cultural attitudes in assessing the performance of different government agencies is *Government Matters: Welfare Reform in Wisconsin* (Princeton, NJ: Princeton University Press, 2004), by Larry Mead. In the book Mead argues quite persuasively, using extensive data, that the biggest determinant of the states that were the most successful in welfare reform was the presence of "moralistic" cultures in which state leaders were expected to explain their actions on behalf of constituents in terms of the general public interest as opposed to more narrow parochial interests.

9. Daniel J. Elazar, *A View from the States*, 3rd ed. (New York: Harper & Row, 1984), 134–137.

10. "Lt. Colonel John Nagel," *The Daily Show with Jon Stewart*, August 23, 2008, http://www.thedailyshow.com/video/index.jhtml?videoId=92011&title=lt.-col.-john-nagl.

11. Anonymous input from reviewer, modified for grammatical context.

12. Thomas A. Schweich, "Generation No," *New York Times*, December 11, 2008, http://www.nytimes.com/2008/12/12/opinion/12schweich.html?_r=1.

13. Anne Webber, "The Short, Strange Political Life of Craig Benson," *The Wire*, January 5, 2005.

14. Anonymous interview with authors.

15. Dwight Ink, "Twenty-first Century Career Leaders," chapter in *Transformational Trends in Governance and Democracy*. eds. Ricardo S. Morse, Terry F. Buss, C. Morgan Kinghorn (Washington, DC: National Academy of Public Administration and M. E. Sharpe, 2007).

16. W. Henry Lambright, *Powering Apollo* (Baltimore: Johns Hopkins University Press, 1995), 95.

17. *New York Times*, July 25, 1959, edited transcript. Available from Turner Learning at: http://cgi.turnerlearning.com/cnn/coldwar/sputnik/sput_re4.html.

18. "We Will Bury You," *Time*, November 26, 1956.

19. Lambright, *Powering Apollo*, 93.

20. James Reston, "Down and Up," *Time*, May 12, 1961, http://www.time.com/time/magazine/article/0,9171,869893,00.html.

21. Special Message to the Congress on Urgent National Needs, delivered by President John F. Kennedy to a joint session of Congress, May 25, 1961, http://www.jfklibrary.org.

22. Lambright, *Powering Apollo*, 101.

23. Ibid., 2.

24. See Patricia Sullivan, "Walter Schirra, Fifth Astronaut in Space," *Washington Post*, May 4, 2007. Variations on this comment have been attributed to many other astronauts as well.

25. Webb and NASA came under attack from Walter Mondale, at that time the junior senator from Minnesota. Senior NASA official George Mueller noted that NASA "probably spent more time on it per unit information gained for doing better in the future by several orders of magnitude than on a whole host of other things that really made it possible to do the program." From NASA web site, edited excerpts from three interviews conducted with Dr. George E. Mueller. Interview #1 was conducted by Robert Sherrod on April 21, 1971, while Dr. Mueller was vice president of General Dynamics. Interview #2 was conducted by Sherrod on March 20, 1973, while Dr. Mueller was president

of System Development Corporation. Interview #3 was conducted on August 27, 1998, by Summer Chick Bergen and assisted by Carol Butler of the Johnson Space Center Oral History Project, from http://history.nasa.gov/SP-4223/ch5.htm#n.

26. From radio show "Washington Goes to the Moon," cited in transcript of interview with Walter Mondale, WAMU radio, May 1, 2001, at http://wamu.org/d/programs/special/moon/mondale.txt.

27. NAPA helped support the research and writing of this book.

28. *NASA: Balancing a Multisector Workforce to Achieve a Healthy Organization*, report of a panel of the National Academy of Public Administration, February 2007.

29. Ibid.

30. Admiral James Loy, interview with the authors, January 22, 2008.

31. Nathan Thornburgh, "The Mess at Ground Zero," *Time*, July 1, 2008.

32. Paul Pastorek, interview with the authors, October 16, 2008.

33. Franklin D. Roosevelt, State of the Union Address, January 4, 1935, from John T. Woolley and Gerhard Peters, *The American Presidency Project* [online]. Santa Barbara, CA: University of California (hosted), Gerhard Peters (database). Available at http://www.presidency.ucsb.edu/ws/?pid=14890.

34. Daniel P. Moynihan, *The Politics of a Guaranteed Income* (New York: Random House, 1973), 443.

35. Nixon's address to the nation on domestic issues, August 8, 1969, from John T. Woolley and Gerhard Peters, *The American Presidency Project* [online], Santa Barbara, CA: University of California (hosted), Gerhard Peters (database), http://www.presidency.ucsb.edu/ws/?pid=2191.

36. Cited in Arianna Huffington, "Where Liberals Fear to Tread," August 26, 1996, at http://www.arianaonline.com/columns/files/082696.html.

37. Cited in "Welfare as They Know It," *Wall Street Journal*, August 29, 2001, A14.

38. Center on Budget and Policy Priorities, "Urban Institute Study Confirms That Welfare Bills Would Increase Child Poverty," July 26, 1996.

39. Larry Mead, *Government Matters: Welfare Reform in Wisconsin* (Princeton, NJ: Princeton University Press, 2004), 3–6.

40. Ibid., 229.

41. Ibid., 2

42. Fast Stream is a service within the Cabinet Office that focuses on attracting and retaining top talent for Senior Civil Service careers. Not only are Fast Streamers heavily engaged in high-profile projects within their departments, they also are eligible for priority hiring in other departments and agencies, as well as endorsed among European and international partners.

Chapter 6, pages 167–195

1. All quotes from Mickey Landry are from an interview with the authors, November 4, 2008.

2. Joseph Berger, "A Post-Katrina Charter School in New Orleans Gets a Second Chance," *New York Times*, October 17, 2007.

3. Paul Vallas, interview with the authors, October 16, 2008. *Pretzel Logic* was a Steely Dan album from 1974.

4. Sarah Carr, *Times Picayune*, June 9, 2008.

5. Anonymous, interview with the authors, October 16, 2008.

6. Pre-Katrina, only 26 percent of Orleans Parish public school children achieved "basic" scores in English. By 2008, the figure was up to 36 percent. Dawn Ruth, "Breaking the Mold," *New Orleans Magazine*, December 2008.

7. Marcia Slacum Greene, "Familiar Territory for New Leader," *The Washington Post*, November 16, 1996, A1.

8. Resignation letter of Julius W. Becton, April 14, 1998, from DCWatch.com http://www.dcwatch.com/schools/ps980414.htm.

9. Bob Levey, "Q&A with Julius Becton," April 14, 1998, "Levey Live" WashingtonPost.com on-line interview from http://discuss.washingtonpost.com/wp-srv/zforum/levey/bob0414.htm.

10. The full Peter Drucker quote is: "Every agency, every policy, every program, every activity, should be confronted with these questions: 'What is your mission?' 'Is it still the right mission?' 'Is it still worth doing?' 'If we were not already doing this, would we now go into it?' This questioning has been done often enough in all kinds of organizations—businesses, hospitals, churches, and even local

governments—that we know it works. The overall answer is almost never 'This is fine as it stands; let's keep on.' But in some—indeed, a good many—areas the answer to the last question is 'Yes, we would go into this again, but with some changes. We have learned a few things.'" See Peter F. Drucker, "Really Reinventing Government," *The Atlantic*, February 1995.

11. Charles Jencks, *New Paradigm in Architecture: The Language of Post-Modernism* (New Haven: Yale University Press, 2002), 9.

12. The story of Pruitt-Igoe can be found in numerous sources. For a good description of the interplay of architecture and function at Pruitt-Igoe, see James Bailey, "The Case History of a Failure," *Architectural Forum*, December 1965.

13. Craig Barnes, interview with the authors, August 2008.

14. Richard H. Thaler and Cass R. Sunstein, *Nudge* (New Haven: Yale University Press, 2008).

15. Texas Sunset Advisory Commission, *Guide to the Texas Sunset Process* (Austin, TX: January 2006).

16. Interview with Tim Graves, former Sunset staff member, Texas Sunset Advisory Commission, January 25, 2008.

17. Saralee Tiede and Kathy Shwiff, "Industries Facing Sunset Review Step Up Lobbying and Donations," *Dallas Times-Herald*, December 2, 1982.

18. "Sunset Holds Reins on State Bureaucracy," *San Antonio Express-News*, June 19, 1983. Felton West and Fred Bonavita, "Sunset Review Process Made Important Changes Possible," *Houston Post*, June 26, 1983.

19. John Edwards, "Sunset Commission Readies to Shine Light on Three Powerful Regulatory Agencies," *Austin Press*, November 11, 1981.

20. West and Bonavita, "Sunset Review Process Made Important Changes Possible."

21. Ibid.

22. The agency's duties were subsequently incorporated into a division of the Office of the Governor. Sunset Advisory Commission, *Sunset Commission Report to the 78th Legislature on the Department of Economic Development*, Austin, TX, February 2003.

23. Thirty-three agencies were abolished outright and twenty-one were abolished with some functions transferred elsewhere.

24. Craig Barnes, interview with the authors, August 2008.

25. The Air Control Board is now part of the Texas Commission on Environmental Quality.

26. Ken Levine, interview with the authors, December 10, 2008.

27. Representative Carl Isett, interview with the authors, June 2008.

28. William P. O'Brien, "Reality and Illusion: The White House and Harry S. Truman," *White House History* 5 (Spring 1999): 6.

29. Robert Breeden, "The Truman Renovation," *White House History* 5 (Spring 1999), www.whitehousehistory.org/whha_press/press_archives/whha_archives-whitehousehistory-5.pdf.

30. Ronald C. Moe, *The Hoover Commissions Revisited* (Boulder: Westview Press, 1982), 25.

31. Senate Republican Conference, "Pick Up the Challenge: II," *Senate Majority News*, October 22, 1948.

32. Robert J. Donovan, *Joe Martin: My First Fifty Years in Politics* (New York: McGraw-Hill, 1960), 191.

33. Peri E. Arnold, *Making the Managerial Presidency: Comprehensive Reorganization Planning, 1905–1996* (Lawrence, KS: University of Kansas Press, 2007), 143.

34. Amity Shlaes, *The Forgotten Man: A New History of the Great Depression* (New York: Harper-Collins, 2007), 28.

35. Ibid., 30.

36. Ibid., 45.

37. Heady Ferrel, "The Operation of a Mixed Commission," *The American Political Science Review* 43, no. 5 (Oct. 1949): 940–952.

38. William E. Pemberton, "Truman and the Hoover Commission," *Whistle Stop* 19, no. 3 (1991), http://www.trumanlibrary.org/hoover/commission.htm.

39. Arnold Schwarzenegger, "Text of Schwarzenegger's Remarks," SignOnSanDiego.com by the *Union-Tribune*, October 8, 2003, http://www.signonsandiego.com/news/politics/recall/20031008-0049-ca-recall-schwarzeneggerremarks.html.

40. John M. Broder, "Schwarzenegger Calls Budget Opponents 'Girlie Men,'" *New York Times*, July 19, 2004, http://query.nytimes.com/gst/fullpage.html?res=9506E1DC133AF93AA25754C0 A9629C8B63.

41. Governor Schwarzenegger's State of the State Address, January 6, 2004, http://gov.ca.gov/speech/3085/.

42. Ibid.

43. Sally Ride, interview with the authors, December 2, 2008. Unless noted otherwise, all statements by Ride are from this interview. Among her numerous roles, Ms. Ride serves as Chair of Deloitte LLP's external Council for the Advancement and Retention of Women, where one of the authors is employed. Please see www.deloitte.com/us/about for a detailed description of the legal structure of Deloitte LLP and its subsidiaries.

44. Rogers Commission, *Report of the Presidential Commission on the Space Shuttle Challenger Accident*, Volume 1, 96, http://history.nasa.gov/rogersrep/v1ch2.htm.

45. Ibid., 93.

46. Ibid., 104.

47. Sally Ride, "Cold Comfort," *Government Technology*, August 8, 2007, http://www.govtech.com/gt/128090.

48. Timothy Curry and Lynn Shibut, "The Cost of the Savings and Loan Crisis: Truth and Consequences," *FDIC Banking Review*, December 2000, http://www.fdic.gov/bank/analytical/banking/2000dec/brv13n2_2.pdf.

Chapter 7, pages 197–218

1. Samuel Bodman, "Establishing a Comprehensive Energy Plan," *Vital Speeches of the Day* 71, no. 21 (August 15, 2005): 642.

2. Ibid.

3. There is a legitimate reason to note the legislative accomplishment of signing a bill. Rather than celebrating the hoped-for results, however, it would be more appropriate to acknowledge the hard work that went into the bill's passage and to set the stage for the hard work of implementation to follow.

4. Donald L. Barlett, James B. Steele, Laura Karmatz, Eric Roston, and Joan Levinstein, "The New Energy Crisis," *Time*, July 21, 2003, 36.

5. Richard Nixon, "1974 State of the Union Address," The American Presidency Project, http://www.presidency.ucsb.edu/ws/index.php?pid=4327.

6. Robyn Kenney, "Energy Policy and Conservation Act of 1975, United States," The Encyclopedia of Earth, http://www.eoearth.org/article/Energy_Policy_and_Conservation_Act_of_1975,_United_States.

7. Barlett, Steele, Karmatz, Roston, Levinstein, "The New Energy Crisis."

8. U.S. Department of Energy, "Energy Timeline, from 1971–1980," http://www.energy.gov/about/timeline1971-1980.htm.

9. Jimmy Carter, "Energy Security Act Remarks on Signing S. 952 into Law," June 30, 1980, The American Presidency Project, http://www.presidency.ucsb.edu/ws/index.php?pid=44684.

10. Barlett, Steele, Karmatz, Roston, Levinstein, "The New Energy Crisis."

11. This law, which provided $3.2 billion in spending authorizations, included incentives for producing energy from renewable sources; easier licensing for commercial nuclear plants; mandatory efficiency requirements for lighting, electric motors, and other equipment; requirements to boost the use of nonpetroleum auto fuels; plans for new research programs at the Department of Energy; new programs to reduce greenhouse gases; and programs to investigate the health effects of electromagnetic fields. "President Signs Energy Bill: Energy Policy Act of 1992 Will Reduce Oil Imports by One-third by 2010," *Science News*, November 21, 1992, at bnet.com, http://findarticles.com/p/articles/mi_m1200/is_n21_v142/ai_12940385. "The Energy Policy Act of 1992: A Budgetary Perspective," Congressional Budget Office staff memorandum, December 1992, http://www.cbo.gov/ftpdocs/62xx/doc6218/doc03a.pdf.

12. George H. W. Bush, "Remarks on Signing the Energy Policy Act of 1992 in Maurice, Louisiana," October 24, 1992, The American Presidency Project, http://www.presidency.ucsb.edu/ws/index.php?pid=21652.

13. Y. Borg and C. K. Brigg, *U.S. Energy Flow—1992*, report by Lawrence Livermore National Laboratory, October 1993, 1, http://www.osti.gov/bridge/servlets/purl/10193434-KAC7zn/native/10193434.pdf.

14. Barlett, Steele, Karmatz, Roston, Levinstein, "The New Energy Crisis."

15. 9/11 Commission, *The 9/11 Commission Report: Final Report of the National Commission on Terrorist Attacks on the United States*, Executive Summary, July 22, 2004, 11, http://govinfo.library.unt.edu/

911/report/911Report.pdf. The commission noted: "The missed opportunities to thwart the 9/11 plot were also symptoms of a broader inability to adapt the way government manages problems to the new challenges of the twenty-first century. Action officers should have been able to draw on all available knowledge about al Qaeda in the government. Management should have ensured that information was shared and duties were clearly assigned across agencies, and across the foreign-domestic divide."

16. Ibid., 266–272.

17. Ibid., 272. "Jane's" reply to the angry email was that she didn't make up the rules, but that "every office of the FBI is required to follow them including FBI NY."

18. Wertheimer's remarks are taken from a presentation at the Deloitte Public Leadership Institute & National Academy of Public Administration conference on Web 2.0, Washington, DC, June 5, 2008.

19. 9/11 Commission, *The 9/11 Commission Report*, 268.

20. CBS News, "Katrina Report Blames Levees," June 1, 2006, www.cbsnews.com, and "Task Force Hope Status Report," June 4, 2006, in online newsletter of the Army Corps of Engineers at http://www.mvn.usace.army.mil/hps/Status%20Report%20Newsletters/SRN_June_4_2006.pdf.

21. Interagency Performance Evaluation Task Force (IPET), "Performance Evaluation of the New Orleans and Southeast Louisiana Hurricane Protection System," June 1, 2006, I-118 and I-31. According to the report: "The majority of the pump stations are not part of the HPS and were not designed to provide capability during large storms. The system did not perform as a system. The hurricane protection in New Orleans was designed and developed in a piecemeal fashion, resulting in inconsistent levels of protection."

22. Letter from the American Society of Civil Engineers External Review Panel to Carl Strock, November 29, 2006, from the ASCE Web site at http://www.asce.org/files/pdf/11292006erpletter.pdf. ASCE External Review Panel stated that it was clear that "the breaching and flooding resulted from multiple, ill-fated choices and decisions that were made at nearly every level."

23. Francis Fukuyama, *The Great Disruption: Human Nature and the Reconstitution of Social Order* (New York: Free Press, 2000), 6–7.

24. See Jim Collins, *Good to Great and the Social Sectors: A Monograph to Accompany Good to Great* (New York: HarperCollins, 2005).

25. Michael Hammer, *Beyond Reengineering* (New York: Harper Business, 1996), xii.

26. See, for example, Stephen R. Covey, *The 7 Habits of Highly Effective People* (New York: Simon and Schuster, 1989).

27. John F. Kennedy speech to joint session of Congress, May 25, 1961, from www.jfklibrary.org.

28. President George H. W. Bush, interview with Chris Wallace, Fox News, viewed on You Tube, date of interview unknown.

29. George W. Bush address to the nation, March 19, 2003, http://www.americanrhetoric.com.

30. Jenna Dorn, interview with the authors, June 2, 2008.

31. Tim Wiest, interview with the authors, March 2009.

32. Derek Turner, interview with the authors, December 2007.

Chapter 8, pages 219–241

1. Godfrey Hodgson, *The Gentleman from New York: Daniel Patrick Moynihan* (New York: Houghton Mifflin Harcourt, 2000), 79.

2. Moynihan's report helped shape district architecture for decades and continues to be an influence today—you can still find Moynihan's guidelines for federal architecture on the General Services Administration's Web site in the guide for buildings and real estate, section 1.2, general design philosophy, http://www.gsa.gov/Portal/gsa/ep/contentView.do?contentType=GSA_BASIC&contentId=12763.

3. President's Council on Pennsylvania Avenue, "Report of the President's Council on Pennsylvania Avenue" (Washington, DC: Government Printing Office, April 1964).

4. George Will, "Majestic Avenue," *Jewish World Advocate*, May 15, 2000.

5. Ibid.

6. President Lyndon Baines Johnson, State of the Union address, January 8, 1964.

7. Federal education assistance included the Head Start program, created for low-income preschoolers in 1965; federal assistance for grade schoolers in low-income areas came in the form of

Title I of the Elementary and Secondary Education Act of 1965; the Higher Education Act of 1965 included scholarships and low-interest loans. The Medicare program (a new feature of Social Security) was created to serve the elderly in 1965. The Medicaid program for the poor came into being a year later.

8. Office of Policy Planning and Research, U.S. Department of Labor, "The Negro Family: The Case for National Action," http://www.dol.gov/oasam/programs/history/webid-meynihan.htm.

9. Lyndon Baines Johnson, State of the Union address, January 10, 1967, LBJ library, www.lbjlib.utexas.edu/johnson/archives.

10. "Light in the Frightening Corners," *Time*, July 28, 1967, http://www.time.com/time/magazine/article/0,9171,837080,00.html.

11. Daniel Patrick Moynihan, *Maximum Feasible Misunderstanding: Community Action in the War on Poverty* (New York: The Free Press, 1969, 1970).

12. Ibid. lxi.

13. Ibid., 168–170.

14. Nicholas Lemann, "Slumlord; Pat Moynihan Has Done Some Great Things—But Betraying the Poverty Warriors Isn't One of Them," *Washington Monthly*, May 1991, from Nicholas Lemann, *The Promised Land: The Great Black Migration and How It Changed America* (New York: Alfred A. Knopf, 1991).

15. Moynihan, *Maximum Feasible Misunderstanding*, Introduction to the Paperback Edition, xxix.

16. Variants of this quote have been attributed to Moynihan in several sources, including Ellen Hume, "Tabloids, Talk Radio, and the Future of News: Technology's Impact on Journalism," Washington, DC, The Annenberg Washington Program in Communications Policy Studies of Northwestern University, 1995.

17. George Will, "Pat Moynihan, R.I.P.," Town Hall.com, March 27, 2003, http://townhall.com/columnists/GeorgeWill/2003/03/27/pat_moynihan,_rip.

18. Ibid.

19. Michael Kramer, "The Political Interest," *Time*, January 31, 1994, http://www.time.com/time/magazine/article/0,9171,980052,00.html.

20. David Saltonstall, "Hillary Clinton Learned 'Hard Lesson' on Health Care, She Wrote to Moynihan," *New York Daily News*, April 16, 2008, http://www.nydailynews.com/news/politics/2008/04/16/2008-04-16_hillary_clinton_learned_hard_lesson_on_h-3.html.

21. Will, "Pat Moynihan, R.I.P."

22. *Anchorage Daily News*, March 27, 1965.

23. The effort also included innovative policies spearheaded by Sen. Clinton Anderson (D–New Mexico) and Johnson's cabinet.

24. All quotes of Dwight Ink not otherwise cited are from a series of four interviews with the authors between January 2007 and November 2008.

25. James Conaway, "The Worker: Dwight Ink: Now for a Few Good Words About Bureaucrats," *Washington Post Magazine*, April 15, 1984, 17.

26. Schlesinger and the State Department instead favored a ban on all nuclear testing in the hopes that the Soviet Union would not violate the treaty through underground tests.

27. 1978 letter from President Carter to Dwight Ink, personal files of Dwight Ink.

28. Dwight Ink, "Managing Change That Makes a Difference," in *Meeting the Challenge of 9/11: Blueprints for More Effective Government*, ed. Thomas H. Stanton (Washington, DC: National Academy of Public Administration, September 2006).

29. Burt Schorr, "Mr. Ink Learns How to Close an Agency," *Wall Street Journal*, October 1, 1981, 29.

30. Conaway, "The Worker: Dwight Ink."

31. Arthur M. Schlesinger, *A Thousand Days: John F. Kennedy in the White House* (New York: Houghton Mifflin Harcourt, 2002), 255.

Index

Acknowledgments

This is the second book the two of us have written together. The first, *Revolution at the Roots*, was written a little more than fifteen years ago. We are now older and hopefully wiser, but still committed to the enduring challenge of trying to make the great experiment of democracy a raging success.

It is a cliché no less than our title, but this book truly was a team effort. We express our most heartfelt gratitude to all those who assisted in the research, data collection, and manuscript review. This book is immeasurably better for their input, and the authors absolve all such participants for any errors, omissions, or faulty reasoning that found its way into the final product—that stuff is all ours.

The financial prospects for public-sector management books are bleak. For this reason alone, two organizational sponsors deserve special thanks. Deloitte allowed Bill to devote significant time to this book in his role heading up the firm's public-sector thought leadership practice, while the National Academy of Public Administration supported John in researching and writing the book on a special grant. The economic support of these organizations is greatly appreciated, but it only begins to tell the story of how they enriched the final product.

No one at Deloitte played a more important role in making *If We Can Put a Man on the Moon* a reality than Bob Campbell, a longtime colleague and close friend. Bob has been advising government leaders for more than three decades. His encyclopedic policy knowledge, combined with his decades of experience leading major government transformation initiatives, gives him a truly unique perspective that we tapped into time and again over a two-year period. In addition to giving generously of his time for interviews and brainstorming, Bob read the manuscript cover to cover twice. His frank and often tough feedback made this a much better book than it otherwise would have been.

Many other Deloitte colleagues played a critical role. A dinner conversation with Greg Pellegrino helped to inspire the initial idea for the book. Greg also provided leadership support at critical times throughout the book project. John Levis, Vikram Mahidhar, Ajit Kambil, and Mark Klein also provided strong and continued support throughout the process. Vikram's sage advice for how to frame the book also proved critical.

Ryan Alvanos and Jon Warshawsky, both extremely talented writers and editors, put in countless hours helping us to improve the book's language and logic. Pakshalika Jayaprakash and Aditi Rao also provided critical editorial support. Tiffany Dovey and Dwight Allen read multiple chapters and offered dozens of thoughtful suggestions. Ashish Singh Gambhir, Alec Kasuya, Anchal Shrivastava, and Shalabh Singh provided top-notch research assistance. Prasad Kantamneni assisted in the survey design and analysis. Terri Prow set up the interviews. Wade Horn provided valuable feedback on the manuscript. Terri Beck, Casey Haugner, Soy Park, and Holly Wilmot coordinated the marketing effort. Thanks also to the following Deloitte colleagues for generously offering their time and insights: Cathy Benko, Peter Brown, Todd Cain, Jason Charter, John Dalrymple, Tom Davis, Simon Dixon, Bill Ezzell, Rick Funston, Brian Green, Ernie Gregory, Marty Goldberg, Ira Goldstein, Carlo Grifone, Janet Hale, Heather Hanford, Dan Helfrich, Anna Hight, Matthew Hudes, Elina Ianchulev, Ira Kalish, Paul Keckley, Keith Leslie, Naomi Leventhal, Paul Macmillan, Michael McMullan, Doug Palmer, Gene Procknow, General Harry Raduege, Sally Ride, Jordan Schiff, Jeff Schwartz, Brian Siegal, Ian Simpson, John Skowron, Ellen Stewart, Branko Terzic, Leif Ulstrup, Peter Wallace, and Tim Wiest.

The other critical partner in this project was the National Academy of Public Administration (NAPA), a nonprofit independent coalition of top public management and organizational leaders, chartered by Congress.

The National Academy is the oldest and most respected organization in the country specifically dedicated to the topic of this book: public management. In numerous ways, it provided insights and access to the collective wisdom of an incredible collection of dedicated, experienced public servants who serve as National Academy Fellows. Thanks especially go to Jenna Dorn, NAPA's dynamic president, former NAPA vice president Frank DiGiammarino (now a key official in the Obama administration), vice president Lena Trudeau, and prominent management expert and Fellow Dwight Ink. NAPA Fellows gave generously of their time as part of the project, both in participating in our survey on execution and through many one-on-one interviews.

When we began the daunting task of reviewing more than seventy-five major public undertakings spanning more than sixty years, we realized that to do it right would require a small army of intelligent, thoughtful individuals who understood government and yet were willing to work for free. The answer was clear: we needed grad students. This work could not have been accomplished without the assistance of both students and faculty from America's leading graduate schools of public policy and administration. More than seventy graduate students participated in the research project, drafting case studies and testing and re-testing our frameworks against these real-world examples. Special mention goes to Kevin Bacon, a faculty member of the Lyndon Baines Johnson School of Government at the University of Texas, whose class did a year-long research project in conjunction with the research for this book. Thanks to Kevin's inspired leadership, the class did some groundbreaking work on executing major transformation initiatives. Kevin also read the entire book manuscript and offered dozens of helpful comments. Thanks also go to Charis Varnum at Columbia University's School of International and Public Affairs, and Alessandro Acquisti and Lynn Pastor at Carnegie Mellon for offering up their students to work on the book project.

The graduate students participating in the book project were: Abed Ali, Carolyn Carnahan, Stephanie Counts, and Elizabeth Krimmel (American University); Basil Al Essa, Kedar Kamalapur, Robert Kaminski, Patrick Mallory, Ryan Menefee, Vasudeva Ramaswa, Mark Rutledge, Deepak Sharma, Mary Sheridan, Arun Varadharajan, Seth Watson, and Marc Wautier (Carnegie Mellon University); Alexander Bock, Helen

Cao, Jorge Cervantes, Almudena Fernandez, Rose Carmen Goldbert, Sudipti Gupta, Jingjia He, Jennifer Holowchak, Akiko Ito, Yasuyuki Matsui, Maminirina Rakotoarisoa, Toru Sashida, Benjamin Villanti, Qian Wu, and Tomohiko Yamamoto (Columbia University); Michael Bergen (Georgetown University); Betty Feng, Daniel Honker, Kathleen Logisz, Lindsey Seelhorst, Audrey Vaughn, and Kristen Warms (George Washington University); John Cassidy, Jarrod Loadholt, and Stella Tsay (Harvard University); Justine Lazaro, Andrew Lee, Melinda Mattes, and Sarah Minor-Massy (University of California, Berkley); Jennifer Breckheimer, Jackie Clemente, and Shafiq Meyer (University of Southern California); Catherine Bendowitz, Elise Braun, and Alyssa Oldani (University of Chicago); Luke Brennan, Greg Campion, Lawrence Crockett, Tom Czerwinski, Erin Daley, Andrew Farmer, Fritz Fitzpatrick, Lori Gabbert Charney, Jennifer Gorenstein, Julia Harvey, Ashlynn Holman, Colleen Kajfosz, Brian Larson, Jason Modglin, Raenetta Nance, Sherry Penson, Sanvita Sample, and Jeff Schulz (University of Texas, Austin).

In addition, Peter Harkness, a good friend and founder of *Governing* magazine, read the draft and provided helpful suggestions. Merrill Douglas and Marty Gottron provided excellent editorial assistance. Other friends and colleagues from the world of business and government were kind enough to review the book, including Charlie Chieppo, Ian Doughty, Robert Knisely, Boyd Peterson, and James Stergios.

Hundreds of current and former public officials and academics were interviewed for this book. Thanks go out to all those who gave their time to be interviewed for the book, and while there is not enough space to thank all of them we did want to highlight several who were especially generous with their time: Luke Blair, Ed DeSeve, Billy Hamilton, Dwight Ink, Representative Carl Isett, Ken Levine, Mayor Ken Livingstone, Admiral James Loy, Tim Murphy, Governor Tom Ridge, Robert Stavins, Derek Turner, James Q. Wilson, and Senator Tim Wirth.

We couldn't have asked for a better editor than Jeff Kehoe or a better publisher than the Harvard Business Press. After we handed in our "finished" manuscript, Jeff helpfully pointed out a number of shortcomings. This wasn't exactly what we had wanted to hear, but it was exactly what we needed to hear, and under his gimlet eye the final product was improved by several notches. We will miss the spirited discussions regarding the ellipsis in the title ("What the heck does dot-dot-dot mean, anyway? It sounds like Morse code."), and we will miss working with Jeff's colleagues from HBP, including Courtney Schinke, Allison Peter, Erin Brown, and Stephani Finks. We feel grateful to have had such a professional team from the world's premier management publishing house behind the book.

Our agent Jim Levine, a former government official, understood from the beginning what we were trying to accomplish with the book. Jim patiently guided us through a reworking of the proposal and enabled you to avoid the inconvenience of reading these words in mimeographed form. Thanks, Jim.

The support of family and friends was critical to both of us. Despite being on constant deadline to finish his own books and screenplays, Dave Eggers was always willing to read chapter drafts and offer the kind of editorial insight that money can't buy. His wife Vendela, yet another author in the family, also provided valuable insights. Younger brother Toph Eggers, a talented screenwriter, also gave many valued suggestions, even if we didn't take the one about giraffes. A number of close friends also helped Bill get through this long journey. Thanks especially to Alex and Luciana for the Brazil getaway when it was needed most; Kevin and Amy for always providing humor at the right moments; and Linda for showing such understanding and support throughout the process—and for the always-scrumptious cooking.

Words cannot do justice to all that Nancy O'Leary means to John. She really is the wind beneath John's wings, as she frequently reminds him. Nancy not only provided valuable insight on the manuscript, but also bore the brunt of the happy task of raising toddlers while her husband worked from a home office. Honey, I love you and I promise the next book will be written from an underground bunker in an undisclosed location. Thanks also to Emily O'Leary, age four, who reviewed the manuscript and whose insightful comment, "Where are the pictures?" led to the inclusion of the drawings of Sisyphus in chapter 5. Thanks also to Lisa O'Leary, age two, whose irrepressible spirit helped her daddy get through it, so she gets a big a moo-tickle. You are all blessings of my life.

We hope you enjoy the book.

About the Authors

An author, columnist, and popular speaker for two decades, *William Eggers* is a leading authority on government reform. As a global director for Deloitte Research, he is responsible for research and thought leadership for Deloitte's public sector industry practice. (Deloitte Research is a part of Deloitte LLP.)

His books include *Governing by Network* (Brookings, 2004), *Government 2.0* (Rowman and Littlefield, 2005), and *The Public Innovator's Playbook* (Deloitte Research, 2009). His writings have won numerous awards including the Louis Brownlow award for best book on public management, the Sir Antony Fisher award for best book promoting an understanding of the free economy, and the Roe Award for leadership and innovation in public policy research.

He is a former manager of the Texas Performance Review and director of e-Texas. He has advised governments around the world, and his commentary has appeared in dozens of major media outlets including the *New York Times*, *Wall Street Journal*, and *Chicago Tribune*. He splits his time between Austin, Texas, and Washington, DC. He can be reached at weggers@deloitte.com.

John O'Leary is a Research Fellow at the Ash Institute for Democratic Governance and Innovation at the Harvard Kennedy School. His writings on public policy have appeared in the *Boston Globe*, *Wall Street Journal*,

San Diego Union-Tribune, and elsewhere. He has held several leadership positions in Massachusetts state government, including Chairman of the Civil Service Commission, Director of the Division of Unemployment Assistance, and Chief Human Resource Officer.

A process engineer by training, Mr. O'Leary has been a Vice President at Scudder Kemper Investments and the Director of Business Process Reengineering at Lycos. He is a 1984 graduate of MIT and holds an MS degree from the University of Massachusetts at Amherst. He can be reached at johnoleary@alum.mit.edu.